I.B.TAURIS SHORT HISTORIES

I.B.Tauris Short Histories is an authoritative and elegantly written new series which puts a fresh perspective on the way history is taught and understood in the twenty-first century. Designed to have strong appeal to university students and their teachers, as well as to general readers and history enthusiasts, *I.B.Tauris Short Histories* comprises a novel attempt to bring informed interpretation, as well as factual reportage, to historical debate. Addressing key subjects and topics in the fields of history, the history of ideas, religion, classical studies, politics, philosophy and Middle East studies, the series seeks intentionally to move beyond the bland, neutral 'introduction' that so often serves as the primary undergraduate teaching tool. While always providing students and generalists with the core facts that they need to get to grips with the essentials of any particular subject, *I.B.Tauris Short Histories* goes further. It offers new insights into how a topic has been understood in the past, and what different social and cultural factors might have been at work. It brings original perspectives to bear on the manner of its current interpretation. It raises questions and – in its extensive bibliographies – points to further study, even as it suggests answers. Addressing a variety of subjects in a greater degree of depth than is often found in comparable series, yet at the same time in concise and compact handbook form, *I.B.Tauris Short Histories* aims to be 'introductions with an edge'. In combining questioning and searching analysis with informed history writing, it brings history up to date for an increasingly complex and globalized digital age.

www.short-histories.com

'*A Short History of the Crimean War* provides an authoritative account of the origins of the conflict, its principal engagements and its geopolitical consequences. Furthermore, the author's thoughtful and erudite discussions of literary and visual materials – together with the careful attention given to the significance of journalism in forming public opinion, and of the key roles played by women – mean that the book also makes a very welcome contribution to current debate on the lasting historical and cultural significance of the Crimean War. An excellent introduction.'

– Philip Shaw, Professor of Romantic Studies, University of Leicester,
author of *Waterloo and the Romantic Imagination*

'Trudi Tate's book, besides giving an admirably concise history of the Crimean War which will appeal to a wide readership, also offers new and thought-provoking insights of undoubted interest to the specialist. Whether it be in her analysis of the role of the British press in reporting the war, her examination of the literary response towards it, or her highlighting of the extent to which criticism of the conduct of the war was largely class-based, Dr Tate pronounces with authority. If one aspect of the book were to be singled out for special praise, however, it would have to be her explanation of how the capture of the Russian fortress of Sebastopol was perceived by onlookers and represented in both print and the new art-form of photography. One does not readily forget the passage where the author vividly summarises the reaction of visitors to the shattered ruins of Sebastopol, a mixture of simple pride at martial achievement – "Look at what we have done!" – and frightened awe as the realisation of the destructive power of industrialised warfare on the cusp sank home for the first time: "*Look at what we have done*". All in all, a book that can be recommended without reservation.'

– Alastair Massie, author of
The National Army Museum Book of the Crimean War

A Short History of . . .

the American Civil War	Paul Anderson (Clemson University)
the American Revolutionary War	Stephen Conway (University College London)
Ancient China	Edward L Shaughnessy (University of Chicago)
Ancient Greece	P J Rhodes, FBA (Durham University)
Ancient Rome	Andrew Wallace-Hadrill (University of Cambridge)
the Anglo-Saxons	Henrietta Leyser (University of Oxford)
Babylon	Karen Radner (University of Munich)
the Byzantine Empire	Dionysios Stathakopoulos (King's College London)
Christian Spirituality	Edward Howells (Heythrop College, University of London)
the Crimean War	Trudi Tate (University of Cambridge)
English Renaissance Drama	Helen Hackett (University College London)
the English Revolution and the Civil Wars	David J Appleby (University of Nottingham)
the Etruscans	Corinna Riva (University College London)
Florence and the Florentine Republic	Brian Jeffrey Maxson (East Tennessee State University)
the Hundred Years War	Michael Prestwich (Durham University)
Irish Independence	J J Lee (New York University)
the Italian Renaissance	Virginia Cox (New York University)
the Korean War	Allan R Millett (University of New Orleans)
Medieval Christianity	G R Evans (University of Cambridge)
Medieval English Mysticism	Vincent Gillespie (University of Oxford)
the Minoans	John Bennet (University of Sheffield)
the Mongols	George Lane (SOAS, University of London)
the Mughal Empire	Michael H Fisher (Oberlin College)
Muslim Spain	Amira K Bennison (University of Cambridge)
New Kingdom Egypt	Robert Morkot (University of Exeter)
the New Testament	Halvor Moxnes (University of Oslo)
Nineteenth-Century Philosophy	Joel Rasmussen (University of Oxford)

the Normans	Leonie V Hicks (Canterbury Christ Church University)
the Ottoman Empire	Baki Tezcan (University of California, Davis)
the Phoenicians	Mark Woolmer (Durham University)
the Reformation	Helen L Parish (University of Reading)
the Renaissance in Northern Europe	Malcolm Vale (University of Oxford)
Revolutionary Cuba	Antoni Kapcia (University of Nottingham)
the Risorgimento	Nick Carter (Australian Catholic University, Sydney)
the Russian Revolution	Geoffrey Swain (University of Glasgow)
the Spanish Civil War	Julián Casanova (University of Zaragoza)
the Spanish Empire	Felipe Fernández-Armesto (University of Notre Dame) and José Juan López-Portillo (University of Oxford)
Transatlantic Slavery	Kenneth Morgan (Brunel University London)
Venice and the Venetian Empire	Maria Fusaro (University of Exeter)
the Vikings	Clare Downham (University of Liverpool)
the Wars of the Roses	David Grummitt (University of Kent)
the Weimar Republic	Colin Storer (University of Nottingham)

A SHORT HISTORY OF THE CRIMEAN WAR

Trudi Tate

I.B. TAURIS

LONDON · NEW YORK

Published in 2019 by
I.B.Tauris & Co. Ltd
London • New York
www.ibtauris.com

PB ISBN: 978 1 84885 861 9
HB ISBN: 978 1 84885 860 2
eISBN: 978 1 78672 555 4
ePDF: 978 1 78673 555 3

A full CIP record for this book is available from the British Library
A full CIP record is available from the Library of Congress

Library of Congress Catalog Card Number: available

Typeset by Free Range Book Design & Production Limited

Contents

List of Maps and Illustrations

Acknowledgements

I am grateful to many people who have helped me to develop this work over many years in Frankfurt and in Cambridge: Rachel Bates, Gillian Beer, Anthony Dawson, Adrian duPlessis, David Feldman, Holly Furneaux, Mike Gait, Sophie Gordon, Irene Hills, Klaus Hofmann, Stefanie Lotz, Alastair Massie, Eric Nye, Gill Plain, Corinna Russell, Susan Sellers, John Tate, Toni Tate, Jennifer Wallace and Bobbie Wells. Thanks to the Royal Collection, Windsor Castle, for permission to reproduce photographs. I am particularly grateful to Douglas Austin and Major Colin Robins of the Crimean War Research Society for their valuable advice and to my editor Alex Wright for seeing the project through. Special thanks to Rosa Tate for making it all worthwhile.

Timeline

1853

31 May	Russian ultimatum to Turkey.
8 June	British fleet approaches the Dardanelles.
2 July	Russian army crosses the Pruth river into Moldavia.
5 October	Turkey declares war on Russia.
28 October	Turkish army crosses the Danube river at Kalafat.
30 October	British fleet enters the Bosphorus.
4 November	Russians defeated by Turks at Oltenitza.
30 November	Turkish naval squadron destroyed at Sinope.

1854

4 January	Allied fleets enter the Black Sea.
8 January	Russians invade the Dobruja (Romania).
10 February	British peace deputation sees the Tsar in St Petersburg.
23 February	First British troops sail for Turkey.
11 March	British Baltic Fleet sets sail.
20 March	French Baltic Fleet sets sail.
28 March	France and Britain declare war on Russia.
5 April	British troops arrive at Gallipoli.
18 April	Turkish victory at Rohova.
22 April	Bombardment of Odessa.
28 May	Embarkation of French and British force for Varna.
26 June	French and British fleets arrive off Kronstadt.

7 July	Russians defeated by the Turks at Giurgevo.
28 July	Russians withdraw across the Pruth river.
13 August	Allies besiege Bomarsund in the Baltic.
16 August	Surrender of Bomarsund.
7 September	Allies embark at Varna for the Crimea.
14 September	Allies land unopposed at Calamita Bay.
20 September	Battle of the Alma.
24 September	Allied flank march around Sebastopol.
26 September	British enter Balaklava.
29 September	French commander, St Arnaud, dies.
17 October	First bombardment of Sebastopol.
25 October	Battle of Balaklava.
26 October	Little Inkerman.
4 November	Florence Nightingale arrives in Scutari with 38 nurses.
5 November	Battle of Inkerman.
14 November	Hurricane in the Crimea.

1855

10 January	Russians feint attack on Balaklava.
17 January	Russian attack on Eupatoria, north of Calamita Bay.
26 January	Piedmont joins the Allies.
31 January	Lord Aberdeen's government falls.
5 February	Lord Palmerston forms the new government.
24 February	French attack on Sebastopol fails.
2 March	Tsar Nicholas I dies. Succeeded by Alexander II.
15 March	Conference of Vienna opens.
4 April	Second Baltic fleet leaves Spithead.
9 April	Second bombardment of Sebastopol.
26 April	Vienna Conference closes.
25 May	Kertch and Yenikale captured.
26 May	Allied naval forces enter the Sea of Azov.
6 June	Third bombardment of Sebastopol. Capture of the Mamelon and the Quarries by the Allies.
16 June	First Russian attack at Kars.
17 June	Fourth bombardment of Sebastopol.

18 June	Main assault on the Malakov and Redan defeated.
28 June	Death of Lord Raglan.
1 July	General Sir James Simpson appointed to command of the British army in the Crimea.
7 August	Second Russian attack at Kars.
9 August	Bombardment of Sveaborg (Finland).
17 August	Fifth bombardment of Sebastopol.
5 September	Sixth bombardment of Sebastopol.
8 September	At Sebastopol, French successfully take the Malakov. British fail to take Redan.
9 September	Russians evacuate the south side of Sebastopol.
29 September	Russian attack at Kars defeated. Cavalry skirmishes at Eupatoria. Omar Pasha's troops embark for Asia Minor.
7 October	Kinburn expedition sails for the mouth of the Dnieper river.
17 October	Allied expedition captures forts at Kinburn.
6 November	Omar Pasha defeats the Russians at the River Ingur, south of the Caucasus Mountains.
26 November	Russians accept surrender of the Turkish forces at Kars.

1856

16 January	Tsar Alexander II accepts Austrian demands.
29 January	Russian guns bombard Sebastopol.
25 February	Paris Peace Conference opens.
29 February	Armistice is signed.
30 March	Treaty of Paris is signed.
27 April	Ratification of the Treaty of Paris ends Britain's participation in the war.

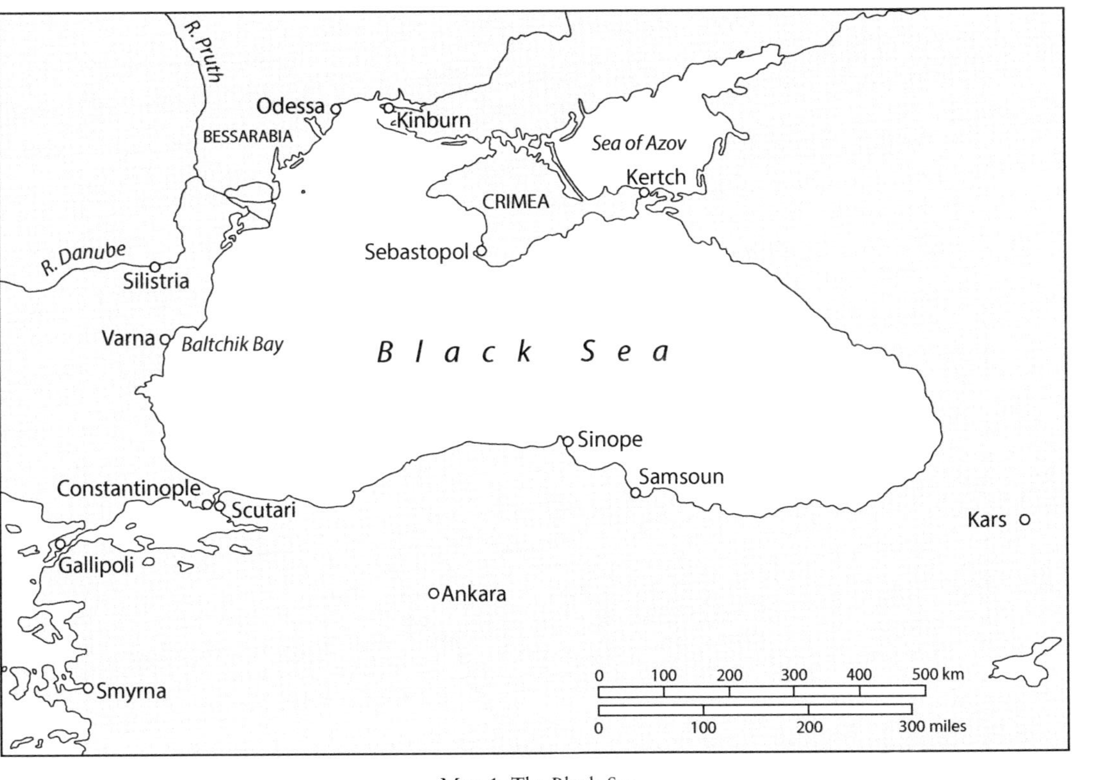

Map 1: The Black Sea

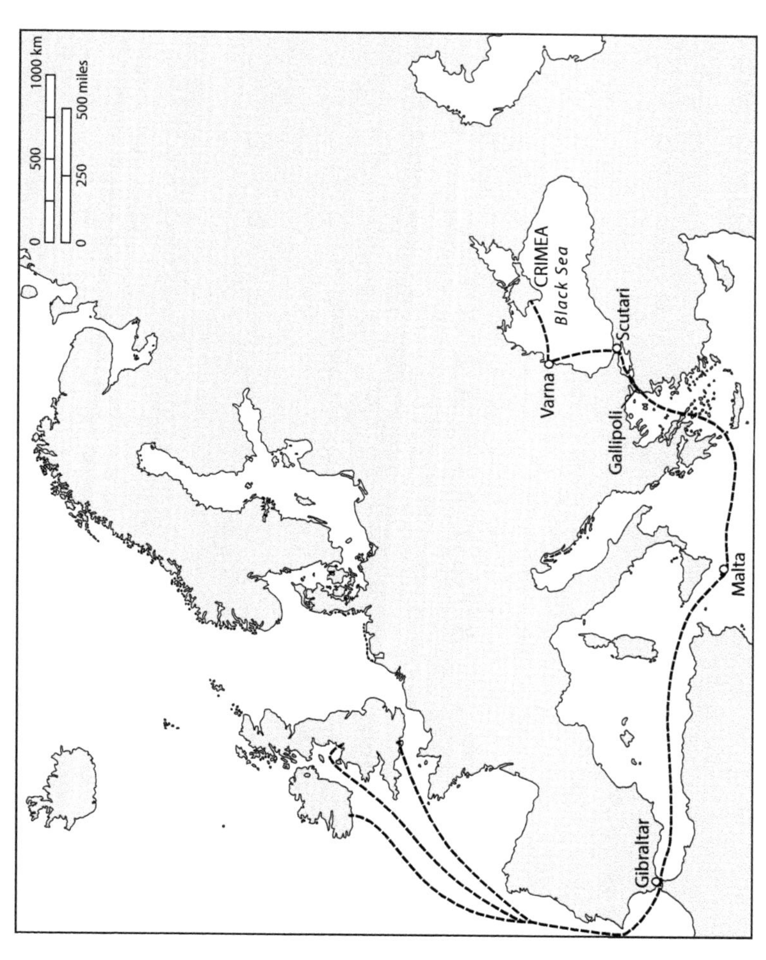

Map 2: The Route from Britain to the Crimea

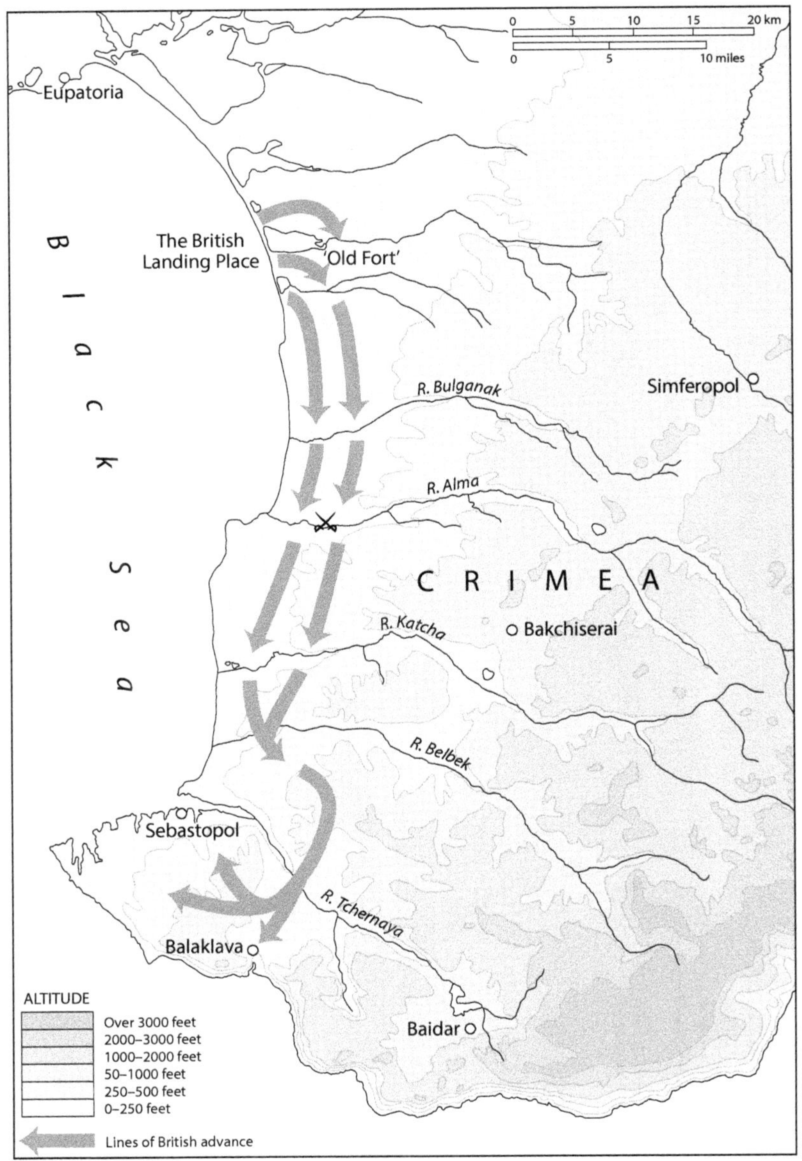

Map 3: The Advance to Sebastopol

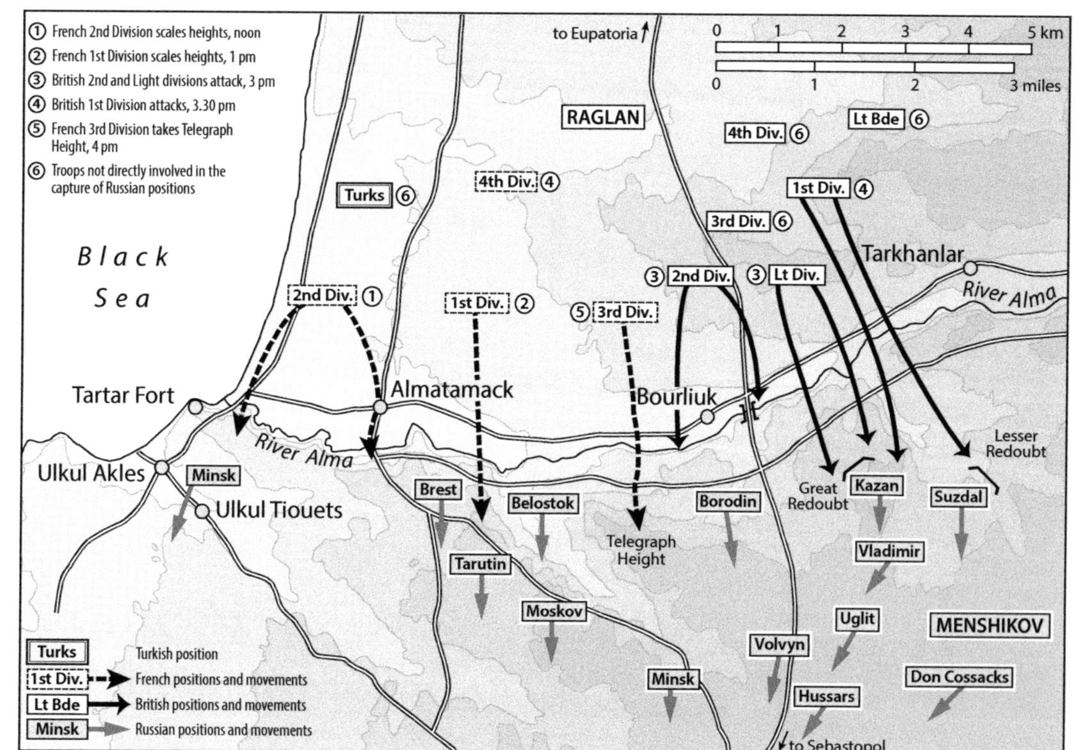

Map 4: The Battle of the Alma

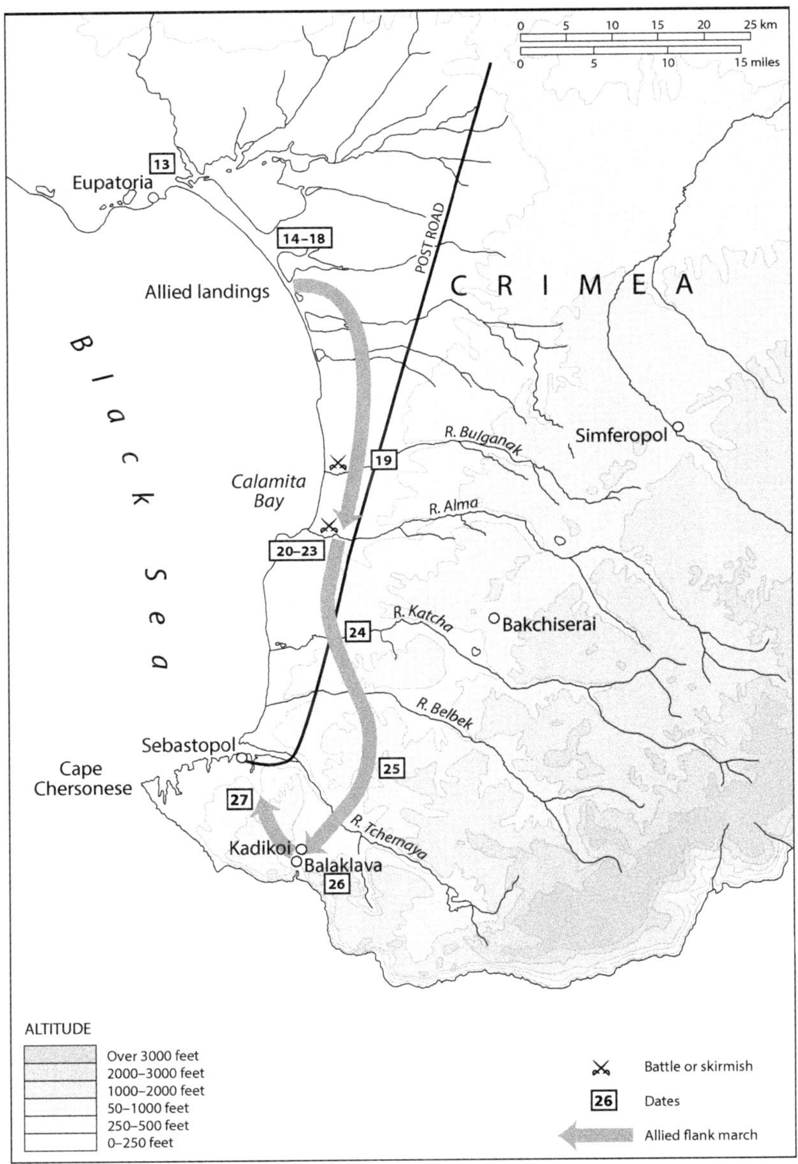

Map 5: The Area of War in the Crimea

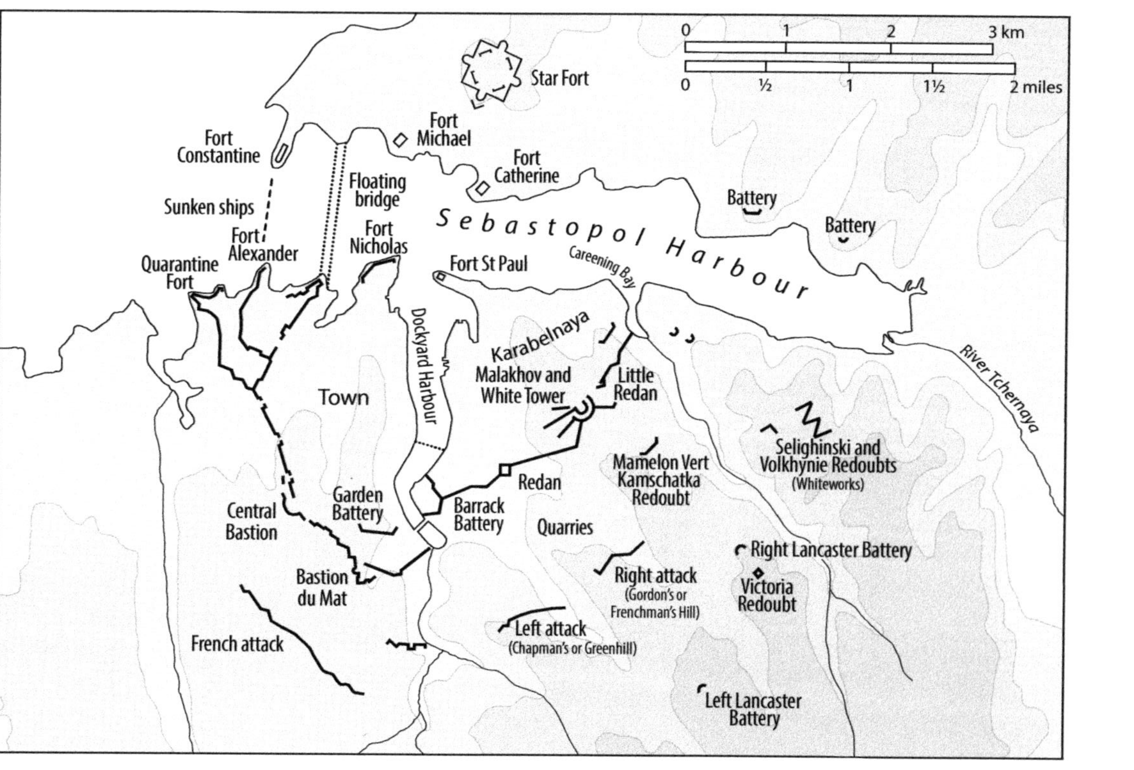

Map 6: Sebastopol Defences

Introduction

One evening in 1855, a ball in Melbourne, Australia, was disturbed by the sudden arrival of a messenger. The music stopped; the dancers waited; the gentlemen conferred. '"*The Russians have landed!*" was the despairing cry.'[1] After a short period of anxiety, the rumour was quashed, but the ball was a failure and the guests quietly dispersed. Stories of this kind were rife throughout the Australian colonies in this period, and had more to do with local political concerns than with the war between Britain and Russia.[2] Yet the incident is characteristic of the far-reaching cultural resonances of the Crimean War (1854–6). The war profoundly affected the domestic politics of the main combatant nations – Britain, France and Turkey on the one side, Russia on the other. It was also important to the other great powers, Austria and Prussia, as well as Sardinia, which joined the war in 1855. And it was felt in places far away – Australia, Jamaica, and India, at least as story, or fantasy. The war was important to the United States, which at this time was a rival to Britain and on good terms with Russia. Had the war continued into 1856, it might well have developed into a world war, setting Britain against the US and drawing in other European powers.[3] As it was, it helped to sow the seeds of the catastrophe of the First World War, 1914–18.

The conflict we now call the Crimean War was known at the time as the Russian War, or the War in the East, and it was fought across a wide geographical area, not just in the Crimea. Important parts of the struggle took place by the Danube, in the Sea of Azov, the Caucasus, the White Sea, the Pacific, and above all in the Baltic. Indeed, the outcome of the war was decided largely in the Baltic, where the British navy blockaded Russian trade and threatened St Petersburg, then the capital of the vast Russian Empire. British history and cultural memory tend to focus on the courage and the suffering witnessed in the Crimea, where approximately half a million soldiers died, the majority of disease and neglect rather than in active combat.[4] These experiences were real, but in the end, they counted for little in terms of the peace settlement.[5] What we remember as the 'Crimean War' is only part of the full history. Indeed, the Crimean War of popular memory is, in certain ways, a fiction. How that fiction was formed in historical and cultural memory is part of the story I tell here.

***

Though the name 'Crimean War' is somewhat misleading, it is the name we've had for more than a century; it is the name we all know. So to avoid confusion, I will continue to use it in this study.

The Crimean War has attracted less interest from historians than other European wars of the nineteenth and twentieth centuries. It was of course a lesser conflict than the Napoleonic Wars (1792–1815) or the First and Second World Wars (1914–18 and 1939–45). For a long time it was remembered as a land war, with the naval actions in the Baltic regarded as unimportant. In fact, we now know that the navy achieved the most effective actions of the war, but these were not reported in much detail at the time, and were not seriously researched by historians until the late twentieth century. Andrew Lambert's pioneering work on the Baltic campaign has given us a tremendous new insight into what happened in the war, and what it might mean.[6] There is an important point for historiography here. For more than a century, historians drew a lot of their information about the war from the newspapers. While William Howard Russell's reports were generally accurate – unlike much reporting from later wars – our reliance upon the press means that the interests of the newspapers have shaped the historical narrative. In particular, because the journalists were at the Crimea, and not much elsewhere during the war, it was the Crimea that was represented in most detail, most discussed, and seen by civilians at the time as most important. But this is a distortion of the military and historical reality. We need a more cautious attitude towards the press. It is hugely valuable as one of the voices at the time, but its significance is too often overstated. The newspapers' attitudes (particularly those of *The Times*) have been allowed to dominate cultural memory, and that has hindered our understanding of the full history.

The Times frequently presented itself as the voice of 'public opinion' and the spokesman for the middle classes. Many people took this claim seriously, including within government, and it has been repeated frequently in histories of the war. In fact, we have very limited knowledge of public opinion in the 1850s. We can find evidence in diaries and letters of the time that some people agreed with *The Times* on certain issues, while some disagreed. Of those who agreed, some felt *The Times* represented their informed views; others felt they had derived their opinions from *The Times* in the first place, and that it could be a dangerous influence. 'Public opinion' was frequently invoked, even blamed, for many decisions made about the war. This was partly true, as the franchise had been extended in 1832, so that about 20 per cent of men could now vote, and more people were able to engage with the events of the day through the press. But it was also a myth and needs to be treated with some scepticism.

The Crimean War has something to teach us now, not least about how we can be persuaded into war, when it might not be in our best interests; and how we remember and misremember warfare, especially when we are observing it from a distance.[7] Today, the history should remind us how hard-won and precious is peace in Europe.

***

This short history takes a fresh look at Britain's involvement in the war, describing the familiar military history alongside the lesser-known but crucial naval history. These narratives are interwoven with discussions of representations of the war, in the newspapers, memoirs, poetry and photography, as well as eyewitness reports in letters and diaries of serving soldiers and medical officers. Read together, the representations can give us some understanding of how the war was *experienced* – as grim reality by those present – and how it was *perceived* or *imagined* by those watching on the spot, and by others far away. I am interested in how the Crimean War affected Britain's sense of itself, its armed forces, and the very idea of warfare. It took place during what we might see as the height of Victorian confidence, just a few years after the Great Exhibition of 1851, in which the tremendous progress of nineteenth-century industry and commerce were celebrated for, among other things, their contribution to peace.[8] On the surface, at least, peace in Europe in the early 1850s was regarded by many people as normal, and warfare some barbarism of the past. The terrible sufferings of the Napoleonic Wars were still alive in cultural memory, and Britain continued to pay the financial costs of those wars for decades afterwards.[9] On the other hand, the Victorians' deep interest in the ancient cultures of Greece and Rome kept them interested in warfare, at least as an abstraction. The ancient past was often used to justify Britain's part in the Crimean War, as well as to oppose it.[10]

The Crimean War was the first war to be photographed; the first to be reported by eyewitness journalists in the press; the first to be depicted by commissioned war artists.[11] It was the first to make use of the telegraph. In short, it was the first war to make use of modern methods of representation. These representations played a vital role in shaping the cultural memories of the conflict.[12]

The eyewitness reports in the newspapers had far-reaching effects. Thomas Chenery's articles in *The Times* in October 1854 about the terrible conditions in the hospital at Scutari moved Florence Nightingale to offer her services to the nation, which were to have a huge impact upon the development of modern nursing. William Howard Russell's articles in *The Times* were enormously influential. They were often much longer than newspaper pieces today, running to 5,000 or 6,000 words. His accounts of the courage and stoicism of the troops contributed to army reform and better pay and conditions for ordinary soldiers. His report of the charge of the Light Brigade was a powerful inspiration for Tennyson's poem, keeping the event powerfully in British cultural memory for a century and more.

The press reports, especially those by Russell in *The Times*, are remarkable, powerful pieces of writing. There was almost no censorship, and Russell took care to get his facts right, both through his own observations and by consulting with others present. He occasionally made errors of fact, and he was not afraid to express a strong opinion.[13] None the less, Russell's reports were, by and large, honest and accurate – much more so than much war reporting since. George Eliot, Dickens or Tennyson reading *The Times*' reports of, for example, the Battle of the Alma in 1854 or the fall of Sebastopol in 1855 had access to much more accurate news than in wartime since, despite (and also because of) the wide reach of television cameras and the internet.

In 1854 there was no censorship of newspapers and no organized propaganda (that did not fully develop until 1914). It took about 12 days, sometimes longer, for reports to get from the Crimea to London, especially in the early days of the war.[14] But when they did arrive they were fairly reliable. Some reports were completely speculative, or simply wrong – such as the false rumour that Sesastopol had fallen, which was reported as fact in early October 1854.[15] But this was the exception, not the rule. One purpose of this book is to suggest that we perhaps should be a little more humble about our own time in comparison to the Victorians. The reports from the Crimea were not instantaneous, but that did not matter. Those on the spot needed information as quickly as possible, to make relevant decisions and plans. But civilians at home didn't need instant accounts of the details of warfare. The Victorians were wise enough to recognize that accuracy is more important than speed if civilians are to play a responsible part in their society at war – whether that be offering moral or practical support to the armed services, or protesting and putting the government under pressure to end a conflict. There are many ways in which civilians are involved in war, not least by paying for it through their taxes, and British governments even in the 1850s needed a considerable degree of consent from the population to take the nation to war. The government did not control the press, and the newspapers, especially *The Times*, were increasingly asserting themselves as a real force in politics. *The Times*' participation in the war was exciting for civilians, but it was also troubling, as the newspaper exercised considerable power without responsibility, all the while claiming the moral high ground. The role of the press in the Crimean War raised questions about the complex effects of representation in wartime which remain with us today.

Russell's brilliant eyewitness reports in *The Times* have proved a rich source for historians, but this has been a mixed blessing.

For more than a century, the histories of the war relied heavily on Russell, and on Alexander Kinglake's eight-volume history of the war, *The Invasion of the Crimea* (1863–87). Russell has been criticized for unfairly blaming Lord Raglan, Commander-in-Chief, for matters that were out of Raglan's control, especially in regard to the failures of supply.[16] Kinglake, who also tells a gripping story, has been faulted for taking the opposite view, and being too uncritical of Raglan. Kinglake's history was commissioned by Raglan's widow in 1856, in the hope of rehabilitating her husband's reputation. Consciously basing his history on the *Iliad*, Kinglake tells the story of the war only up to July 1855, and the death of Lord Raglan. The war itself continued through the fall of Sebastopol in September 1855 until the peace treaty was signed in the spring of 1856.[17]

Many aspects of the management of the war were much criticized, both at the time and since, and it is remembered as an heroic but ultimately pointless undertaking; a tragedy of suffering to no great effect. I have some sympathy with this view; it was certainly a tragedy for most of those involved, and it does seem reasonable to argue that the checking of Russian expansion could have been achieved by less brutal means. For Baumgart, it was worse than 'perfectly useless' (p. 216). Yet, as Baumgart himself shows us, the war had significant effects. It altered the balance of power within Europe and coloured diplomatic relations over the following decades. It weakened Russia's power, reducing its influence on Eastern Europe for nearly a century, until 1945. Russia's comparative weakness from 1856 in turn made it possible for Germany to unify into a single nation, which it achieved in 1871, with long-term consequences for all of Europe.

Still, as Sweetman notes, 'One fundamental question persists': was all the suffering for the victory of 1856 worthwhile? Over the next decade or so, the Russians repudiated all the important elements of the peace treaty. So what was gained in the long term? Possibly very little. Later in the century, new conflicts emerged in the Balkans which were to lead to the First World War. These too were side effects of the Crimean War, sustaining the Ottoman Empire for a few more decades. Nations seeking independence from Turkey could achieve this only by war and revolution. Had the transitions to independence been supported by international negotiation, rather than ad hoc, through warfare, much suffering might have been prevented. 'If the Crimean War had not been fought,' remarks Sweetman soberly, 'would this European catastrophe [the First World War] have been avoided?' (p. 16). By contrast, Lambert suggests that in containing Russian power for nearly a century, the war did achieve something worthwhile. But it came at considerable cost, and it helped to sow the seeds of the much greater conflicts of the twentieth century.[18]

We are now more aware of the fact that the Crimean War was fought on several fronts, importantly in the Baltic Sea, although it is the Crimean theatre which was most discussed at the time, and which has persisted in the cultural imagination, while other aspects of the war have been almost entirely forgotten. Why has this happened? The reasons lie, I suggest, in the representations of the war as it occurred, especially in the press. Every day for nearly two years, the British newspapers were filled with reports and discussions about the Crimea, the 'seat of war in the East'. Weeklies such as the *Illustrated London News* (*ILN*) published maps, drawings and etchings taken from photographs. The world's first modern war correspondents provided eyewitness reports from the Crimea, which were published, without censorship, in the daily press. For the first time, photographers went to a war zone, among them Roger Fenton and James Robertson. Many other artists (some of them serving in the army) produced watercolours, sketches and other representations of the conflict and its effects. In an essay now regarded as one of the founding texts of modernism, Charles Baudelaire wrote enthusiastically about the work of Constantin Guys, 'The Painter of Modern Life' (1863). Among the works praised are Guys' paintings of French troops at the Crimea: '*tableaux vivants* of an astonishing vitality, traced from life itself, uniquely picturesque fragments'. 'No newspaper,' declared Baudelaire, 'no written account, no book has unfolded so well, in all its painful detail and melancholy scope, the great epic poem of the Crimea.'[19]

These representations in the press inspired many others, including a lot of war poetry, which drew its ideas and images directly from the newspaper reports, and was itself often published in the press. This in turn raised questions about the very status and purpose of literature.[20] Methods of representation and the politics of war intersected in curious new ways. This is true of all wars, perhaps, but it became more visible, and raised new questions, in the mid-nineteenth century. 'War' had an awkward relationship to the idea of modernity during this period, and the questions it raised continue to shape our understanding of wars, and of representation. On the one hand, peace was regarded as the highest achievement of nineteenth-century culture. After Waterloo (1815), Britain was at peace (at least nominally) for 40 years. War was perceived by many people as regressive and a threat to industrial progress. More widely across Europe, the great powers avoided war among themselves from 1815 until the 1850s because their governments feared that major wars encouraged revolution.[21] The war in the Crimea contributed to a significant change in attitude; in effect, it made warfare *thinkable* again. As Hobsbawm argues, by the 1860s the great powers in Europe realized they could start and stop wars almost at will, a power that statesmen such as Bismarck exploited most effectively (p. 98).

In Britain, alongside the realities of mid-Victorian prosperity and peace, there were serious problems. Vast numbers of industrial workers shared too little of the nation's wealth. Other nations were starting to challenge Britain's naval power, its empire, its share of world markets.

After 40 years of peace, the Crimean War was for many people a shock and an enigma. The ostensible causes – defending liberalism against autocracy; or defending the Christian holy places – in reality meant setting one empire against another. The original causes were a trivial quarrel over custody of keys to a church in the Holy Land. But this was not a real reason for the conflict. The main cause of the Crimean War was the complex 'Eastern Question': the continuing struggle over who would reap the benefits of the decline of the Ottoman Empire, a process which had far-reaching effects across much of the world.[22]

THE EASTERN QUESTION

All the European powers, great and small, were concerned with the Eastern Question. Since the mid-fourteenth century, the Turks had conquered a huge area across Asia, Africa and Europe, from

Egypt to the Alps.[23] The Ottoman Empire was strong for about 300 years, then began to decline, starting with the siege of Vienna in 1683. This process of decline and retreat was to last for more than two centuries. As Turkish power weakened, many struggles for power and autonomy emerged: in Greece, the Balkans, the Middle East, the Caucasus and elsewhere. The effects of Ottoman decline are still felt in unresolved tensions and conflicts today in these regions. It was a key problem for all the European great powers throughout the nineteenth century, each seeking to secure the best legacy for themselves, and to disadvantage their rivals. Tensions were especially high between Russia and Turkey, who went to war every 20 years or so between 1806 and 1877.[24] In each case, apart from the Crimean War, Russia won all of these conflicts and took territory from Turkey, as it had been doing for a very long time, including the annexation of the Crimea by Catherine the Great in 1783. In the 1850s, Russia was keen to secure more Ottoman territory for itself, in order to gain control of the Black Sea and ensure access to the warm waters of the Mediterranean. Britain was determined to stop Russian expansion and to protect its routes to India.

Britain was still the most powerful nation in the world and Russia was its nearest rival. Relations were also uneasy between Britain and its old enemy, France. After the defeat of Napoleon in 1815, the balance of power in Europe had managed to maintain the peace for 40 years, though there were many underlying tensions and conflicting interests. Despite the tensions, many people across Europe were keen to maintain the peace. In Britain, the wonders of its own industrial might in, say, 1850 were not necessarily valued for their military potential (unlike the idea of the 'military-industrial complex' a century later). The Victorian period in Britain was a great age of reform, in education, medicine, law, administration and many other areas of civic life. Going to war was not necessarily a prominent part of this Victorian vision, although the fascination with ancient Greece and Rome meant that fantasies of war and glory were never too far away, and could be mobilized when needed.[25] And once war came, it was obvious that Britain's industrial power had enormous military capacity. Modern shipping, steel, coal, industrial labour, manufactured goods, even the railways could all be turned to military purposes. This in turn would lead, eventually, to industrial warfare and the devastating wars of the twentieth century.

The Crimean War is notorious for the failures in administration, especially in the first harsh winter of 1854–5 outside Sebastopol. The British newspapers were full of shocking reports of men and horses starving in the camp, while tons of supplies rotted, a few miles away, on the Balaklava dockside. Failure in supply, and above all the antiquated bureaucracy of the Commissariat (which controlled food and land transport), caused much avoidable suffering.[26] Many of these problems were to be resolved in the spring of 1855, not least by the construction of a railway line at Balaklava. Clearly this was helpful in solving particular problems, but, more than this, it was a crucial turning point, bringing modern industrial power and creativity squarely into the service of war. Perhaps this has always been the case: perhaps every new piece of technology has been regarded by some people as a potential weapon. But it seems to me that this attitude was less prominent in the mid-Victorian age, which had other priorities.[27] Lessons had been learned from the terrible sufferings of the Napoleonic Wars. Being modern and industrialized surely meant being civilized; or at least too modern for war. But this did not last, and the reverberations of the Crimean War were to be felt for a century and more. We still live in the world it helped to create: the world in which our industrial might, our creative powers and our communications are all in some ways implicated in the modern war machine, only now it is so naturalized that we hardly notice it. Revisiting the Crimean War helps to make these issues visible again.

One lesson from the Crimea learned by some, at least, was to direct more resources into armaments and war preparations; to be preparing, always, for the next war. Historians such as Andrew Lambert argue that the hugely expensive naval arms race in the mid-nineteenth century was decisive in winning the war against Russia and containing Russia's expansive ambitions. Lambert suggests that it also helped to maintain a steady if uneasy peace between Britain and France after the war. This view shaped thinking long afterwards, especially in the Cold War period.

After a long period of peace, the Crimean War proved that a major war was, after all, still possible. And despite the vivid reporting which revealed some of the horrors of war, the representations paradoxically demonstrated that war was, in a way, still bearable, especially for those far away – that modern society can be horrified, even sickened by daily reports of war, yet can continue to function normally. In our own time – perhaps since the first Gulf War of 1991, with its deeper roots in the American involvement in Vietnam – we find ourselves constantly consenting to war, just by living our ordinary lives. As Susan Sontag has argued, modern life in the developed world is full of images of wars elsewhere. For millions of people, such images are now part of daily life, in the mainstream media and also circulated across social media, often with little, if any, factual or historical context, and sometimes with a startling degree of inaccuracy.[28] What these images mean, and how they affect our nations' decisions in relation to military action (if at all), is increasingly hard to say. It is very difficult to get one's ethical bearings in relation to war and its many representations today. That confusion, like the representations themselves, has its modern roots in the Crimea.

1

THE DRIFT TO WAR AND THE BATTLE OF THE ALMA

As the Ottoman Empire became weaker and continued to lose parts of its vast territory, what would take its place? Would the various peoples living under Turkish rule find independence, or would they be absorbed into another empire or sphere of influence? Russia had a long history of interest in the Eastern Question and by the middle of the nineteenth century had secured a considerable amount of former Ottoman lands, including the Crimea, which had been annexed in 1783 by Catherine the Great. The retreat of Ottoman power began at the end of the seventeenth century. More than 100 years later, by the 1820s, the Eastern Question had become a matter of interest to all the European Great Powers. In 1844, the Tsar made a state visit to Britain, received a warm welcome from Queen Victoria and discussed the future of the Ottoman Empire with the Foreign Secretary, Lord Aberdeen. He and Aberdeen agreed that Britain and Russia would always consult before taking action in relation to Turkey.

Early in 1853, when Aberdeen was now Prime Minister, Tsar Nicholas raised the Eastern Question with the British envoy, Sir George Hamilton Seymour. In a famous phrase, he suggested that the 'sick man of Europe' was nearly dead, and his inheritance ought to be shared out, with Britain and Russia taking significant portions of the spoils. He expected Britain to agree, but British leaders were quite worried about Russian expansion. The official British response was vague, and the Tsar felt this meant some kind of agreement. He was surprised and disappointed to find that within a year, Britain had turned against him. A number of influential British leaders, notably Lord Palmerston (1784–1865, who became Prime Minister during the war), felt strongly that Russia was a threat to British interests and to European stability, and had for many years expected – and planned – that one day the two nations would go to war. This wasn't a particularly widespread view, but it had some influential adherents, including Sir James Graham, First Lord of the Admiralty. Opposed to Palmerston, but very critical of Russia, was David Urquhart, who argued for closer trade and relations with Turkey.[1] Expressions of Russophobia were familiar in the press, and could be mobilized if a conflict developed.

Punch, for example, criticized the 'wily Czar' in the early 1850s, calling him 'the worst Sovereign'; 'o'erweening', full of 'wicked wit'; 'like a base marauder / Threatening force'.[2] In December 1853, *Punch* published 'The Autocrat's Anthem': 'For Law and Ruth, and Faith and Truth, / With my jackboot's heel I'll spurn 'em!' In January 1854, it suggested that the 'Russian Bear' needed his nails cut.[3] *Punch*, like other papers, frequently criticized the Russian autocratic system, and sometimes suggested that the Tsar was mad.[4] Similarly, the *Illustrated London News* described the Tsar as 'insane' from too much power. It argued that, as a tyrant, he was, paradoxically, also a slave: 'He is the slave of those evil passions which tyranny invariably fosters in the hearts of tyrants. He is the slave, also, of the traditional policy of his family. He is the slave of Peter the Great and the Empress Catherine [...].' Russia's autocratic system was a 'public nuisance' in Europe, and must be opposed.[5]

All this helped to make war seem like a reasonable, necessary response to an intolerable situation. Russia was presented as a bully, menacing Turkey and threatening the stability of Europe and the Middle East.

DISPUTES OVER THE HOLY PLACES

Palestine had been under Ottoman Muslim control for hundreds of years, but other religions had access to their sacred sites. Different groups claimed rights over certain holy places, and complex arrangements had been agreed with the Ottoman authorities over the years. There were struggles between Catholic Christians and Orthodox Christians over control of particular holy sites in Bethlehem and Jerusalem. Who should be allowed to restore the Church of the Holy Sepulchre, and which group should hold the keys to a disputed church in Bethlehem?[6] In the early 1850s, the arguments became bitter. *Punch* complained that 'It is absurd, and yet awful to think, that all Europe should be kept on the *qui vive* about a key of no real value, which, in fact, nobody cares about.'[7] The squabble was an excuse rather than a real cause for war, but the French and Russian leaders behaved as if these disputes really mattered, and undoubtedly some adherents took them very seriously.[8] And the disputes did stand for legitimate concerns over religious rights and respect for others, alongside the prestige of the great powers. The religious quarrels were both real and a fiction, used quite cynically to manipulate and exploit. The French appealed to the Sultan to support the Catholics; the Russians argued in support of the Orthodox Christians. Within the churches, tempers flared and blows were exchanged. The Sultan attempted to placate both sides, but this made the situation worse.

In February 1853, the Tsar sent a mission to Constantinople led by Prince Menshikov, a military veteran of the Napoleonic Wars, very experienced in war and administration but inflexible and lacking in tact. He had served in the Napoleonic Wars in 1812 and in the Turkish Wars in 1828–9, in which a war injury left him castrated and very hostile to Turkey. He seemed a provocative choice of ambassador, more likely to stir up conflict than keep the peace. Menshikov put a series of unreasonable demands to the Sultan, demanding a Russian right of intervention on behalf of the 10 million or so Orthodox Christian subjects in the Ottoman Empire. The demands were refused and Menshikov departed on bad terms in May 1853. Now Russia and Turkey were on the road to another open conflict. They had been at war at regular intervals, every 20 years or so, for more than a century. This dispute could arguably have been defused by diplomacy, and diplomacy continued throughout the war, eventually helping to shape the settlement. But not enough was done to address the crisis as it unfolded. Each power worked for its own concerns, rather than for the larger good. And some were not averse to war. Britain felt it had no choice but to support Turkey. Britain and France, long-standing enemies in the past, allied themselves against Russia, though their war aims were quite different.

After the Napoleonic Wars had ended in 1815, Britain was the most powerful country in the world. Russia was seen as a real threat to that power. Russia had been expanding over the previous two centuries, taking in adjoining lands. It was regularly at war with the Ottoman Empire, usually acquiring Ottoman territory as a result. Palmerston wanted not just to halt Russian expansion, but to push back the boundaries of the huge Russian Empire: Finland would return to Sweden, for example; Crimea and Georgia to Turkey; and the Baltic provinces would go to Prussia. The aim was to keep the Ottoman Empire intact for a few more decades. Palmerston argued that he did not care about preserving Turkey so much as keeping Russia out of Turkey, and out of Norway and Sweden, too.[9] Palmerston had further grand plans to contain Russian power, but when the war ended these were never realized. As well as preserving the balance of power in Europe, Britain was concerned to protect its large empire and the sea routes, especially to India.

When Turkey declared war against Russia, Lord Aberdeen was prime minister of Britain. He was keen to maintain the peace and did not support Palmerston's plans against Russia. The press exerted enormous pressure in favour of war and against Aberdeen, who felt unable to resist the pressure to go to war. (Further pressure would later lead him to resign as prime minister. In January 1855 he was replaced by Palmerston.)

Louis Napoleon, who had been elected president of France in 1848 before proclaiming himself Emperor Napoleon III in 1852, was looking to overturn the Vienna Treaty of 1815, signed in the wake of the final defeat of the previous Emperor Napoleon. He also sought to improve his standing within France by winning favour with the Catholic Church, hence his active support for the Catholic cause in Palestine. He saw the war with Russia as providing opportunities to change the balance of power in Europe, weakening the reactionary Holy Alliance of Russia and Austria, reclaiming Polish independence from Russia and making substantial changes in Italy and the Balkans. He envisaged the war as moving beyond the Crimea into Central Europe.

Russia originally hoped that going to war would further weaken the Ottoman Empire and give Russia better access to warm water ports in the south. The Tsar also wanted to encourage an uprising against Turkey among the Balkan Christians. He hoped Austria would join the war, suggesting that Austria might acquire Serbia and Herzegovina as the Ottoman Empire retreated. But Austria's ruler, the Emperor Franz Joseph, feared revolution and did not support the Tsar's war plans. Austria never joined the war but played an important role in the diplomatic negotiations. Nor did Prussia support Russia, and the Tsar soon found himself in a defensive war rather than on the attack against Turkey.

On 31 May 1853, Russia issued an ultimatum to Turkey, threatening to occupy the Danubian Principalities of Wallachia and Moldavia (now Romania and Moldova). Meanwhile, the French and British were starting to mobilize their fleets in support of Turkey. In mid-June, both fleets arrived at Besika Bay at the entrance to the Dardanelles. Russia moved into the principalities in July. Despite these movements, diplomacy was continuing and war was by no means inevitable. But then, on 5 October 1853, Turkey declared war against Russia. The Turkish army crossed the Danube river at Kalafat in late October and, on 4 November, defeated the Russians at Otenitza. Meanwhile, the allied fleets entered the Bosphorus on 30 October. This action violated the 1841 Treaty of London which closed the Dardanelles to all warships. This was another step towards war.

SINOPE

In November a small Turkish flotilla anchored at Sinope (on the Black Sea, on Turkey's northern coast), where it was destroyed by a much larger Russian fleet on 30 November. Some 3,000 Turkish sailors were killed and their wooden ships destroyed by the Russians' explosive shells. The Russians also destroyed the harbour and bombarded the town. The event was in fact a legal act of war, but it was presented in Britain as a massacre.[10] The *Illustrated London News* reported on 31 December:

> This was a fearful moment! The sea of fire, the roaring of the artillery, the continual explosions, and the fragments of human bodies which were hurled about in all directions in the air formed one of the most fearful spectacles man ever beheld.[11]

Its editorial took an even stronger view:

> The odious and treacherous butchery committed by the Russians at Sinope is far more than sufficient to justify the Turkish Government in refusing any terms of compromise, or of listening to any negotiation, until the outrage shall have been avenged. But Mahomedan Turkey shows itself far more Christian in its conduct than the so-called Christian Emperor of the Russians.[12]

Many newspapers took a similar view, increasing the pressure upon the British government to make a formal declaration of war. *Punch* wrote indignantly of the 'Russian butcher', 'Russian slaughtering' and the 'Tragedy of Sinope'.[13] *The Lady's Newspaper* commented that 'The disaster at Sinope has been terrible [...] The Russians behaved with great cruelty [...] The Turks fought with the energy of despair.'[14] For *The Times*, Sinope was a 'catastrophe', a 'deplorable event', a scene of 'havoc and destruction' and a 'disgrace', in which the Russians used 'an enormous disproportion of force' against the Turks, who fought with 'the greatest courage and spirit'.[15]

Was it peace or war? As Lord Clarendon told Parliament, 'we are drifting towards war'. On 27 February 1854, the Tsar was warned by France and Britain that Russia must leave the principalities. He did not respond, and, in late March, France and Britain declared war on Russia. This was greeted with dismay in some newspapers, and with enthusiasm in others, particularly *The Times*. For the *Illustrated London News*, war came as a curious kind of relief. It acknowledged that many people were very frightened of war. They knew how earlier generations had suffered in the Napoleonic conflicts, and had been paying for those wars for many years.

Nations and generations born and nurtured in peace, that know nothing of war but the burdens which it has entailed upon them, and the miseries which it inflicted upon their forefathers, cannot but look with dread upon its renewal in their time and in their own persons.

'But,' it argues, 'these feelings seldom last beyond the hour when war is known to be inevitable.' Once war is declared, there is relief. Worry is replaced with 'positive satisfaction'. 'The anxiety is no longer to prevent war, but to go into it manfully, and fight it out heroically.' Curiously, the effort to prevent war is seen here as more distressing than actual warfare.[16]

Meanwhile, in January–February 1854, a delegation of Quakers made a journey to St Petersburg to try to persuade the Tsar to maintain the peace. The Tsar assured them he was committed to peace, and hoped the Quakers might be able to influence the British government. But they had no official standing or influence with the government and were much mocked in the British press.

THE FOUR POINTS

After many months of discussion, official war aims were agreed between Britain, France and Austria, summed up as Four Points in August 1854:

1. The Russian guarantee of the Danubian Principalities was to be replaced by a European Guarantee.
2. The Danube was to be a free river.
3. The Five Power Treaty of 1841 was to be revised in the interests of the balance of power.
4. The Christian subjects of the Sultan were to be placed under European and not Russian protection.[17]

The war aims were vague, but their implications were complex, as all the interested parties tried to protect their different concerns: Austria wanted to preserve the conservative order, while France hoped to change the European balance of power in its favour, encouraging revolutions where they served French interests. Britain was determined to protect its large empire and its control of the seas as well as to maintain what was left of the Ottoman Empire, at least for now. These and other interests exerted a complex of pressures on the balance of power, and had significant effects on many nations and peoples, in the Caucasus, the Balkans, Poland and many other places, not least the Crimea.[18]

For the newspaper *John Bull*, the conflict had already begun by January 1854. 'The fact is that Russia is actually making war in earnest in every direction, and by all the means in her power,' it argued, while Britain was merely 'sitting still', hoping to preserve the peace. 'As if, forsooth, it were possible to be at peace with a country which is at war with us!'[19]

Britain's declaration of war was greeted with enthusiasm and much self-congratulation by the newspapers. This is often read as the authentic voice of the people, but in fact we do not know what most British people felt about going to war. There is simply no record of most people's views, and we can never know precisely how popular the war was. There were expressions of support, and of dissent, too. One of the best-known voices against the war was the Quaker MP John Bright (1811–89). In a speech given to the Peace Society conference in Edinburgh in October 1853, Bright argued:

Now, what is it that we really want here? We wish to protest against the maintenance of great armaments in time of peace; we wish to protest against the spirit which is not only willing for war, but eager for war; and we wish to protest, with all the emphasis of which we are capable, against the mischievous policy pursued so long by this country, of interfering with the internal affairs of other countries, and thereby leading to disputes, and often to disastrous wars.
[...]
What is war? I believe that half the people that talk about war have not the slightest idea of what it is [...] In a short sentence it may be summed up to be the combination and concentration of all the horrors, atrocities, crimes, and sufferings of which human nature on this globe is capable [...] You who lived during the period from 1815 to 1822 may remember that this country was probably never in a more uneasy position. The sufferings of the working classes were beyond description, and the difficulties, and struggles, and bankruptcies of the middle classes were such as few persons have a just idea of. There was scarcely

a year in which there was not an incipient insurrection in some parts
of the country, arising from the sufferings which the working classes
endured.[20]

In February 1855, Bright spoke about the war's devastating effects
on the families of the men who were serving:

> I am certain that many homes in England in which there now exists a
> fond hope that the distant one may return – many such homes may be
> rendered desolate when the next mail shall arrive. The angel of death
> has been abroad throughout the land; you may almost hear the beating
> of his wings.[21]

He was also very critical of Parliament's failure to stand up to
pressure from the newspapers:

> If every man in this House, who doubts the policy that is being pursued,
> would boldly say so in this House and out of it, it would not be in
> the power of the press to mislead the people as it has done for the
> last twelve months [...] We are the depositaries of the power and the
> guardians of the interests of a great nation and of an ancient monarchy.
> Why should we not fully measure our responsibility? Why should we
> not disregard the small-minded ambition that struggles for place? and
> why should we not, by a faithful, just, and earnest policy, restore, as I
> believe we may, tranquility to Europe and prosperity to the country so
> dear to us? (7 June 1855)

But the drift to war proved unstoppable.

DEPARTURE TO WAR

In February 1854, the British government appointed Lord Raglan
(1788–1855) as Commander-in-Chief of the British Expeditionary
Force.[22] As a young man, he had served with Wellington in the
Peninsular War, and then at Waterloo in 1815, where he had lost
an arm. After 1815, he had a wealth of experience as a staff officer,
administrator, MP and diplomat. He spoke good French, had a
reputation for accuracy in his work, and had a track record of

dealing tactfully with difficult people and situations. However, he was 65 now, and some felt that his military experience was too long ago to be useful. He was physically fit, had learned a lot from his time with Wellington, but had never been a military leader in the field. He was to be blamed for many of the problems in the Crimea, most of which were not his fault.

In February and March, the first allied troops departed for Turkey. They were at Gallipoli on the Dardanelles by March and April 1854. Austria mobilized its troops near the frontier of the Danubian Principalities and the Russians withdrew early in July 1854. Though Austria never officially joined the war, it had considerable influence upon the shape of events, as, to a lesser extent, did Prussia.

In late May the French and British troops sailed to Varna. The days were very hot and the nights were quite cold. Food supplies were limited, and the water was unclean. The troops' health began to decline and many, especially the French, became ill with cholera. After much discussion, the allies decided to attack Russia in the Crimea by mounting a rapid raid upon Sebastopol, the Russians' major military port in the area. As it turned out, the raid would become an 11-month siege, costing hundreds of thousands of lives with enormous suffering on all sides.

TO THE CRIMEA

The allied ships departed from Varna before sunrise on 7 September 1854. 'The moonlight was still floating on the waters,' writes Kinglake, 'when men, looking from numberless decks towards the east, were able to hail the dawn. There was a summer breeze blowing fair from the land' (II, p. 148). The troops were relieved to be moving at last, though no one knew quite where they were going. Odessa? Sebastopol? Speculation was rife. The French and British commanders could not agree on the best landing place. Raglan went to inspect the west coast of the Crimea. The British fleet was already at sea with the embarked army. After some negotiation between Raglan and French commander, St Arnaud, the allies sailed to Calamita Bay. The troops would be landed just south of Eupatoria, on a sandy beach some 30 miles north of Sebastopol.

It wasn't an easy trip. Conditions were crowded, there was a shortage of food and water, and people were still falling sick with cholera. It could kill with alarming speed. Fanny Duberly records the sad fate of a British officer, 'seized but on Friday with diarrhoea, which turned to cholera on Saturday, and on Sunday the body was left in its silent and solemn desolation'. On the crowded ship, the sick man was placed in the saloon, with just a screen to separate him from officers dining, their meal accompanied by the 'ghastly wrangle' of his dying hours.[23] A staff officer, Lieutenant-Colonel Calthorpe, reported about 90 British deaths and 300 seriously ill on the trip; the French lost even more.[24]

The allies had hundreds of ships carrying more than 60,000 troops to war. The fleets looked impressive, and threatening, with a forest of masts moving amidst clouds of smoke billowing from the steam-engined vessels. But the French and British ships that set off together moved at different paces; after a while the ships were spread out across a wide area, leaving them rather exposed. According to Russell, the vessels covered a front of nine miles, 'and after we had anchored, stragglers arrived every hour for two or three days'.[25] Fortunately for the allies, the Russian commander Prince Menshikov did not attack the fleet, preferring to face the armies on land. Even as the allies approached the Crimean coast, precise landing plans were still uncertain. As Royle remarks, one might expect such decisions to have been made well in advance, but Raglan often found himself making decisions on the hoof. To confuse matters further, he had little information about Russian troop strengths or movements.

On 13 September the large fleet arrived at Eupatoria, a prosperous trading port of about 9,000 people. Menshikov felt he could not spare troops to defend it, so the local officials offered a formal surrender, and a small allied force occupied the town the next day. They promised to treat the local people fairly, and gave residents permission to leave if they wanted to. Eupatoria had a mixed population of Russians, Greeks, Jews and Armenians living alongside the majority population of Crimean Tatars.[26] Many residents had already left the area, especially the Russians, who were somewhat afraid of the indigenous Tatar population. Some Tatars did support the invaders, but most did not. Even before shots were fired, refugees were fleeing inland from the coasts to the regional capital, Simferopol, and beyond. The Tatars were seen by some Russian authorities as an internal enemy, and were persecuted during the war. The war eventually caused a mass exodus of some 200,000 Tatars from the Crimea.[27] As Kozelsky argues:

> The war changed Crimea in ways that were far more devastating than the damage caused by the siege of Sebastopol. [During the war] Crimea was governed by martial law that was imposed by officials who had little prior knowledge of the peninsula. Businesses were destroyed; productive populations became refugees, and native populations were displaced. (p. 867)

And while the allies' official intentions towards non-combatants might have been peaceful, in practice civilians were not well protected. Both the Russians and some of the allied troops seized food from the villages they occupied around the River Alma, and showed little respect for the locals or their property. The Russian soldiers stripped the vineyards and orchards, many of them enjoying the rare luxury of fresh fruit for the first time.[28] Neither side was very concerned by the losses or sufferings of the local people. Reports from each nation at the time tend to blame the others for incidents of looting and violence towards civilians, and not much was done to stop them.[29] And it was difficult to prevent soldiers taking civilians' food when the armies were short of supplies.

The next day, 14 September, the two fleets arrived at their points of disembarkation on Calamita Bay. 'We are "an army of occupation" at last,' remarked Russell in *The Times* (p. 43). The French troops were landed in two days. The British took four days, partly because, unlike the French, they had more than 1,000 cavalry horses to bring ashore, in worse weather conditions. The horses were frightened as well as hungry, and not all of them survived the landing, as Fanny Duberly recorded:

> English troops disembarking in a heavy surf. The landing of the horses is difficult and dangerous. Such men as were disembarked yesterday were lying all exposed to the torrents of rain which fell during the night. How it did rain! In consequence an order has been issued to disembark *the tents*. The beach is a vast and crowded camp, covered with men,

horses, fires, tents, general officers, staff officers, boats landing men and horses, which latter are flung overboard, and swum ashore. Eleven were drowned to-day.[30]

Similarly, Captain Nigel Kingscote (great-nephew and ADC to Raglan) wrote in a letter to his friend, Staff Surgeon Henry Mapleton:

> No opposition to our landing most fortunately or we should have been in a mess, as, though the first day was fine until about 6 pm, yesterday there was a dreadful serf [sic] and very dangerous for landing horses. I am sorry to say your grey pony was drowned as the brute swam from shore instead of to it.[31]

The first night on land was wet and miserable – 'blowing and raining torrents' remarked Kingscote. But at least the army was on solid land, even if drenched with rain. Meanwhile,

> ... the poor marines and sailors in the men-of-war boats were towing large rafts, with horses, guns, and detachments of artillerymen, amid a heavy swell from the sea, that was now running high – it was as dark as pitch, the horses almost mad with excitement, kicking and plunging. A number of poor fellows found a watery grave, rafts being upset in the heavy surf while attempting to land, the sea dashing with all its majestic force upon the sandy beach, although we could not see it.[32]

Huddled under blankets or coats, with no shelter and little sustenance, some men tried to make fires from the remains of broken rafts. The next day the unloading continued. In all, approximately 63,000 men and 128 guns were landed. The allies had no form of land transport with them, and had to hire (or buy, or seize) wagons and transport horses from the locals. There was never enough transport or logistical support, and this caused continuing problems.

Though miserable, they still looked impressive from a distance, as Polish officer Captain Robert Hodasevich, who served (somewhat unenthusiastically) in the Russian army, recorded:

> On reaching our position on the heights [on 15 September] one of the most beautiful sights that it was ever my lot to behold lay before us. The whole of the allied fleet was lying off the salt lakes to the south of Eupatoria, and at night their forest of masts was illuminated with various-coloured lanterns. Both men and officers were lost in amazement at the sight of such a large number of ships together, especially as many of them had hardly ever seen the sea before. The soldiers said, 'Behold, the infidel has built another holy Moscow on the waves!' (p. 35)

Where were the Russians? The allies did not have much reliable intelligence, and were at the point of landing quite vulnerable, had the Russians decided to attack. But Menshikov did not try to oppose the invasion. Apart from sending a few Cossacks to observe the landing, he kept his army at a distance. Up until now, Menshikov had been quite certain that the allies would not invade the Crimea so late in the year. The Crimean winters could be harsh and the Black Sea very stormy. Invasion in September would surely be folly. When the enemy had appeared on his very doorstep, at Eupatoria, Menshikov suspected this was merely a probe or a distraction. As the allies landed their huge forces at Calamita Bay in the following days, Menshikov believed, not unreasonably, that their goal must be the port of Sebastopol, and he concentrated most of his 33,000 infantry, 3,400 cavalry, 2,600 gunners and 116 guns on the south bank of the River Alma, intending to stop the allies from reaching Sebastopol.

The aristocratic, inflexible Menshikov was much criticized afterwards for failing to oppose the allies' landing. In character, he was confident to the point of arrogance and lacked the capacity for self-reflection. Hodasevich goes so far as to call him 'a very unfit Commander-in-Chief', who took little interest in the condition of his men, allowing the officers to exploit them for personal gain (p. 30). There is no doubt some truth in these criticisms, but it is perhaps also fair to say that he was hampered by the inefficiencies in the Russian military structure, by a poor system for gathering intelligence, and a lack of modern weaponry. For now, however, he was in an advantageous position. The allies were short of crucial supplies and did not know the area well. They were indeed moving their large force south to Sebastopol, though the precise plan of action had not yet been decided.

The morning of 19 September was bright and sunny. The armies assembled and the march south began. The Turkish troops were led by Suleiman Pasha, while the French divisions under St Arnaud were commanded by Generals Canrobert, Bosquet and Forey, and Prince Napoleon (cousin to the French Emperor Napoleon III). Lord Raglan commanded the British army, which included the 1st Division of infantry under the Duke of Cambridge; the Light Division under Sir George Brown; the 2nd Division under Lieutenant-General George de Lacy Evans; the 3rd Division under Major-General Richard England; the 4th Division under Major-General George Cathcart; and the cavalry, commanded by Major-General Lord Lucan. To get to Sebastopol, they had to cross four rivers. The French and Turkish troops moved on the right of the march, next to the coast, while the British were on the inland side, on the exposed left flank. Five regiments of British light cavalry covered the British forces: two ahead, two on the flank, and one in the rear. Quarrelsome cavalry leaders Lord Lucan and Lord Cardigan (commander of the Light Brigade) were both riding with the cavalry.

The troops were supported by the ships, as Russell reported on 19 September:

> The right of the allied forces was covered by the fleet, which moved along with it in magnificent order, darkening the air with innumerable columns of smoke, ready to shell the enemy should they threaten to attack our right, and commanding the land for nearly two miles from the shore. (p. 56)

This was reassuring, even if the British were actually beyond reach of the fleet's protection. And the armies themselves 'presented a splendid appearance':

> The effect of these grand masses of soldiery descending the ridges of the hills rank after rank, with the sun playing over forests of glittering steel, can never be forgotten by those who witnessed it. Onward the torrent of war swept; wave after wave, huge stately billows of armed men, while the rumble of the artillery and tramp of cavalry accompanied their progress. (p. 56)

The beautiful morning turned into a terribly hot day. The march became an ordeal, the men struggling in their heavy uniforms and desperately thirsty, with no fresh water for miles around.

> We had not gone far under that boiling hot sun that shone above us with increasing intensity, [wrote NCO John Fisher] when like sheep after a long journey may be seen our brave men dropping down here and there gasping for thirst [...] Some of the men was punished or threatened for leaving the ranks that same day although choking with thirst.[33]

Some fell out with heat exhaustion. Some were weak from the illnesses of Varna and the voyage and had to be carried off on stretchers. 'It was a painful sight,' wrote Russell, 'a sad contrast to the magnificent appearance of the army in front, to behold litter after litter borne past to the carts, with the poor sufferers who had dropped from illness and fatigue' (p. 56). The parade-ground uniforms – tight, hot tunics and heavy shako caps – added to the difficulties in the late summer heat.

That afternoon, they arrived at the first of the four rivers, the Bulganek. Men and horses were much relieved to get a drink. Some Cossacks were sighted on the other side, and Raglan sent an advance guard of cavalry led by Lord Cardigan to investigate. As the British group advanced, the Russians retreated across a valley to higher ground. Some fire was exchanged, causing some casualties. Then an order came from Raglan to retire. He could see that beyond the Cossacks was a group of some 6,000 Russians, and did not want the cavalry to risk heavy casualties at this early stage of the conflict. Cardigan and Lucan reluctantly withdrew, followed by jeers from the Cossacks. More mocking was heard from the British infantry. Raglan's caution was arguably on this occasion quite sensible, but the incident left the cavalry commanders frustrated and resentful, building up tensions that were to cause further problems later, at Balaklava.

This first skirmish was inconclusive, and the allies knew they would soon have to face the Russians in full force. Menshikov had a simple plan: to try to stop the allies from reaching Sebastopol. He had placed his forces in a strong defensive position a few miles south, at the River Alma. Menshikov believed he could hold the allies there and beat them in three weeks, driving them out of the Crimea in humiliating defeat.

As the allied camp settled down to sleep on the night of 19 September, the two principal commanders had a meeting. There are different accounts of what was agreed. In some accounts, St Arnaud, now very ill, proposed a pincer attack: the French and Turks on the Russians' left (by the sea), the British inland, attacking the Russians' right, turning them around. The aim was to cut off the Russians' supply and reinforcements, and to prevent them from withdrawing. Raglan listened politely and appeared to agree with the French plan. The French 2nd Division under Bosquet would lead; the other allied troops would follow two hours later. The nearby ships would provide covering fire. Another view of the meeting is that the British thought the plan agreed was that the French on the right approaching the undefended sector would advance, climb the (low) heights, and then 'roll-up' the Russian position and as they did so the British would advance against the strong Russian centre.[34] Many of the allied leaders had served in the Napoleonic Wars, 40 years earlier; but for their young troops, this would be their first real experience of warfare, and they looked forward to it with a mixture of excitement and dread.

THE BATTLE OF THE ALMA: 'THAT TERRIBLE HILLSIDE'[35]

The allied armies rested overnight and resumed the march the next morning, 20 September. It was another beautiful day. By about midday, they reached the River Alma. It was a striking piece of landscape which was soon to enter history and mythology as the site of one of the few set-piece battles of the war. Lieutenant-Colonel Calthorpe wrote of the side facing the French:

> The river Alma is a winding stream, and at this time of year of no great depth. Here and there are pools, but generally speaking the water was not more than knee-deep. Its banks are very steep, varying in height from four to 10 feet, and on both sides are either copses or vineyards, and occasionally groves of trees of larger size, of which the common poplar is most frequently met with. On the northern side (our side) of the river, the enemy had cut down and removed all trees and brushwood

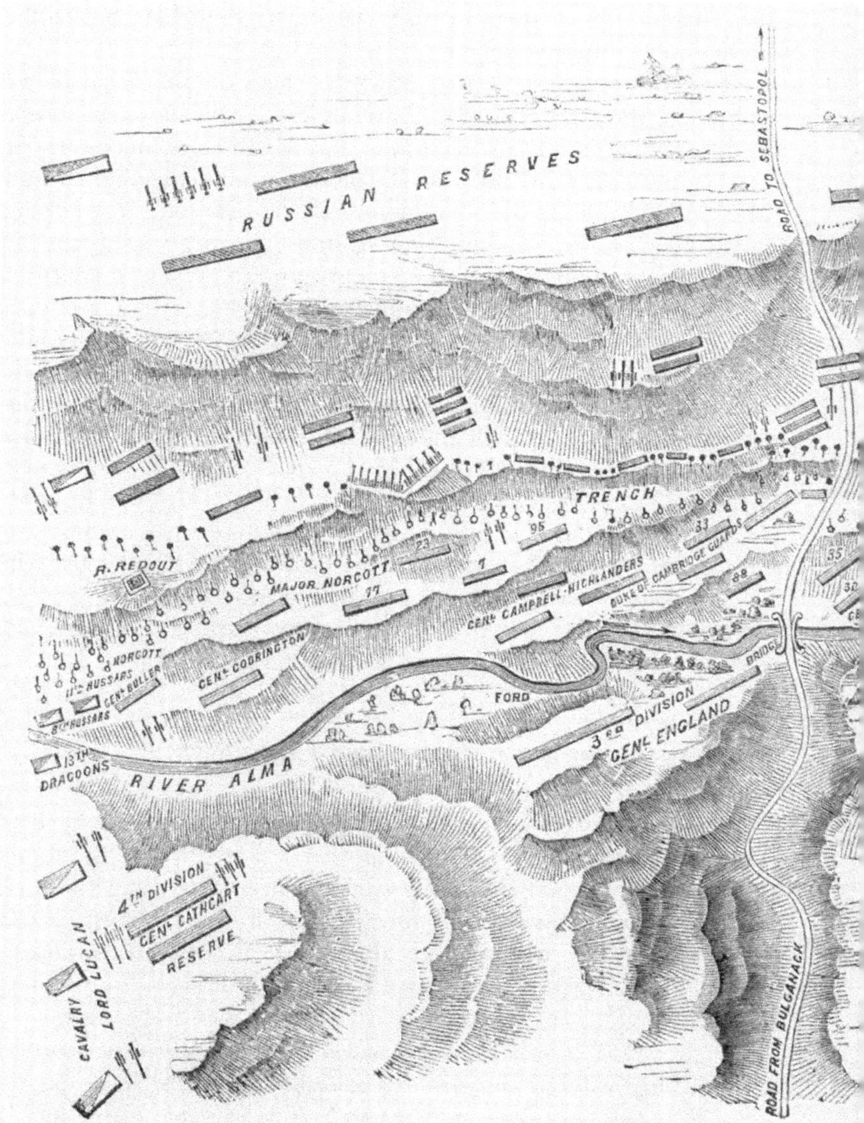

ROAD TO SEBASTOPOL

RUSSIAN RESERVES

TRENCH

R. REDOUT

MAJOR NORCOTT

23

95

7

33

77

GEN. CAMPBELL-HIGHLANDERS

DUKE OF CAMBRIDGE GUARDS

98

35

NORCOTT

11TH HUSSARS

GEN. BULLER

GEN. CODRINGTON

8TH HUSSARS

FORD

BRIDGE

3RD DIVISION GEN. ENGLAND

13TH DRAGOONS

RIVER ALMA

CAVALRY LORD LUCAN

4TH DIVISION

GEN. CATHCART

RESERVE

ROAD FROM BULGANACK

Fig. 1: Plan of the Battle of the Alma, *Illustrated London News*, 28 October 1854

that could in any manner make cover for our men during the attack. There were two villages on that side of the river; one about a mile from the sea (Malamak), opposite the centre of the French army; and the other (Bourlick [Bourliouk]) two miles higher up, and just in front of our right. Both of these villages were small, not exceeding 50 houses each, but still giving admirable cover for the riflemen of the enemy.

On the other (south) side of the river,

… extending from the sea nearly to the village of Bourlick, is a range of heights, at places almost perpendicular, resembling cliffs varying from 300 to 500 feet above the sea. On the top the ground is level, and not unlike what we had been marching over for the last two days; at a distance of half a mile from this edge, and about two miles from the sea, was an unfinished stone tower, probably intended as a telegraph station. Round this the enemy had constructed a low parapet, in which they had placed some field guns: this was again protected by large masses of infantry. Such was the position in front of our allies, and so strong was it by nature, that the Russians had not thought it necessary to strengthen

Fig. 2: Scene in the French Camp after the Battle of the Alma,
Illustrated London News, 14 October 1854

it further than I have stated, except indeed by having large numbers of infantry on the south side of the river, thrown out as skirmishers.[36]

The Russian position facing the British was equally formidable:

The heights I mentioned as being opposite the village of Bourlick from that point recede, running back for some distance, and then returning towards the river a mile higher up, thus forming a vast ravine, something in the shape of an inverted V. The ground in front of the English, on the other side of the river, rose more gradually, forming species of plateaus or terraces as it ascended the ravine. The enemy had taken advantage of these terraces to place their guns of position.[37]

The landscape gave the Russians a superb natural advantage, as Hodasevich remarked:

The position chosen by Prince Menschikoff on the Alma, for the purpose of meeting, and, as he fondly hoped, of defeating the invaders of the Crimea, was a position of great strength: his army was disposed on the heights above the river, the banks of which are very steep and planted with trees on either side, which rendered the passage very difficult. (p. 58)

Menshikov had built two fortified earthworks above the village of Bourliouk, known as the Greater and Lesser Redoubts, and he gave careful thought to the placing of his troops, concentrating many of them on Kourgane Hill. His position was well defended, but he made a fatal error, neglecting to defend the western part, by the sea. There, the very steep, barren cliffs seemed to Menshikov to be inaccessible, so he placed few troops on that side of his position. Nor did he check the area properly; if he had, he would have discovered a narrow path leading up the cliff face. It would be a difficult path for attacking troops, but not impossible.

As a group of Russian spectators from Sebastopol gathered on Telegraph Hill (fortified with champagne) to watch the battle, the allied leaders consulted. The plan had changed somewhat since the previous day. Raglan did not feel the British were strong enough for a flank attack. Rather, the French should advance on the right, then the British would make a frontal attack on Kourgane Hill, which meant, as Royle remarks, that 'the tactics would evolve as the battle progressed', which was not very encouraging.[38] Around 1 pm, the first allied troops were ordered to advance. The French troops led by Bosquet moved ahead first. The British 2nd and Light Divisions were in front, with the 3rd Division behind the 2nd on the right and the 1st Division supporting the Light Division on the left. In reserve were the 4th Division; the cavalry protected the open flank.[39]

Meanwhile, the French were making good progress. Leaving their backpacks by the river, Bosquet's troops, many of them Zouaves with plenty of fighting experience, crossed the river, and found their way easily up the narrow cliff road. Few Russians were in place to oppose them; after a short struggle, these were easily driven back. 'Prince Menschikoff had left this line unguarded, because he regarded it as absolutely impassable even for goats,' reported the *Illustrated London News* afterwards. But 'He did not know the Zouaves.'[40] A Zouave memoir published in 1856 recalled:

> [W]hen the first cannon of battle had resounded, towards one o'clock in the afternoon; the Zouaves of the Bosquet division cross the Alma, in water to the waist, and grapeshot from waist to head; scale the steep cliffs amid avalanches of bullets, then having regained a lofty height which Menschikoff regarded as inaccessible, folded their arms, smiling in pity, before that Russian army, once the terror of Europe, now flying vanquished and eternally humiliated![41]

The Russians were surprised and impressed by the Zouaves' speed and skill. Further inland, other French divisions were moving forwards successfully, putting the Russians under tremendous pressure.

Raglan wanted to wait until the French had made adequate progress before ordering his troops to advance. According to Russell, a message came to Raglan 'that the French had crossed the Alma, but they had not established themselves sufficiently to justify us in an attack'.

> The infantry, therefore, was ordered to lie down, and the army for a short time was quite passive, only that our artillery poured forth an unceasing fire of shell, rockets, and round shot, which ploughed through the Russians, and caused them great loss. They did not waver, however,

and replied to our artillery manfully, their shot falling among our men
as they lay, and carrying off legs and arms at every round. (p. 61)

Amidst this carnage the men kept their nerve. At around 3 pm,
Raglan ordered the infantry to advance. Gowing described how
the survivors pressed on.

We still kept advancing and then lying down again. Our men's feelings
were now wrought up to such a state that it was not an easy matter
to stop them. Up to the river we rushed and got ready for a swim,
pulling off knapsacks and camp kettles. A number of our poor fellows
were drowned, or shot down with grape and canister – which came
amongst us like hail – while attempting to cross. Our men were falling
now very fast. Into the river we dashed, nearly up to our arm-pits, with
our ammunition and rifles on the top of our heads to keep them dry,
scrambled out the best way we could – the banks were very steep and
slippery – and commenced to ascend the hill. (p. 17)

The Russians stuffed straw into the houses and set fire to the
abandoned village of Bourliouk, creating smoke in order to inhibit
the advance of the British 2nd Division, but some of it blew back
and hindered the Russians, too. The village was 'in continuous
blaze for 300 yards' in front of de Lacy's Division, forcing them to
change their formation, and leading to considerable confusion.[42]
The Light Division was drifting to the right, encroaching upon the
2nd Division; other groups of soldiers were starting to overlap.

By now the scene was chaotic, but none the less it was clear that
the Russians were starting to lose the battle, despite the advantage
of their position. The Minsky regiment on the Russian left were
in retreat from the Zouaves. Surprised by the allies' success in
coming so close, so quickly, Menshikov seems to have panicked,
riding about confusedly, trying to direct reinforcements, no longer
in control. According to some eyewitnesses, Raglan maintained a
deliberately calm demeanour, riding well ahead of his troops to a
position on Telegraph Hill where he could see both the advancing
British and the Russians' response.

Despite the heavy Russian fire, the British continued to advance,
but at considerable cost, as de Lacy Evans describes. He led his 2nd
Division around the burning village of Bourliouk,

> [...] to endeavour to force, by that direction, the passage of the river &
> the Bridge. But this was not easily done, for we were completely under
> the Enemy. Every man & every movement exposed to their view, & to a
> continuous shower of every species of Cannon Shot or Missile, directed
> with too accurate aim, such perhaps as few of the most experienced
> soldiers have witnessed.[43]

Similarly, Russell's account in *The Times* described the difficulty
of the advance:

> The British line [...] was struggling through the river and up the heights
> in masses, firm indeed, but mowed down by the murderous fire of
> the batteries, and by grape, round shot, shell, canister, case shot, and
> musketry, from some of the guns of the central battery, and from an
> immense and compact mass of Russian infantry. (pp. 61, 62)

'Sharp, angular, and solid,' wrote Russell, 'the Russians looked as
if they were cut out of the solid rock' (ibid.). Like Russell, many
observers at the time were struck by the sight of the vulnerable
allied bodies doggedly advancing in the face of 'murderous fire'.
Even the Russians' old-fashioned muskets could do horrible damage
to a human body.

Gradually, the British troops were gaining ground from the
Russians around the Great Redoubt. At about 3.30 pm the Guards
Brigade and Highland Brigade (1st Division) went into action.
Meanwhile, things nearly went disastrously wrong for the Light
Division. Russian commander Prince Gorchakov sent one of his
regiments to attack the British on their left flank. As 3,000 Russians
approached, bayonets fixed, someone in the British lines mistook
them for French soldiers. An order went out to hold fire, then to
retire, and soon many of the British troops were heading quickly
down the hill, away from the battle. They believed they were
following instructions, but it was a mistake, and they blundered
into the Guards Brigade who were coming up the hill. Despite this
piece of luck in their favour, the Russian commanders were unable
to seize the initiative. The infantrymen were locked into a hard
struggle. Watching from his vantage point, Raglan ordered two
9-pound artillery pieces to be fired at Russian positions above.
In another turn of luck, an early shot hit a Russian ammunition

wagon. The Russian artillerymen started to fall back; their reserves were attacked and weakened. Russian Commander Prince Gorchakov did not think a counter-attack would succeed. The British pushed forward and secured Kourgane Hill. The French had taken Telegraph Hill. By 4 pm, the Alma was won.

The allied armies were exhilarated by their success, but exhausted, and the commanders decided against pursuing the retreating Russians to consolidate the victory. This decision was much criticized afterwards – had the Russians been followed, and more thoroughly beaten, so it was argued, the conflict might have ended after the Alma. As it turned out, the war would continue, under the most gruelling conditions, for more than a year.

BRITISH CASUALTIES

The battle left more than 5,000 dead and many more wounded. There was some immediate aid at hand, but injured British soldiers who required sustained care were transported 300 miles across the Black Sea, to Scutari, where part of a huge army barracks had been converted into a hospital. The voyage took four days and many of the wounded died along the way.

From 9 October, *The Times* published a series of reports from the hospital at Scutari. Written by *The Times*' correspondent at Constantinople, Thomas Chenery (though often wrongly attributed to Russell), these articles were to have some of the most far-reaching effects of all the newspaper reports from the war. Chenery's first report appeared alongside the first full accounts of the Battle of the Alma. He revealed that the number of men who became sick was far higher than anyone had expected, creating considerable problems of transport and care. The overcrowding on the ships made the health situation worse.[44] 'Numbers arrived sickly and weak [from Varna] on the beach of Kalamita Bay,' wrote Chenery, 'and the dreadful night of the 14th [of September], during which the whole army stood knee deep in mire, beneath a pouring rain, had an immediate effect on many who were comparatively healthy. It was found that 1,500 of the British force were unfit for the hard work which was to be expected every day.' These were sent to Scutari in the hope they would recover and return to service; and many did. But the transport and care of the sick men was 'disastrously mismanaged', and many men died needlessly (p. 82).

Many who made it to the Bosphorus would recover well, but conditions in the hospital were primitive, and soon degenerated, with disastrous effects upon the patients. The doctors and hospital administrators insisted that they were adequately prepared for the expected influx of patients, but this was far from true. A few days later, Chenery wrote more critically. 'It is with feelings of surprise and anger that the public will learn that no sufficient preparations have been made for the proper care of the wounded.' There was a shortage of doctors, dressers and nurses, and not even a sufficient supply of linen for bandages. 'The greatest commiseration prevails for the unhappy inmates of Scutari, and every family is giving sheets and old garments to supply their want. But, why could not this clearly foreseen event have been supplied?'[45] This was to become a frequent question throughout the war. Underlying the problems were an antiquated system of administration, and many years of Treasury reductions to the army medical service's budget.[46]

Chenery was shocked by the poor provisions made for nursing the soldiers:

> At the commencement of this war a plan was invented, and carried out, by which a number of Chelsea pensioners [veterans of previous wars, some very old] were sent out as an ambulance corps to attend on the sick. [... These old men] have been found in practice rather to require nurses themselves than to be able to nurse others. At Gallipoli and Bulgaria they died in numbers, while the whole of them were so weak as to be unable to perform the most ordinary duties.[47]

These 'worn-out and aged cripples' were simply not strong enough to care for 'the sick who lie by hundreds in the wards of a vast hospital, and require unceasing care by night and day'. The wounded soldiers nursed themselves: 'The soldiers attend upon each other, and directly a man is able to walk he is made useful in nursing his less advanced comrades, but the few pensioners are not of the slightest use.' Similarly, convalescent patients were needed to bring the hundreds of new sick and wounded from the transport ships to the hospital.

In the light of Chenery's reports, *The Times* editorial on 12 October made a direct appeal to its middle-class readers:

> Every man of common modesty must feel, not exactly ashamed of himself, but somehow rather smaller than usual, when he reads the strange and terrible news of the war. Here we are sitting by our firesides devouring the morning paper in luxurious solitude [...] It is true we are paying double income-tax [...] but, on the whole, the suffering is sadly vicarious. These poor fellows are going through innumerable hardships [...] [But what] are we doing for the cause we have so much at heart? Is it right that these poor fellows should bear the whole of the burden? [...]
>
> Is it fit that the soldier should suffer everything, and we not at all? Or rather, is it fit that he should suffer anything that it may be in our power to remove? [... If] we only wish to do something, we have no doubt that something may be found to be done [...]
>
> There are no nurses at Scutari; at least, none for the English, though the French are attended by some Sisters of Mercy from a neighbouring convent.

With so few to care for them, patients could not even get enough water to drink. *The Times* had a practical suggestion:

> We now have the opportunity [...] of sending [the soldiers] a few creature comforts. Four or five thousand pounds would do a great deal even among as many men [...].[48]

This appeal had an immediate effect. The next day, several letters appeared in *The Times*, offering financial help. Robert Peel (son of the former Prime Minister) proposed 'the immediate exercise of private benevolence', which he suggested could raise £10,000 in one week. He sent a cheque for £200, hoping that others would do the same, so that comforts could be sent to the troops with all speed. Two other letters on the same page offered donations.[49] And so *The Times*' Crimea Fund was established. It received a lot of support from readers, but it was a mixed blessing. It was perhaps as much self-promotion for the newspaper as actual help for the troops, some of whom complained that Commissariat workers or staff officers kept much for themselves.[50] *The Times* was fulsome in its own praise, considerably overstating how much it contributed to the hospital at Scutari, for example, and using the existence of the fund as a weapon in its attacks upon the government and the army.[51] The newspaper reports from Scutari were powerful and evidently moved many people to take action or to give donations. That said, we need to be cautious not to overestimate the effect of the press on the actual experience of the war. Its tendency to vastly inflate its own impact at the time has coloured historical accounts ever since.

Some of the most damning reports about conditions at Scutari were not published at the time. When British MP Augustus Stafford visited the hospital in early November 1854, he wrote a frank account of what he saw. He was particularly shocked by the state of the earth closets (the 'necessaries'). The original barracks at Scutari had been built for Turkish soldiers who, he explained, had clean toilet habits, preferring to wash rather than use paper. The toilet room was provided with taps, and the waste pipes were quite small. In the summer of 1854, soldiers in the barracks broke off the taps. When the barracks was turned into a hospital, the taps were not repaired; nor was there a flow of water into the toilets. As a result, he writes:

> [...] the pipes soon choked up; and the liquid faeces, the evacuations from those afflicted with diarrhoea filled up the pipes, have floated up over the floor and come into the room where the necessaries are, extend and flow into the ante-room and were more than an inch deep when I arrived there this morning.

The patients could not avoid this horrible waste.

> Men suffering from diarrhoea, who have no slippers and no shoes on, as this filth advances, come less and less near to the [toilets] and nearer and nearer the door, till at last I found them within a yard of the ante-room performing the necessary functions of nature; and in consequence the smell from the place was such that I could find no epithet to describe its horror.[52]

Appalled, Stafford discussed the matter with Dr McGrigor and a senior army officer. He learned that junior doctors had already raised the matter several times. One problem was that the complicated administrative system made it very hard to discover which department had responsibility for the toilets. Dr McGrigor found that each department he approached said that another department was in charge. So nothing was done, and the doctor was very worried about the spread of gangrene and hospital fever in such conditions. Stafford sent his report to John Delane, editor of *The Times*, who did not feel it was suitable to publish, but forwarded it to government war ministers, the Duke of Newcastle and Sidney Herbert, who were already very concerned about the conditions at Scutari, but, due to the cumbersome administrative arrangements, unable to improve them as they would wish.[53]

That said, the published reports were disturbing enough, and had important effects. One response was to become iconic in British history, and remains one of the most valued achievements of the war. Florence Nightingale (1820–1910), then Superintendent of the Hospital for Invalid Gentlewoman, an experienced nurse and administrator, offered her services to the nation. Minister at War Sidney Herbert asked her to lead an official group of nurses, supported by the government, to help the sick and injured troops. By late October she had recruited 38 nurses, and they were on their way to Scutari. This was one of the most far-reaching effects of the Battle of the Alma.

Florence Nightingale already had a lot of experience in nursing and was dedicated to the development of nurse training in Britain. Her experiences at the war gave her a wealth of knowledge and insight which she drew upon for the rest of her life. Against considerable resistance from the hospital doctors, Nightingale worked tirelessly to improve the standards of hygiene, welfare, administration, procurement and rehabilitation of patients.[54] While managing the nurses, working hard on procurement and dealing with political struggles, she also wrote a huge number of letters from Scutari.[55] She crossed the sea from Scutari to the Crimea several times to inspect the medical conditions there. She became very ill with 'Crimean Fever' but kept working at Scutari and was affected by the illness for many years after returning to England. She continued to write through her illness and made a huge impact on the shape of nursing which is still felt today. Right from the beginning, Nightingale was much reported in the press for her work at the war. Much of the newspaper adulation was rather foolish, and annoyed her, but her fame arguably helped to change perceptions about women's capacities for high-level administration, hard work, resourcefulness and thinking, all under the most difficult of circumstances. For the cultural critic Stefanie Markovits, the war promised to regenerate heroic masculinity, but its greatest hero turned out to be a woman.[56]

RUSSIAN CASUALTIES

When they retreated from the Alma on 20 September, the Russians left their thousands of dead and injured behind. Russell estimated that the wounded Russian infantry, when brought in for medical treatment, covered more than an acre. An anonymous medical officer describes his work, looking after the wounded Russians on the battlefield, in a letter to *The Times*:

> No description I could give would realize the horrors of war – the dead, the dying, horses, guns, carriages, *pêle-mêle* – headless trunks, bodies minus arms or legs, mutilation of every sort and kind, – that my blood almost freezes at the recollection. Every available hut was improvised into an operating theatre, and under every disadvantage we performed the most formidable surgical operations.[57]

Under such conditions, with little food or shelter, many of the wounded Russians would not survive. On 23 September Russell noted, 'Alas! That plain is covered with the wounded Russians still. Nearly sixty long hours have they passed in agony on the ground, and now, with but little hope of help or succour more, we must leave them as they lie.' 'Many men died of cholera last night,' he writes:

> My sleep was disturbed by the groans of the dying, and on getting up in the morning, I found that the corpse of a Russian lay close to the tent in which I had been permitted to rest. He was not there when we retired to rest, so that the wretched creature, who had probably been wandering about without food upon the hills ever since the battle, must have crawled down towards our fires and there expired in the attempt to reach them; several men had died close to our tent during the night. (p. 68)

Timothy Gowing described collecting the wounded, 'both friend and foe':

> Ours were at once put on board ship and sent to Scutari; some hundreds of the enemy were collected in a vineyard on the slopes. The dead were buried in large pits — and a very mournful and ghastly sight it was, for many had been literally cut to pieces. It was a difficult matter really to find out what had killed some of them. Here, men were found in positions as if in the act of firing; there, as if they had fallen asleep; and all over the field the dead were lying in every position it was possible for men to assume. Some of those who had met death at the point of the bayonet presented a picture painful to look upon; others were actually smiling. Such was the field of the Alma. (p. 22)

And among these bodies, the field of battle was strewn with the ghastly detritus of war, as Russell recorded on 22 September:

> The quantity of firelocks, of great coats, of bearskin caps, of shakos, of Russian helmets and foragers, of knapsacks (English and Russian), of cross and sling belts, bayonets, cartouch-boxes, cartridges, swords, lying all over the hills, exceeded all computation, and round shot, fragments of shell smeared with blood and hair, grape-shot, Minié balls, and bullets were under the foot and eye at every step. (p. 66)

There is a horror of wrecked and abandoned *things*, scattered among the worse horror of torn and suffering human flesh. Many witnesses comment upon such sights, unsure what to make of the sheer waste and misery all around them. 'Oh, war, war! the *details* of it are horrid,' wrote George Paget.[58]

On 23 September, the French and British moved on from the Alma. They passed hundreds of Russian wounded who were abandoned on the battlefield. British army medic Dr Thompson remained behind to help them, but he died of cholera just a few days later.[59]

THE ALMA IN BRITAIN

Raglan's brief battlefield dispatch arrived in London on 1 October, having travelled to the British Ambassador at Constantinople who sent it to Belgrade, where it was telegraphed to London. His full dispatch, written on 21 September, took much longer to arrive. It travelled by steamer and train, arrived in London on 8 October and was published in *The Times* on 9 October. On that date and for many days afterwards, *The Times* was full of official dispatches; journalists' eyewitness reports; letters from officers, medical staff and some ordinary soldiers; as well as opinionated editorials and commentaries. In the period between the battle itself and the arrival of the reports (20 September to 8 October), *The Times* had only fragments of information, many unverified (and often incorrect), as well as plenty of speculation, not least by its own writers. There was a false rumour that Sebastopol had fallen, and this was reported all over the press as a likely fact for a few days in early October.[60] There were other false stories as well. Generally, however, *The Times* in 1854 was careful to distinguish between what was known to be true and what was rumour or speculation – much more so, in fact, than much war reporting in the twentieth and twenty-first centuries.

This first proper battle of the war was long to be commemorated in both Britain and France. For Russell, Alma was 'a name that will ever be memorable in our history' (p. 68). The girl's name Alma enjoyed a popular revival in the 1850s, and many streets and pubs were named after the event. To this day one can find streets named Alma in London, Luton, Sheffield, Vancouver, Fremantle and many other towns all over Britain and the Commonwealth; and a few Alma Arms survive around Britain. In Paris, streets, hotels and a metro station carry the name Alma, while a statue of a Zouave stands under the famous Pont d'Alma.

The eyewitness narratives of the Alma in *The Times* are powerful, moving and disturbing. Britain was really at war now, after 40 years of relative peace, and people thousands of miles away at home were given a shocking glimpse of its reality, not just in *The Times*, but across many newspapers and journals. The *Illustrated London News* published a special Alma supplement on 14 October, which included a long account of the entire battle (much of which was lifted directly from *The Times*), an article on Russian prisoners of war in Britain, plus illustrations, obituaries and commentary. It published several poems about the Alma in the latter part of October.

The first of these appeared on 14 October, a few days after the first news reports. 'The Heroes of the Alma' by 'C. M.' is subtitled 'For music', and it opens with a call to celebration:

> Ring the joy-bells – chime on chime!
>> England conquers as of yore!
> Ring for Alma's heights sublime,
>> Union Jack and Tricolor![61]

The poem has three stanzas, the first and last of which express joy and triumph, while the middle stanza is more sombre:

> Sound the requiem – deep and clear!
>> England weeps her children slain,
> Mourns with sympathy sincere
>> Heroes lost, but not in vain.

But the mourning does not last long, as the stanza concludes:

> Yet – be the tears of sorrow dried!
>> We owe their babes a glorious debt;
> And grief is vain if it forget
> The claims of those who died.

The poem calls upon the nation to acknowledge 'a glorious debt' to the dead as well as to their descendents. (This sense of obligation did not always translate into actual help for soldiers' families.) This idea was not new, but it came newly into focus after the Battle of the Alma, when detailed accounts of the soldiers' experiences of their first real battle were available not long after the event, and could be read by their families. Many people who could not read had access to newspaper reports, which were read aloud in pubs and other public places all over the country.

A week later, the *Illustrated London News* published 'Alma' by Mrs T. K. Hervey, printing it on the same page as the official list of killed and wounded in the battle. Hervey's poem begins to speak, somewhat paradoxically, by claiming to be speechless:

> O for a voice to utter what the startled lands proclaim;
> A voice to reach to heaven like the leaping of a flame!
> Like those who breathe the mountain's breath, throned on its starry peak,
> Our lifted souls stand thrilled and mute – we gasp, but cannot speak.[62]
> (stanza 1)

The poem goes on to imagine civilians going about their daily lives – 'this world's dull work' – in a state of high excitement, 'with pulses at full beat'. People are so moved by the war news that they do not notice even the most beautiful elements of their surroundings; not 'how pale the moon', nor 'how red the sun departs'. All thoughts are with 'this great victory' which is 'knocking at our hearts'. In the first stanza, the 'startled lands' of the Crimea 'proclaim' the allied victory; by stanza three, landscape everywhere seems to speak of the event:

> Where'er a hill looks up to heaven, where'er a river runs,
> There Nature's proud memorial speaks to England of her sons.

Like 'C. M.', Hervey was conscious of knowing considerable detail about the war from the press; of witnessing it from a great distance. Civilians found this troubling as well as interesting. Hervey imagines a strong physical reaction among the nation's readers, as they take in the new stories from the war:

> O nobly dared – thrice nobly done! We have no word for more
> Who watch from far the tempest's rack, safe housed upon the shore;
> The Alma waters blind us as they swim before our sight,
> And our reeling brain grows dizzy as we picture Alma's height. (stanza 4)

And as they think about the battle, people wonder who has survived, who is dead ('Whose sword is yet within his grasp? – whose face is to the ground?', stanza 10). This news hasn't yet arrived. The population at home has both too much information and too little. Hervey struggles to deal with this paradox, her poem of celebration constantly threatening to fall silent (despite its verbose style):

O, empty breath, and barren speech – how weak ye sound, and vain!
What greetings shall await them who return to us again?
Our straining eyes shall know them not, too dazzled when they come,
And our voice shall sound no welcome, for the joy that strikes us dumb!
    (stanza 11)

The problem of knowing a lot about the battle and very little about individuals who served was keenly felt by the families of soldiers. A poem in the *Illustrated London News* on 28 October by popular novelist Dinah Mulock Craik dramatizes precisely this problem. 'By the Alma River' is spoken by the wife of a soldier, as she puts her young son to bed.[63]

Willie, fold your little hands;
Let it drop, that 'soldier' toy:
Look where father's picture stands, –
Father, who here kissed his boy
Not two months since, – father kind,
Who this night may – Never mind
Mother's sob, my Willie dear,
Call aloud that He may hear
Who is God of battles, say,
'O, keep father safe this day
By the Alma river.'

The poem is set when news of the battle has first reached England (9 October). The town's bells ring 'for victory'. But there are 'no knells', she reflects, 'For the many swept away, – / Hundreds – thousands!' She is waiting anxiously for further news, wondering

Who they were that fought and *fell*
By the Alma river.

As she puts the child to bed, she tries to imagine what the father might be doing:

Come, we'll lay us down, my child,
Poor the bed is, poor and hard;

Yet thy father, far exiled,
Sleeps upon the open sward,
Dreaming of us two at home:

She admits that she does not care who wins the war: 'Any flag i' the wind may roll / On thy heights, Sebastopol'. She hopes desperately that the next day will bring 'news of joy' that her husband has survived. The poem concludes in quiet resignation:

[...] – Child, say thy prayer
Once again; a different one:
Say, 'O God, Thy will be done
By the Alma river.'

Craik's poem is both sentimental and poignant, imagining something of the profound anxieties experienced by the families of serving soldiers. This was felt across classes, as Fanny Duberly mused in her journal on 19 September: 'I wonder if, among the annals of a war, the sickening anxieties of mother, wife, and sister ever find a place. Let us hope the angel of compassion makes record of their tears.'

Queen Victoria and Prince Albert shared this concern for soldiers' families and in October 1854 the Royal Patriotic Fund was established with Prince Albert as president. It coordinated the raising and distribution of funds for the widows and orphans of men killed in the war. By summer 1855, more than £1,000,000 had been raised. In May 1855, an auction of art and other items was held to raise money for the fund. Several members of the royal family contributed paintings or drawings.[64]

While the families waited and wondered after the Alma, government ministers and army commanders exchanged urgent messages about what to do next. Meanwhile, the army was on the move, southwards, towards Sebastopol. And towards winter, 'Generals January and February', Russia's most powerful defenders.

2

THE SIEGE ESTABLISHED AND THE BATTLE OF BALAKLAVA

Sebastopol, whose name is interpreted as 'venerable city', 'imperial city' or 'city of glory', was the main port for Russia's Black Sea fleet. In 1854 it was a garrison town, with many elegant classical buildings constructed in the 1830s.[1] The site of Sebastopol had a long history, from the ancient Greek settlement of Chersonese, through to the Byzantine and Ottoman empires. The city of Sebastopol was founded in June 1783,[2] when Catherine the Great seized the Crimea from Turkey. In 1804 it was chosen as the main naval base for the Russian Black Sea Fleet. Development went on through the early nineteenth century. Dissatisfied with the first naval works, the Russians employed a British engineer named Upton who undertook a massive building project. *The Times* called him the 'Fortifier of Sebastopol'. 'He procured immense iron works at Birmingham and by dint of science, labour, and expense, he made [Sebastopol] what it is.'[3]

After the Alma, the allied armies remained for two days as the wounded were collected and embarked on the ships and the dead were buried. Action was also paralysed as the French commander St Arnaud was by now terribly ill. The armies marched south on 23 September, towards Sebastopol. They had little reliable information about the Russians' strength there, and needed to settle on a plan. On 24 September, the leaders met to discuss their options. St Arnaud was deteriorating and died aboard ship. General Canrobert took over the French command.

The march south was arduous and a risky operation, as Captain Nolan noted in his journal:

> Our army drawn out to a narrow thread by the difficulties and impediments in the road could have been cut through by a bold & resolute Enemy. Our men were exhausted, our artillery horses actually dropping down & dying on the roadside [...].[4]

There was very little water, and some men collapsed on the march from sickness and thirst.

Some of Raglan's advisers, such as Admiral Lyons and Generals Airey and Cathcart, felt the allies should seize the moment and attack Sebastopol immediately, before the Russians could organize their defences. Others, such as the chief engineer Burgoyne, urged a more cautious approach. So did the French commanders. Raglan himself preferred an immediate attack, but caution prevailed. Some commentators argued afterwards that, had the allies attacked Sebastopol immediately, they would have taken it quite easily. Some Russian sources from inside Sebastopol later confirmed this view. The allies made a flank march around the city to approach it from the south-east.

A classic siege was now mounted, with parallel trenches and batteries painstakingly dug, slowly creeping forward towards the town. When the trenches had been dug, a heavy bombardment would take place before any assault was made on the city. It took several days to unload and set up the heavy guns of the siege artillery. The Russians made good use of this time to fortify Sebastopol with a complex of defensive earthworks, under the direction of engineer Eduard Totleben, described by Russell as 'the illustrious defender of Sebastopol'.[5]

From the direction of the sea, Sebastopol was strongly defended. But it was vulnerable from the land. Eight bastions had been planned in the 1830s, but these were not complete by the time the war began. In late September, the garrison in Sebastopol held only 16,000 men, too few to defend the four-mile front on the southern side of the city. A further 28,000 reinforcements arrived in early October. On the advice of Totleben, Menshikov took the bold step

Fig. 3: Roger Fenton, View of the Lines of Balaklava from Guard's Hill, 1855

of sinking several of the Russian ships in the mouth of Sebastopol harbour, to keep the allied fleets out. This freed up many Russian sailors to contribute to the city's defence, which they did very ably.

Totleben brought the ships' guns into the land defences and constructed formidable and highly effective earthworks which were rebuilt and reshaped in response to the allies' actions. He was one of the first military thinkers to treat a fortress 'not as a walled town, but as an entrenched position, closely linked with the offensive and defensive capacities of an army and as equally susceptible to tactical changes'.[6] Meanwhile, Menshikov assembled a large army outside the city, on the high ground to the east, which posed a serious threat to the allied flank.

On 26 September, Raglan arrived at Kadikoi, a village near Balaklava harbour, which was set on a narrow inlet, on the southern coast of the Crimea. Balaklava was chosen as the British base. At this stage it was hoped – assumed – that Sebastopol would fall quite soon, and Balaklava looked suitable for the purpose of

Fig. 4: Roger Fenton, The Ordnance Wharf at Balaklava, March 1855

supplying the British forces, as *The Times*' editorial commented approvingly on 6 October:

> Balaklava is a harbour on the south coast of the Crimea, situated seven miles in a direct line from Sebastopol, and 11 miles to the east of Cape Chersonese. [... The mouth of the harbour is] only 30 yards in width, but it will contain 12 sail of the line. The site is one of the most beautiful in the East and it derives its name from the 'Belle Chiave' of the Genoese, who founded the little town at the bottom of the haven, and built the fort on the adjoining cliff. The port is formed by a deep inlet [...] in the rocks, with water sufficient to float the largest ships in perfect security; it is completely protected from every wind, and may be regarded as a dock for all the purposes of disembarcation.[7]

In fact, Balaklava's 'romantic and strange-looking little harbour' proved hardly adequate for the long siege.[8] It had one steep

Fig. 5: James Robertson, Harbour of Balaklava, 1855–6

unmetalled road to the plain which soon became slippery in the winter mud and snow, making the transport of supplies for the troops immensely slow and difficult. It was to be remembered as a place of bitter deprivation and suffering for thousands of British troops, not to mention their horses and pack animals, many of whom died during that harsh winter. But for now, in the late summer sunlight, it looked both beautiful and promising. It was taken with very little resistance. The French settled at Kamiesch Bay, nearer to Sebastopol and their own camps, which proved a better base.

Establishing the siege was a daunting task, and some wondered if it could succeed, as Brigadier-General Richard Airey wrote in a letter:

We have now been here before Sevastopol 12 days – We have made little advance or progress – each day adds to our difficulties and the nearer we approach, the more insurmountable do they appear – The people at home are much in error, if they imagine that because our landing and Battle of Alma have been successful that we are much nearer a successful result, in our Entry into Sevastopol –

Our inability to prevent the Enemy from communicating exteriorly from the North, protected by Fort Constantine gives them every facility to strengthen themselves by reinforcements & the heavy armament of their New Batteries – every day they have new guns in position.[9]

The shortage of troops meant that the town was never completely invested. The allied troops laboured hard, digging trenches and bringing their weapons in place. Russell observed British sailors hard at work dragging ships' guns and howitzers up the hilly roads early in October (p. 89). But as Sebastopol could not be fully surrounded and was open to the north, as Airey pointed out (above), the Russians were able to take in material to strengthen their defences and to move troops in and non-combatants out. With the harbour blocked by the sunken ships, a dedicated population, and their heavy weapons in place, the Russians were well positioned to defend their city and they had their fleet's store of ammunition and reserve cannon close at hand.

Meanwhile, with the huge influx of troops, the continuing sickness and the poor transport, Balaklava soon degenerated into 'a filthy, revolting state', as Russell wrote on 5 October. 'Lord Raglan has ordered it to be cleansed, but there is no one to obey the order, and no one attends to it' (p. 92).

While the Russians constructed their defensive earthworks, the allies dug trench systems outside Sebastopol. As Colin Robins explains, the trenches began parallel to the enemy and were dug methodically closer and closer, with batteries placed appropriately.[10]

On 10 October, Russell described some French works:

Towards sunset, four battalions, numbering 2,400 men, marched to the front on our left, and at nine o'clock they commenced work. Before daybreak they had finished a ditch, parapet and banquette, 1200 metres long, at a distance of 900 metres from the enemy's line; and so little did the Russians suspect the operation, that they never fired a gun to disturb them. Each man worked and kept guard as one of the covering parties in turn till daybreak, and by that time every man had finished his half metre of work, so that the 1200 metres was completed. (p. 95)

The British were also busy, as Captain William Radcliffe writes:

> The working parties generally number 500 men on each attack. [The right and left attack] are guarded by an arm'd covering party more than double their number to prevent the enemy making Sortie to destroy the works.

The men worked long hours:

> This makes the duty very hard for all of us as we are seldom off duty, 12 hours out of 36 but all work most cheerfully, well knowing the sooner we open our Fire the sooner 'twill be over & it is most astonishing what can be done in one night. I came off duty this morning at 4 a.m. after 24 hours guard in the trenches. I'll endeavour to give you a short account of that 24 hours. We marched from Camp (got our tents 3 days ago) before daylight, but did not get to the works soon enough for we were seen from the Batteries, and they showered Shot & Shell at us [...] When we got under the Breastwork that had been thrown up in the night we were pretty well under cover, but were obliged to lie down all the time for this of course was the target for the Enemy's Artillery day & night & the trench was only half made.

They had an ingenious system for protecting themselves:

> However a few men were placed on the look out their head a few inches above the work, to give notice when they fired, by watching the smoke from their Guns by day & the flash by night & calling out 'Shot' when all in the Trenches lie down & get under cover of the breastwork till it has pass'd & then resume their work [...] Neither Officer or men are allowed to go to sleep for a minute, all sit up or lie with their *Arms* within *hands* ready in a moment to repel an attack.[11]

But the hard ground was difficult to dig, as Airey explained:

> We cannot entrench, the ground being a mere thin coating of earth 3 or 4 inches, & sometimes bare, on rock. – Our only means is filling gabions from the rear, and all this under a tremendous fire, that our men hardly like facing, nor is it fair to place them under – our position is terribly extensive, and our forces weakened every day by cholera [...].[12]

When they came off duty, the British troops often did not have enough food, and for about two weeks they had no tents, either. The weather was turning wintry. 'The cold for the last two nights has been intense,' wrote Russell on 10 October, 'the wind being bitterly sharp and high, and blowing freshly from the north. It has brought with it colds, fevers, ague; it pierces one's bones even in the warmest tents, and it has produced an increase to our large list of sick' (p. 96). By late October, the British army could muster only 16,000 fit men.

THE FIRST BOMBARDMENT

After all this preparation, the bombardment of Sebastopol finally began on 17 October. The day opened with the Russians firing 'furiously' on all the allied batteries at 6 am. The allied barrage began at 6.30 am. 'The cannonade on both sides was most violent for nearly two hours,' wrote Russell:

> Our left attack consisted of four batteries and 36 guns; our right attack, of 20 guns, in battery. There were also two Lancaster batteries and a four-gun battery of 68-pounders on our right. The French had about 46 guns. (p. 96)

A 'fearful rain of shot and shell,' noted Fanny Duberly, 'which poured incessantly on the forts and batteries of Sebastopol.'[13]

At 10.30 am, the French suffered a direct hit to their main ammunition magazine, and soon stopped firing. The British continued with their heavy guns, eventually breaking down the defences of the fortification known as the Redan, to the point that it was weak enough to assault. But the French were not ready to attack and Raglan felt the British could not take it alone. No one had expected that such an assault would be possible, so no plans had been made. The generals were too far apart in the field to meet and make a new decision. As so often happened, communication links were weak and opportunities missed. The Russians, again much relieved, rebuilt the defences of the Redan overnight, directed by Totleben.

One problem throughout the war was that Raglan had been directed by the government to cooperate as fully as possible with the French. He diligently tried to follow this instruction, but different national aims, St Arnaud's illness, the distance between the allies, weak communication links and other practical problems caused some poor decisions to be made in an attempt to put allied harmony above military requirements.

Meanwhile, as the first bombardment raged, the allied fleets attempted the impossible task of attacking the sea forts of Sebastopol. With the harbour blocked, they could not get very close. As Russell noted earlier (3 October), 'We have already found by experience that heavy as our ships' guns are, the Russians, by giving their heavy metal great elevation, are able to throw further from their batteries than we can from our decks' (p. 90). Indeed, the allies found they could not do much harm to the Russians or their forts, but they received many hits from Russian shells. By the end of the day, all the British ships had suffered some damage, with *Britannia* hit some 40 times and *Agamemnon* more than 200. Many sailors were killed or injured. It was a courageous effort, to little effect.

The first bombardment continued for several days, but was a failure. The allied troops were disappointed. 'Would that we had been permitted to go strait [sic] at the Town, the day after we arrived here,' wrote Major George Mundy (33rd Regiment). 'I feel convinced that we should have been able to force our way right into the Town, with very little assistance as the Enemy were then panic stricken & there were then but very poor fortifications on this side.' Now, it was too late: 'we have been delaying here so long that we have permitted them to erect the most formidable entrenchments which our Guns seem to have but very little effect upon'.[14] This was a common view. Back in Britain, people were becoming worried about the course of the war. The failure of the bombardment deepened the sense of dissatisfaction and unease.

Under pressure from all sides, Raglan was increasingly worried about the security of Balaklava. He deployed the Cavalry Division of 1,500 men plus 1,200 marines and the 93rd Regiment in an attempt to protect the British base and its lines of communication to Sebastopol. Raglan had good reason to worry. On 7 October, large numbers of Russian troops moved across the Chernaya river and on to the Balaklava Plain. As the days passed, the Russian threat got stronger. Menshikov occupied a village in the Chernaya

Valley on 13 October, and a further 25,000 Russians under General Liprandi arrived close by on 23 October. The next day, a warning came from a spy that the Russians would attack on 25 October. After several false alarms in recent days which had led to overworked and tired men deploying at night, Raglan decided not to react. But this time the threat was real.

THE BATTLE OF BALAKLAVA

Friday, 25 October 1854. It was an eventful day. It started at 5.00 am when the Russians under Liprandi fired upon a redoubt on Canrobert's Hill. This was one of several redoubts manned by Turkish troops, using borrowed British cannon. The 500 Turkish troops at no. 1 redoubt held their ground bravely without support for more than two hours under heavy bombardment, eventually being driven out by Russians with bayonets. The Turkish troops in other redoubts followed, leaving the British cannon behind, though most of the solitary British gunners looking after each gun 'spiked' his cannon before he left. This was the first of four military actions that day.

Raglan was up early and watched the attacks from a high position on the Sapoune Heights. Having observed the Turks' struggles in the redoubts and the loss of the guns, Raglan ordered the 1st and 4th Divisions to move from their position outside Sebastopol to help defend Balaklava. This took a long time, as Massie notes, because the 4th had just come in from a night in the trenches, and their commander Cathcart was reluctant to put them into action again (p. 79). The delay gave the Russians an opening to attack. Frustrated by the delays, and expecting a full-scale attack, Raglan moved the cavalry division away from their position in front of Balaklava, intending to use them later.

Now the only troops defending Balaklava were Colin Campbell's 93rd Regiment, plus some Turkish troops, located on a low hill in front of Kadikoi. The Russian cavalry seized the moment, advancing 'in great strength & with great boldness', as one eyewitness recalled.[15] As the Russian cavalry came over the hill, writes Russell, 'they perceive the Highlanders drawn up at the distance of some half mile, calmly waiting their approach' (p. 109).

Campbell's men had moved away to avoid artillery fire, but when the Russian cavalry charge began, they moved back to the low hill and started firing. 'The Russians [...] drew breath for a moment,' writes Russell,

> [...] then in one grand line dashed at the Highlanders. The ground flies beneath the horses' feet; gathering speed at every stride, they dash on towards that *thin red streak tipped with a line of steel* [...] As the Russians come within six hundred yards, down goes that line of steel in front, and out rings a rolling volley of Minié musketry. (p. 110)[16]

Despite the firing, the charge continued:

> The distance is too great; the Russians are not checked, but still sweep onwards through the smoke, with the whole force of horse and man [...] With breathless suspense everyone awaits the bursting of the wave upon the line of Gaelic rock; but ere they come within a hundred and fifty yards, another deadly volley flashes from the levelled rifle, and carries death and terror into the Russians. They wheel about, open files right and left, and fly back faster than they came.

The Russians retreated, but the action was not over. Most of their cavalry now began to move from the North Valley to the South Valley, across the Causeway Heights. Meanwhile, the British Heavy Brigade was on its way to support the 93rd, which took it across the path of the approaching Russians. The Russians were observed, wrote Russell, 'at an easy gallop, towards the brow of the hill. A forest of lances glistened in their rear' (p. 110). The British trumpets gave warning. A crowd gathered to watch from the heights. The British cavalry wheeled left. The Russians attempted to envelope the British. Brigadier-General Scarlett led his small Heavy Brigade right into the centre of the Russian cavalry.

'As lightening flashes through a cloud,' wrote Russell, 'the Greys and Enniskilleners pierced through the dark masses of Russians.' It was a desperate fight at close hand. 'By sheer steel and sheer courage', the British prevailed. Within five minutes, according to Russell, the Heavy Brigade had defeated a force twice its size (p. 111). There were few casualties on either side, but it made a great impression as a spectacle. Nigel Kingscote, watching with Lord

Raglan, described it as 'the most exciting thing I ever saw or shall see again'. The men come to close blows 'beautifully'; they do their work well, and look 'beautiful'.[17] The term 'beautiful' turns up in many of the eyewitness accounts of the war, used to describe moments of high skill, of technological success, or of extreme brutality. In this case, it is the tremendous courage at close quarters, and perhaps the use of old technologies (horses and swords) which observers find so moving. The 'stars in heaven / Paled, and the glory grew', wrote Tennyson many years later.[18]

Senior officer Lord George Paget remembered:

> The dense masses of Russian cavalry, animated and encouraged doubtless by the successes of the morning [...] — advancing at a rapid pace over ground the most favourable, and appearing as if they must *annihilate* and swallow up all before them; on the other hand, the handful of red coats, *floundering* in the vineyard, on their way to meet them.
>
> The clatter of the swords against the helmets, the trampling of the horses, the shouts! – in short, the din of battle [...] still rings in one's ears! One body must give way. The heaving mass must be borne one way or the other. Alas, one has but faint hopes! For how can such a handful resist, much less make head through, such a legion? Their huge flanks lap round that handful, and almost hide them from our view. They are surrounded and must be annihilated! One can hardly breathe! Our second line (half a handful) makes a dash at them! One pants for breath! — one general shout bursts from us all! It is over! They give way! The heaving mass rolls to the left! They fly! Never shall I forget that moment.[19]

These accounts of the Heavy Brigade are powerful, and the event was strongly registered by those present. But it was immediately eclipsed by the final action of the day: the charge of the Light Brigade. This disaster was to go down in history as one of the most memorable events of the war. Yet it had very little military significance. Its most potent meanings were cultural, and it also had curious political implications, as I will discuss shortly.

THE CHARGE OF THE LIGHT BRIGADE

While the Heavy Brigade engaged with the Russians, the Light Brigade was waiting close by. Earlier in the day there had been some confusion between Lucan and Cardigan about Raglan's orders, which were not very clear. (The two men were brothers-in-law who thoroughly disliked one another; Cardigan often ignored Lucan's orders.) Now, Raglan could see the Russians were unsettled by the events of the day and had left the South Valley. This was a good time to take action. The infantry from Sebastopol were not in position yet, so Raglan decided to make use of the cavalry. He sent an order to Lord Lucan, instructing him to advance. Again the order was misunderstood, and the cavalry did not move.

Annoyed at Lucan's inaction, Raglan sent another order, which would launch the fateful charge. He regarded the matter as urgent, and chose as his messenger Captain Nolan, a cavalry expert and excellent horseman who despised Lucan. Nolan rode at high speed down the sheer escarpment and delivered the written order to Lucan:

> Lord Raglan wishes the cavalry to advance rapidly to the front – follow the enemy and try to prevent the enemy carrying away the guns – Troop Horse Artillery may accompany – French cavalry is on yr. left – Immediate.[20]

The guns were British weapons, lost when the Russians had attacked the Turkish redoubts earlier in the day. But from his position below, Lucan could not see them. 'When Lord Lucan received the order from Captain Nolan,' wrote Russell in *The Times*, 'he asked [...] "Where are we to advance to?" Captain Nolan pointed with his finger to the line of Russians, and said, "There are the enemy, and there are guns, sir, before them; it is your duty to take them", or words to that effect, according to the statements made since his death.' Here, too, there are conflicting accounts of what took place, but the evidence suggests that Nolan had pointed in the wrong direction.[21]

Lucan reluctantly passed the order to Lord Cardigan. 'The noble earl,' writes Russell, 'did not shrink', and he led the cavalry in what he believed to be the direction of the order, towards a Cossack horse artillery battery of eight 'half-pood' guns, facing down the valley.[22]

The historian Alan Palmer writes that 'Cardigan, resplendent in his blue and cherry-coloured uniform with gold trimmings across the chest and shoulder, took up his proper place ten yards ahead of the brigade, and ordered 673 men and horses to advance' (pp. 129–30). They had to cover a distance of about a mile and a quarter.[23]

More than 600 set off; fewer than 200 could be mustered at the end of the day. 'You have lost the Light Brigade!' said Raglan to Lucan that afternoon. In fact, the final death toll was not as high as was feared, and the major loss was of horses. Historian Mark Adkin calculates a total of nearly 300 soldiers (45 per cent) killed, wounded or taken prisoner. Of these, around 110 died in the charge or later – a surprisingly low figure under the circumstances, though this was not known at the time. Early reports suggested that 300 to 400 were dead. The wounded men and horses had a difficult night: it was bitterly cold and there was a shortage of food, shelter and medical care. Some of the men died later from wounds or disease. Many of the horses were shot or died from cold, starvation or exhaustion.[24]

What went wrong? Was Raglan's order ambiguous, or was it misunderstood? For Colin Robins, the order itself was as foolish as any interpretation.[25] Was the error caused by topography? Precisely who said what and what it meant has never been fully established. And what the charge itself meant was a matter of dispute, both at the time and since. Were the cavalry commanders heroes or idiots? Did the charge advance the British cause or hinder it? Who, if anyone, was to blame? The charge raised questions of knowledge and interpretation that were to trouble both the literature and the politics of the 1850s.

REPRESENTING THE CHARGE

The first reports appeared in *The Times* some three weeks later, on 13 and 14 November 1854. All the newspapers were soon full of eyewitness accounts, official dispatches, letters, analyses and debates. The charge was celebrated and lamented in poetry, paintings, lithographs and cartoons. By early 1855, the story of the Light Brigade had been absorbed into middle-class entertainment: you could visit a diorama of the charge at the Royal Gallery of

Illustration, sing 'On to the Charge', and dance the Cardigan Galop. (All of these entertainments are advertised in *The Times* in January and February 1855.) Some of the representations of Balaklava were by witnesses or participants in the action. Others were produced far away, in England, by people who had seen nothing of the event. We might expect the most powerful and lasting works to be the eyewitness reports. Certainly Russell's reports in *The Times* were gripping and had far-reaching effects. But the work which has persisted longest in cultural memory was not eyewitness journalism, but poetry; written not at Balaklava, but on the Isle of Wight, by a poet who had never seen a battle.

Poet Laureate Alfred Tennyson was fascinated by the war. From his home at Faringford on the Isle of Wight, he could hear the sound of cannon practice across the water at Portsmouth and see the troop ships departing for the front. Tennyson followed the progress of the war closely in *The Times* and was particularly moved by the story of the Light Brigade. A few weeks later, he published one of his most memorable poems.

> Half a league, half a league,
>   Half a league onward,
> All in the valley of Death
> Rode the six hundred.
> 'Forward, the Light Brigade!
> Charge for the guns!' he said:
> Into the valley of Death
> Rode the six hundred.
>
> [...]
>
> Cannon to right of them,
> Cannon to left of them,
> Cannon in front of them
>   Volleyed and thundered;
> Stormed at with shot and shell,
> Boldly they rode and well,
> Into the jaws of Death,
> Into the mouth of Hell
>   Rode the six hundred. (stanzas 1 and 3)[26]

Hallam Tennyson later remembered his father sitting down to write about the charge immediately after reading Russell's electrifying prose, but in fact there was a gap of about two and a half weeks. The poem appeared in the *Examiner*, a weekly newspaper, on 9 December 1854, under the initials 'A.T.'. Astute readers recognized the author; the poet Sydney Dobell wrote to Tennyson that 'no man living but yourself could have written the first verse and the "cannon" verse'. For John Forster, editor of the *Examiner*, Tennyson was the only poet who could do justice to the war, for only he could match the 'pitch' of the soldiers' actions in writing.

'The Charge of the Light Brigade' was an immediate success in Britain. In August 1855, an army chaplain requested that the poem be printed on single sheets and distributed to the troops at the Crimea. 'It is the greatest favourite of the soldiers, half are singing it and all want to have it in black and white.'[27] Tennyson was delighted and quickly arranged for a thousand copies to be sent to the British troops outside Sebastopol; a further thousand followed later. Soldiers who had witnessed the charge, and were still suffering the privations of trench warfare, were it seems moved by a poem written far from the action – a work based not on experience, but on articles in the newspaper. Why is this important? The popularity of Tennyson's 'Charge' tells us something about the power of representation in wartime. At its best, poetry can speak of, and appeal to, the *fantasy* investment in war.

In military terms, the Light Brigade was widely thought to have been destroyed for no good reason and yet afterwards, throughout the war, the Russian cavalry dared not confront British horsemen. Commentators were struck by the disparity between the deed and the outcome: 'Never did cavalry show more daring to less purpose'; 'Causeless as the sacrifice was, it was most glorious'; 'Never was exploit more useless, and never more brilliant'. It seemed to be completely pointless, and many people regarded the event as emblematic of the incompetence of the army leadership. Yet, at the same time, the charge was seen as a unique act of martyrdom – what *The Times* called 'a splendid self-sacrifice' – played out in front of a large audience.

> Two great armies, composed of four nations, saw from the slopes of a vast amphitheatre seven hundred British cavalry proceed at a rapid

pace, and in perfect order, to certain destruction. Such a spectacle was never seen before, and we trust will never be repeated [...]

It is difficult not to regard such a disaster in a light of its own, and to separate it from the general sequence of affairs. Causeless and fruitless, it stands by itself, as a grand heroic deed [...].[28]

Like many commentators of the day, *The Times* was fascinated by the charge as a spectacle – an event which, it remarks extravagantly, took place 'under the eyes of the whole world'. Similarly, the *Morning Chronicle* asks breathlessly 'whether the history of the world affords a similar instance of daring bravery'.[29] 'All the world wondered,' writes Tennyson:

> Flashed all their sabres bare,
> Flashed as they turned in air
> Sabring the gunners there,
> Charging an army, while
>   All the world wondered (stanza 4)

Why was the event so astonishing to contemporaries? Partly because of the physical courage displayed by the men who rode, in strict formation and with perfect discipline, into the mouths of the Russian guns. And partly because the cavalry itself was a remarkable spectacle. Not only did the men have splendid, colourful uniforms, but the cavalry was still perceived as an elite aristocratic institution. The commander of the cavalry, Lord Lucan, Earl of Bingham, had bought his command for £25,000. Lord Cardigan, the commander of the Light Brigade, was also an earl; his private yacht was moored in the Bay of Balaklava. More generally, Lord Raglan and many other high-ranking officers were of noble birth or had close links with the aristocracy. Both the newspaper reports and Tennyson's poem are acutely conscious of the significance of class in the charge of the Light Brigade. And both are shaped by middle-class hostility towards the aristocracy, though neither takes a simple view of the matter.

THE ARISTOCRACY AND THE MIDDLE CLASS

What underlies these representations of the aristocracy in 1854? According to David Cannadine, after a flourishing period between 1780 and the 1820s, the aristocracy's power was much diminished and under further attack in the mid-nineteenth century, following the Reform Act of 1832. Nonetheless, in the 1850s, they were still a force to be reckoned with in politics, and they faced a lot of pressure from the increasingly powerful middle class.[30] War was the aristocracy's oldest profession, and by 1854 the army was regarded as the last bastion of aristocratic power, though by now very many officers were not in fact aristocrats.[31]

Two opposing views emerged during this period. On the one hand, the war was regarded as an opportunity for the aristocracy to recover some of its lost prestige. Many people felt that middle-class commercialism had begun to dominate all aspects of British life. Success in the war might reintroduce values associated with the aristocracy, such as heroism, selflessness, sacrifice, tradition, devotion to an ideal. On the other hand, those who favoured reform were frustrated that the army was still run according to traditional principles. These were not efficient in a modern war. The army leadership was regarded (not always fairly) as notorious for its bungling. At the very least, the men needed adequate food, shelter and medical care if they were to be fit for battle, but the aristocratic leaders were seen as hopelessly incompetent at these practical aspects of the war. As *Punch* remarked sharply, war involved 'a good deal of sheer *business*'. In order to fight, the army needed to be as well organized as a successful manufacturing industry or railway company.[32] To this way of thinking, the army should be modernized along industrial lines. This in turn would have the happy effect of diminishing the aristocracy's control over the army, to the benefit of the middle class.

The Crimean War gave new impetus to the struggle between the middle and upper classes, and this was played out with great intensity in the newspapers. *The Times* in particular regarded itself as 'the organ and representative of bourgeois power' during this period; the voice of the middle class, struggling to establish themselves as the dominant force at all levels of British life. 'The [Crimean] war came to be regarded as test of the aristocracy's power to rule in the modern world,' says *The Times*' official history, and it clearly took the view that they had failed. But, as Sweetman points out, some of the criticisms of the army leaders, especially Lord Raglan, were quite unfair, blaming them for matters over which they had no control.

> At the outset of the war, the artillery and engineers were responsible directly to the Master-General of the Ordnance, not the Commander-in-Chief at the Horse Guards, who controlled the infantry and cavalry. Two legally distinct British armies therefore existed [...] The civilian Ordnance Department supplied military equipment, while the Commissariat (a Treasury department) looked after food and land transport; Raglan relied on them without commanding them.[33]

Many of the problems faced by the British army were structural, especially in the early months of the war. And we need to be aware that bourgeois critics had their own class interests, and stood to benefit from the aristocracy appearing incompetent leaders of the army. The worse the army looked, the greater the impetus for reform, and the better for middle-class aspirations to control the machinery of the state.

At the same time, opposing views carried considerable weight. By the 1850s, commerce and industrialization had brought enormous changes to British society. The railways, large-scale mining and manufacturing, and other modern innovations had moved millions of people out of the countryside and into the cities, and had made Britain the wealthiest and most powerful nation in the world. But industrial modernity had also produced foul slums, bad health, social injustice, adulterated food and many other hardships, especially for poorer people. The march of commerce brought harm as well as good, and some hoped that the war would be able to check some of its excesses, and would bring other values to the fore.

Should war become a branch of commerce, people wondered. Clearly, middle-class business skills could help the army to modernize. But if the British military services were reformed along commercial or industrial lines, what would inspire the soldiers to heroic and daring deeds? Would they be willing to suffer intense hardship and discipline and risk their lives in the name of commercial efficiency? Could commerce represent 'the nation' as the aristocracy had done in the past? The old system produced martinets such as Cardigan – flamboyant, bullying, a man who loved his regiment as much as (perhaps better than) his family, and spent £10,000 a year of his own money in clothing them. His men might not have liked him much, but they respected his military bearing and would follow him into the mouth of hell, as the charge of the Light Brigade had shown. Could the middle class produce this kind of obsessive, charismatic leader – or would meritocracy lead to mediocrity, and lose wars?

Somehow, modernizers needed to retain some traces of aristocratic values in the army even as they challenged those values and removed the aristocrats themselves from positions of power. The aristocracy still had something powerful to offer the nation – it provided an idea, a glamour, a devotion to duty. The aristocrats' supposed sangfroid (or stupidity) made them fearless, like Cardigan, who, according to the *Morning Chronicle*, was 'magnificent in his cool contempt of danger'. The tradition of aristocratic military leadership went very deep, and had a long and successful history, most recently against the French in the Napoleonic Wars. It could not be discarded lightly. Ultimately, however, the Crimean War failed to revive aristocratic prestige, partly due to the incompetence of the military leadership, and partly – perhaps largely – due to middle-class pressure, especially in the newspapers. The war increased the power of the commercial middle class, and brought some of their values into the armed services. As Olive Anderson argues, this was a decisive period in the consolidation of middle-class consciousness.[34]

In this political context, *The Times'* reports and Tennyson's poem about the charge of the Light Brigade are quite uncomfortable and uncertain about the event. What did it mean? Why did it produce directly opposing emotions – admiration and mockery; inspiration and despair? The ambivalence at work here has its roots in middle-class attitudes towards the aristocracy, the glamorous, heroic fools who (supposedly) ran the army. Russell in *The Times* calls the cavalry 'rash and reckless' but 'gallant fellows who prepared without thought to rush on [to] almost certain death'. The aristocracy are represented as men of action – spontaneous, brave, reckless, thoughtless – men with bodies rather than minds.

ENTHUSIASM OF PATERFAMILIAS,
On Reading the Report of the Grand Charge of British Cavalry on the 25th.

Fig. 6: 'Enthusiasm of Paterfamilias', *Punch*, 25 November 1854

Yet *The Times*' reports also present a spectacular martyrdom which only the aristocracy could provide. Russell describes how they sweep 'proudly past, glittering in the morning sun in all the pride and splendour of war'. 'A [...] fearful spectacle,' he adds, 'of men who are about to be annihilated by their own rashness.' Russell is respectful of, even as he mocks, the vision of Britain's ancient leadership sending itself to its own death. Like *The Times*' editorials, the eyewitness reports are deeply ambivalent towards the spectacle and suffering of the aristocracy, and this ambivalence is also expressed in Tennyson's poem. Both kinds of writing are drawing upon – and entering into – political debates about aristocratic power in Parliament as well as in the army.

Britain in 1854 was faced with a paradox. The first major war for 40 years showed that army reform was urgently needed. Yet those reforms might destroy precisely the strengths that were regarded as essential for military success. Tennyson's 'The Charge of the Light Brigade' enacts this paradox. It celebrates the cavalry, and also mourns its demise; it cherishes the aristocratic elements even as in some sense it shares *The Times'* desire to destroy them. And the emotion is further complicated by the fact that the cavalry had destroyed itself by the very values that the poem seeks to preserve. These complexities would have been familiar to readers at the time, as the nation struggled with questions of reform. How could the good aspects of the past be preserved, and the bad expelled? What happens if the good goes, too; what will remain?

To look at it another way, while there were powerful reasons to reform the army administration, the army's problems were not really based on class, but in bureaucratic structures which had long needed reorganization. The war itself was supposedly fought (at least at first) to protect the rights of religious groups, a claim made by both sides. Similarly, the focus on the British aristocracy's supposed power and incompetence could be seen as a pretext to further extend and consolidate middle-class power, not least in the press. And the class hostilities were themselves used very effectively by *The Times* to increase its own power.

Tennyson's 'The Charge of the Light Brigade' was taken up at all levels of society, by soldiers as well as civilians, and it circulated among people of all classes in later wars. Particularly striking is the way in which the cavalry were perceived as both victims and martyrs, as poet Richard Trench puts it, 'With a battlefield for altar, and with you for / sacrifice'.[35] As victims, they provide an imaginary point of focus for other groups who feel oppressed by a powerful but incompetent authority. 'Some one had blundered.'

> 'Forward, the Light Brigade!'
> Was there a man dismayed?
> Not though the soldier knew
>   Some one had blundered.

The clumsiness or stupidity of the authority which blundered – in its thinking, its words, the order it issued – is set against the perfect discipline of the cavalry, which is the body of action, not thought or speech:

> Their's not to make reply,
> Their's not to reason why,

> Their's but to do and die:
> Into the valley of Death
>   Rode the six hundred. (stanza 2)

The poem, like the news report, half-imagines – or wishes – that action might be unambiguous. The physical act of the charge arrests, or prevents, interpretation. At the same time, Tennyson recognizes that action, too, produces contested meanings. Two contradictory impulses drive Tennyson's poem: to interpret, endlessly, and to bring an end to interpretation. It must stop; it cannot stop.

According to Mark Adkin, a cavalry charge has a remarkable degree of momentum. 'Once launched, nothing short of the death of horse or rider could halt the frenzied gallop [...] Men and animals were swept inexorably forward. As somebody once said, "It is difficult to be a coward in a cavalry charge"' (pp. 4–5). Writers on the Light Brigade are fascinated by the unstoppable momentum of living bodies. But it also horrifies them. The war employs some of the technology, and the social organization, of the Napoleonic past; but flesh and blood and sabres are faced with increasingly powerful cannon and guns – exploding 'shrapnel shells filled with powder and bullets' and roundshot which 'could slice men in half or disembowel horses'.[36]

The poetry finds it difficult to register this mechanical violence. 'Then they rode back, but not / Not the six hundred', says Tennyson, but he is unable to describe precisely what happened to those who fell, even though some of the newspaper reports are surprisingly explicit about the physical effects of the war. (Some of the accounts of the fall of Sebastopol in September 1855, for example, are disturbingly graphic. See Chapter 4, below, on Sebastopol.) In the 1850s, the British newspapers, which were uncensored, gave some detailed accounts of the bodily suffering of war, while the literature said very little about it. By the First World War, the situation was reversed: the press was rigorously censored and it was *only* in literature that the violence of war could be described.

Above all, Tennyson's poem expresses an ambivalent sense of mourning – an attitude we find in many cultural memories of this war. And Tennyson is troubled by the difficulties of interpretation. What did the action mean? In the end, he is not sure; the Light Brigade can be honoured and remembered, but not understood. The action can be mourned, but not interpreted. The poem submits to its own injunction not to reason why, and it registers both pleasure and muted terror at its own passivity. Finally, Tennyson expresses a melancholic yearning – for a history that is lost even as it occurs, for something more profound than the contemporary world of commercial efficiency. These concerns still speak to us today.

3

SCUTARI, INKERMAN AND THE SIEGE

TO SCUTARI

After Balaklava, many of the sick and wounded were transported to Scutari for medical attention, arriving at the same time as Florence Nightingale docked from England, on 4 November. 'Bad news from Balaklava,' she wrote from the ship *Vectis*, as she waited to disembark. 'You will hear the awful wreck of our poor cavalry [...] 400 wounded arriving *at this moment* for us to nurse.'[1] Though the conditions in the hospitals were being discussed in the newspapers, Nightingale was not convinced that people could really imagine what it was like. 'But oh! you gentlemen [doctors] of England,' she writes in a letter, '[...] can have little idea from reading the newspapers, of the horror & misery (in a military Hosp*l*.) of operating upon these dying and exhausted men.'[2]

The hospital was vast, and rapidly filling:

> We have now four miles of beds – and not eighteen inches apart. We have our quarters in one Tower of the Barrack – and all this fresh influx [of patients] has been laid down between us and the Main Guard in two corridors with a line of beds down each side, just room for one man to step between, and four wards. (p. 37)

Nightingale was deeply moved by the great courage of the ordinary soldiers, who 'bear pain and mutilation with unshrinking heroism'. She writes that many had had limbs amputated, and faced a serious risk of infection and death. There was a great shortage of everything the nurses needed.

> Not a sponge, nor a rag of linen, nor anything have I left. Everything is gone to make slings and stump pillows and shirts. The poor fellows have not had a clean shirt nor been washed for two months before they came here, and the state in which they arrive from the transport is literally *crawling*. I hope in a few days we shall establish a little cleanliness. But we have not a basin nor a towel or a bit or soap nor a broom – I have ordered 300 scrubbing brushes. But one half [of] the Barrack is so sadly out of repair that it is impossible to use a drop of water on the stone floors, which are laid upon rotten wood, and would give our men fever in no time. (p. 38)

Ten days later, little progress had been made in getting the men or their clothes washed. When they arrived, she writes to Sidney Herbert on 25 November, only 30 men were washed each night in 'slipper baths'. At this rate, each of the 2,300 men will be washed only once in 80 days. 'The consequences of all this are Fever, Cholera, Gangrene, Lice, Bugs, Fleas [...] from the using of one sponge among many wounds' (p. 39). The problem was that there was no central authority to manage the different parts of the hospital and its suppliers. Nightingale recognized the need for complete reform of the administration of public services. In February 1855, she wrote angrily about the appalling lack of organization at Balaklava:

> Had there been any body to draw the novel inference that after autumn comes winter, – that roads would be wanted to bring the provisions etc. from Balaklava to the camp, the sick from the camp to Balaklava – that forage is necessary to keep horses alive as well as men, & that where the forage is, there should be the horses also, Scutari would never have existed on the gigantic scale of calamity it does now. But we have kept our horses in camp, our forage at Balaklava & the horses have died in bringing up their own food.[3]

At Scutari, Nightingale had access to reasonable funds, both her own private money and private charity raised by *The Times*, as well as War Office resources which she used to procure some of the things she needed. *The Times*' fund was useful, but the newspaper irritated Nightingale by vastly overstating its contribution:

> The 'Times' is playing a most unfortunate game. I am told it is always writing to prove that it has done everything – the Gov*t*. nothing [...] It never suggests any remedy, but simply says it supplies me with money. Even this is not true – as not above one half of the things supplied by me come from the 'Times' fund. (p. 85)[4]

The Times' high estimation of itself has persisted in cultural memory, but needs to be treated with some scepticism.

LITTLE INKERMAN

The allied armies dreaded the approach of winter. They were keen to establish the siege before the cold weather set in, while the Russians hoped to drive them out of the Crimea entirely; or, failing that, to keep them at arm's length outside Sebastopol. On 26 October, the day after Balaklava, the Russians sent a force out of Sebastopol against the British right flank, in a small area around Inkerman. As Downham points out, this ground was very important, but was not adequately fortified.[5]

Several thousand Russian infantry attacked, but the British drove them back, killing and wounding several hundred, and taking about 100 Russian prisoners.[6] 'The Russians were utterly routed,' writes Russell, 'and fled in confusion.' This short battle lasted a few hours and became known as Little Inkerman. It raised the British spirits, showing their strength and courage against the enemy, but it also encouraged the Russians, who realized the weakness of the British position. As the Russians prepared to return, the British continued their grinding labour in the trenches. 'We make very little way,' writes Russell, 'and it is evident this cannot last. The men are worn out' (pp. 117–18). More was to follow a few days later.

INKERMAN

'The Battle of Inkerman admits of no description,' wrote Russell, calling it 'the bloodiest struggle ever witnessed since war cursed the earth' (p. 123).

Following their probe on 26 October, the Russians decided to attack the British position at the eastern end of the siege, above the town of Inkerman. They knew these lines were weakly defended, due to a shortage of troops. Under considerable pressure from the Tsar, Russian leader Prince Menshikov hoped that a massive push might end the siege and drive the allies out of the Crimea. Some 19,000 Russian troops would come out of Sebastopol, and another 16,000 would march in from the other side of the Tchernaya river. A further 3,000 would make sorties against the French, while 22,000 under Prince Gorchakov would make a feint against Sapoune Ridge. As British officer Edward Hamley explained in *Blackwood's*, 'Few great battles require less military knowledge to render them intelligible than this. The plan of the enemy was, after having succeeded in placing their guns unopposed in the required position, to pour on one particular point of our line which they knew to be inadequately guarded.' Then the Russians intended to 'press on at the same point with overwhelming masses of infantry.'[7]

On 5 November, the Russians launched a full-scale attack on the British sector, on the heights above the ruined town of Inkerman. The ground here was rough, broken and sheer, with tall heights separated by deep ravines, which were covered with very thick brushwood. The fighting raged across this difficult terrain for about eight hours and left a deep impression upon all who witnessed it. 'I do not think "Guy Fawkes' Day" was ever celebrated by more Gunpowder and fire,' remarked officer Frederick Dallas.[8]

The Russian attack began before dawn, in heavy rain and fog. 'It had rained almost incessantly the night before,' writes Russell, 'and the early morning gave no promise of any cessation of the heavy showers which had fallen for the previous four-and-twenty hours. The fog and vapours of drifting rain were so thick as morning broke, that one could scarcely see two yards before him' (p. 119). 'Cold mist rose from the valley, and hung heavily above the plains.'[9] Around 4 am, reported Russell, the British on the heights heard the church bells in Sebastopol 'ringing drearily through the cold night air' (p. 119). This was not unusual. A few British pickets registered the sound of wheels and Russian activities below, but again, such sounds were common enough and did not excite attention.

> No one suspected for a moment that enormous masses of Russians were creeping up the rugged sides of the heights over the Valley of Inkermann, on the undefended flank of the Second Division. (p. 120)

Under cover of the church bells, the Russians quietly moved heavy artillery and thousands of troops through the darkness, up to the heights. Around 6 am, the first shots were fired when they confronted some British pickets on Shell Hill. The British were greatly outnumbered, and fought hard, despite problems with wet charges in their weapons. The noise of the shots alerted other British troops, who soon realized that there were huge numbers of Russians, many more than on 26 October, and that a serious attack had begun. The British 2nd Division was now commanded by Major-General Pennefather, replacing Sir George de Lacy Evans who was ill. Pennefather took the decision to keep the fighting well forward, 'feeding the pickets' with reinforcements. In the thick fog, the small numbers of British troops gave the impression of being a much greater force.

What followed was a very intense day of battles over a small area. 'Rarely has such an artillery fire been so concentrated, and for so long, on [such a] confined space,' wrote Hamley (p. 242). Overall, some 40,000 Russians fought against 7,400 British and 8,200 French. For much of the day, the men could see very little, but fought fiercely, often at close quarters with the enemy. No one could see more than a tiny section of the conflict at any moment, but all were aware of its ferocity. As the *Illustrated London News* commented, this was 'the hardest-fought action that has taken place for many years'.[10] It was not a single battle, but a complex of events: 'a series of dreadful deeds of daring, of sanguinary hand-to-hand fights, of despairing rallies, of desperate assaults', all taking place across the rough terrain, wrote Russell, 'in glens and valleys, in brushwood glades and remote dells, hidden from all human eyes' (p. 123). Tens of thousands of troops participated in the event, yet very few actually saw anything beyond their own immediate location. Those present remembered Inkerman as weirdly invisible; the genuine 'fog of war'.

While there were many incidents of face-to-face combat using old-fashioned bayonets, this was also a battle of modern weaponry. The Russian artillery was used to terrible effect, mutilating and killing many allied soldiers and horses. Even the Russian muskets, which were older and technically inferior to the allied weapons, could do ghastly damage, as Hamley describes. Facing a range of guns hurling musket-balls, he writes, 'it is difficult to stave off the thought that, in the next instant, your arm or leg may be dangling from your body a crushed and bloody mass, or your spirit driven rudely through a hideous wound' (p. 242). In response, the allies used their own heavy weapons and rifles to devastate the Russian ranks. The Russians tended to fight most effectively in big, close columns, but the terrain made this formation difficult to sustain, and at close range they were very vulnerable to the allies' fire. The British fought in thin lines. 'At every point alike the assailants found scanty numbers, but impenetrable ranks,' wrote Hamley. 'Before them everywhere was but a thin and scattered line opposed to their solid masses and numerous skirmishers, yet beyond it they could not pass' (p. 242). Like many witnesses, he praised the Russians as 'bravely led', and fighting with tenacity and courage. The British found the new Minié rifle highly effective, reported Russell, 'the king of weapons' (p. 127), cutting swathes through the Russian ranks. French leader General Bosquet brought troops to help the British, but his offer of help was at first rejected by Cathcart and Brown. Later the French gave valuable support, though Inkerman is remembered most vividly as the British 'soldiers' battle'.

Significantly outnumbered, the allies found it a very hard day. 'On our part it was a confused and desperate struggle,' wrote Hamley. In the fog and confusion, 'every man was his own general'. The situation required the men to fight without much direct command. 'The character of the battle throughout the day had been most curious,' argues John Downham, 'with low-level leadership, individual initiative and sheer bloody-minded courage making up on the British side for lack of numbers, ammunition and generalship. In truth, due to the limited visibility, little control could be exercised by senior commanders on either side.'[11] And the conflict was constantly shifting. 'The tide of battle ebbed and flowed, not in wide waves, but in broken tumultuous billows.'[12]

Battles and skirmishes raged well into the afternoon, in some instances with the same piece of ground being taken several times. One of the most notorious struggles took place over a place known as the Sandbag Battery, a site with no guns and no military value, which was taken and retaken by British and Russian troops in turn. 'In the space of about three-quarters of an hour the battery changed hands four times', the soldiers desperate, even frenzied, in the intensity of their attacks.[13] Many died in the close fighting, the survivors trampling over them to continue the struggle. The piles of bodies there afterwards were a horrible sight, disturbing even battle-hardened French commander General Bosquet. '*Quel abbatoir!*'

After five hours of hard fighting and huge losses, the Russians felt they had gained very little. The British had used the difficult terrain and their well-positioned artillery to good effect, and the Russians felt they were running out of options. Eventually, around 1 pm, after the arrival of a strong French contingent, Russian commander Dannenberg decided to withdraw his troops. As they withdrew, the Vladimir battalions made one last aggressive move against the British, but many in their dense columns were killed by allied artillery. Commentators at the time and since have argued that one last push from the allies at this point would have really weakened the Russians and perhaps even ended the war. But by now, the British were too depleted by the day's battles, and French leader Canrobert was unwilling to risk the French troops without strong British support. And so, many felt, another opportunity was missed.

AFTERWARDS

After the fighting was over, survivors surveyed the field of battle. It was a ghastly spectacle. 'The scenes on the battle-field were awful' wrote the *Illustrated London News* correspondent. 'I sickened over them, and have been ill ever since.'[14] The numbers of killed and injured were enormous, with more than 10,000 Russian casualties, 2,300 British and around 900 French.[15] 'I should say that the loss at Alma was trifling compared with this,' wrote Frederick Dallas

(p. 46). Mrs Duberly could not bear to go and look. 'The thought of it made me shudder and turn sick' (6 November 1854, p. 100). Russell described the sad scenes two days later, on 7 November, as litter-bearers, French and English, toiled painfully up the hillsides, clearing the wounded and the dead (p. 131). The slaughter was 'immense' wrote Hamley in *Blackwood's* magazine. The dead Russians 'lay thick in the coppice. Every bush hid a dead man [...] All the field was strewn.' 'The sides of the hill [...] were literally heaped with bodies.' The dead men were laid out in ranks: 'Few sights can be imagined more strange and sad in their ghastliness.' Meanwhile, thousands of wounded men lay in the bushes all around. Some had to wait two days before they were carried to safety. In all, wrote Hamley uncertainly, it was 'a gloomy though a glorious triumph'.[16]

While Hamley and Russell were uneasy, and at times quite critical of the army leadership, many other British newspapers and journals hailed Inkerman as simply a great victory. For the *Illustrated London News*, it was 'one of the greatest victories ever achieved by this nation over a foreign foe'.[17] Similarly, for the *Daily News*, 'The annals of war may be ransacked in vain to find a victory more gallantly won.' While regretting the 'considerable' loss of life, the paper celebrated 'the advantage gained over the enemy, and the moral effect produced upon his forces', concluding that 'the deadly game is clearly going in our favour'.[18] Even today, military historian John Downham points out the ambiguities of Inkerman, yet regards it as still 'one of the very finest feats of arms in the long and eventful annals of the British Army'; a 'great heritage'.[19]

What did the battle of Inkerman achieve? Both sides claimed some kind of victory, but one could argue that in reality they both lost. The battle weakened both sides, but produced no decisive result, leaving the armies to settle drearily into the siege of Sebastopol. It was now two months since the allies had landed in the Crimea. Having failed to launch a major assault in September, many felt that they were facing a city which, as Romaine commented, was now 'ten times stronger', in terms of its earthworks and cannon, 'than when we began to attack it'.[20] None the less, as winter set in, the Russians could do little more than keep the allies at bay, while the allies could only keep the pressure on the Russians inside Sebastopol – though the city was always open on the harbour side.

The Russians also had a substantial field army stationed outside Sebastopol, threatening the allies from beyond the Tchernaya river. As Colin Robins argues, Menshikov's decision to move his army out of the city was very effective. 'He was able to move freely behind the besieging forces and the besiegers were themselves, in effect, besieged.'[21] Now the allies' main task was simply to keep themselves alive through the winter. This was not easy, especially for the British, who found it increasingly difficult to get supplies from the port of Balaklava to the British camp, some six or seven miles away. In the winter of 1854–5, this was less a war than a struggle to survive.[22]

Immediately after the battle of Inkerman, Raglan and Canrobert made the decision to pause the siege preparations until work had been done to strengthen the right flank. Some British commanders, such as General de Lacy Evans, felt it would be wisest to withdraw from the Crimea at this point, to avoid wintering there, but Raglan was determined to continue.[23] Now his immediate worry was to improve supplies and transport for the troops. These were hugely difficult problems to solve, not least because he had no control at all over crucial elements of supply or transport.[24] And, almost immediately, a new disaster struck.

THE STORM

On 14 November, a mighty storm swept across the Crimea. General Richard Airey was out on his horse at 2.30 am, when all was so still and quiet that he could hear the clocks in Sebastopol. Then at about 6.30 am the storm broke out. Nothing could withstand its force, he writes:

[T]here was not a tent left standing – in 5 minutes the sick were exposed to all its fury – it was also bitterly cold – the glass suddenly falling 25° – it was not possible to light a fire – and altogether the scene of desolation was more than can be imagined. – You will read of our loss in Ships, and Stores with dismay – in fact a greater disaster could scarcely have befallen the Army [...] The loss of the 'Resolute' with our Ammunition, and of the 'Prince' with our Stores, is almost fatal.[25]

Woken in his tent, Russell watched with alarm as the wind rose, his tent flapped open and eventually collapsed on top of its inhabitants. Outside, the ground was turning to mud, and the air, too:

> Mud – and nothing but mud – flying before the wind and drifting as though it were rain, covering the face of the earth as far as it was visible. Meanwhile the storm-fiend was coming, terrible and strong as when he smote the bark of the Ancient Mariner [...] The whole head quarters' camp was beaten flat to the earth, and the unhappy occupants were rushing through the mud in all directions in chase of their effects and clothes [...]. (p. 136)

The force of the wind was immense. Large wagons were overturned; 'men and horses were knocked down and rolled over and over'; 'ambulance wagons were turned topsy-turvy' (p. 136).

> The Marines and Rifles on the cliffs over Balaklava lost tents, clothes – everything; the storm tore them away over the face of the rock and hurled them across the bay, and the men had to cling to the earth with all their might to avoid the same fate. (Russell, p. 136)

Many men and animals disappeared in the storm. Dallas wrote sadly of his horse, 'He was very thin I must say, & I honestly believe he was blown away, for I have never seen him since.'[26] The men who survived were in a bad state:

> The tents remained down for 24 hours. The Commissariat declared that they could not supply food owing to the state of the roads, & since then the men have hardly had enough to support life, all this time having to go every alternate 24 hours to the Trenches, where they lay half clothed, half starved, & worked to death.[27]

The area occupied by the 2nd Division was now 'bare and desolate', the rows of neat white tents torn away, the ground turned into 'sticky mud as black as ink', the tents in muddy heaps.[28]

The storm was a serious blow, creating havoc on land, and worse disasters at sea. Many ships carrying crucial supplies had recently arrived and were waiting to unload. Some 21 ships were destroyed in the gale, their contents strewn around the bay, their crews killed.

Fanny Duberly observed the harbour 'filling fast with masts, spars, dead bodies, rum casks, dead cattle, hay, vegetables & every item of wreck'.[29] Several ships had precious loads of winter clothing for the troops as well as 20 days' supply of food 'for all the horses in the army, and many of the men', as Russell reported angrily (p. 147). The *Prince* had been carrying winter stores, including 40,000 boots and warm uniforms, all of which were lost. Russell noted that the vessels had been anchored in a place known to be vulnerable to terrible storms; much more could have been done to protect them. This failure of management caused even greater suffering for men and horses, many of whom died of neglect and starvation over the winter. Hamley writes in *Blackwood's* of the pitiful plight of many horses:

> Perhaps the most painful feature in the dreary scene was the number of dead and dying horses scattered, not only round the cavalry and artillery camps, but along the various roads [...] Some had fallen and died from fatigue, some perished from cold, some from starvation. Once down, a horse seldom rose again. After a few faint attempts he lay still, except for a feeble nibbling at the bare ground [...].[30]

'What will the people of England say to all this?' wondered Frederick Dallas bitterly (p. 50).

THE SIEGE

The battles discussed so far – Alma, Balaklava, Inkerman – are given considerable prominence in most military histories of the war. But, as Colin Robins points out, for most of the men who served in the Crimea, these events were not the 'real war'. The majority of ordinary soldiers spent most of their time not in action, but in the trenches and tents outside Sebastopol. For them, the real war 'was the desperate ordeal, day after day, of trench warfare. The horrifying conditions of the first winter were harder to bear by far than the bullets and bayonets faced at Alma or Inkerman.'[31] The men often lacked the basic necessities of life. Shelter was rudimentary, or even non-existent. There was a shortage of warm clothes and blankets. Often it was impossible to get dry, impossible to get warm. The men were required to work long, hard hours, digging the trenches, but often there was nothing to eat or drink when they came off duty. Underfed, cold and wet, they soon got sick and many died from starvation, sickness, or neglect. 'Thus was the finest army in the world steadily destroyed,' writes Robins, the sense of unnecessary loss still painful to witness, long after the event.[32]

Dunscombe describes the men's misery on the day of the great storm:

> In the trenches at the New Battery since 4.30 pm last night; to describe the day we spent is impossible; it rained, hailed and snowed the whole day and night; besides all this it blew a perfect hurricane; the whole time I was there, I had nothing to eat or drink, as on account of the severity of the weather our rations could not be sent to us; the men suffered so severely from cold, hunger, and wet and every privation that out of 160 we took with us last night to the entrenchments, we only brought away 98 of them this evening; all the others remained behind either dead, dying or so bad with the cramps that they were not able to walk home [...].[33]

Similarly, Dallas wrote in a letter that, since Inkerman, 'we have been having bad weather & its effects upon our poor men has been fatal beyond belief'. The men die 'of want, overwork, & insufficient Clothing, combined with sleeping (not much of that by the way) on the wet soaking ground'. The officers were generally better off; most had shelter and they could usually buy food. 'The greatest trial here is seeing the sufferings of our men, without being in any way able to alleviate them. They are positively worked to death' (p. 51).

One of the greatest problems for the British was the lack of transport. With the horses and pack animals dying off, and the road from Balaklava harbour deep in mud, plus the profound incompetence and bureaucracy of the Commissariat, it was often impossible to move food and supplies the few miles from the harbour to the British camp, as William Romaine complained on 1 December:

> The worst of the matter is that our carriage has failed us and the men do not get all their rations regularly and when they return wet

through as they always do from the trenches, there is no wood to cook with & a long way to get water [...] They have no change of clothes and their great coats are like cobwebs. There are now some jerseys & socks at Balaklava, but no transport for them and they don't or can't send the soldiers to the rear to get the clothing that is ready for them – so the men are wet for days & nights together, get diarrhoea & cholera go into hospital & are dying at the rate of from 70 to 90 per diem.[34]

Later in December, he wrote bitterly that 'Heaps of all kinds of stores sent by the liberality of Government are arriving but there is no place to store them or land them & nobody to issue them' (p. 57); 'many things desperately needed by the men do not reach them'. Many of the goods which arrived at this time ended up lost, undelivered, or rotting on the quayside, while men and horses were dying of cold and hunger a few miles away.[35] Britain was the richest and most industrialized country in the world, able to send a wealth of goods to its troops in Balaklava. But the bureaucracy and incompetence at the end of the line, especially by the Commissariat, made all this worthless, turning it into waste.

INSIDE SEBASTOPOL

What did the siege look like from the other side? Not much from this point of view was published in English during the war, though dispatches from Russian leaders such as Gorchakov sometimes appeared in the press. However, a book in English did appear in 1856, when Polish officer Captain R. Hodasevich (Chodasiewicz), who served in the Russian army, published his memoir of the siege, *A Voice from Within the Walls of Sebastopol*.[36] Another fascinating account of the siege was produced by one of Russia's greatest writers, Leo Tolstoy, who was then a young officer in the Tsar's army. He was in Sebastopol in late 1854 and January 1855, and wrote three powerful stories about the siege, each piece a mixture of reportage and fiction.[37] The *Sebastopol Sketches* were published in Russian in 1855–6, but were not really known in Britain for another generation, when they were translated into French in 1886 and English in 1887.[38]

Tolstoy's account from the inside begins with a view from the outside, at dawn:

> The light of daybreak is just beginning to tint the sky above the Sapun-gora [Sapoune Heights]. The dark surface of the sea has already thrown off night's gloom and is waiting for the first ray of sunlight to begin its cheerful sparkling. From the bay comes a steady drift of cold and mist. There is no snow – everything is black – but the sharp morning frost catches at your face and cracks beneath your feet, and only the incessant, far-off rumble of the sea, punctuated every now and again by the booming of the artillery in Sebastopol, breaks into the morning quiet.[39]

All those who wrote about Sebastopol were struck by its beauty, none more so than Tolstoy. The city is built above a natural harbour with 'glittering azure water' (p. 42). Approaching from that water, one could see 'the beautiful, radiant structures of the town, visible on the opposite shore and tinted pink by the rays of the morning sun' (p. 42). It was December 1854.

The city had been under constant attack since October. Yet within its walls, civilians appeared to live fairly ordinary lives, moving around in an everyday manner (p. 44). The visitor might have felt quite disappointed at the apparent normality on the city's streets. But close by, on the defences of the besieged city, were very different scenes. Before turning to the military action, however, Tolstoy directed his gaze to the Assembly Hall, now a military hospital. There, he says, you will 'see the defenders of Sebastopol and witness spectacles both sad and terrible, noble and comical, but which will astonish and exalt your soul' (p. 44).

> No sooner have you opened the door than you are assailed without warning by the sight and smell of about forty or fifty amputees and critically wounded, some of them on camp beds, but most of them lying on the floor. (p. 44)

Tolstoy imagines walking through the hospital, talking with patients, observing their suffering and their stoicism. All around were injured civilians as well as soldiers and sailors, some recovering, others dying. In an adjoining room were the surgeons, 'with pale, gloomy physiognomies, their arms soaked in blood up to the elbows, deep in concentration over a bed on which a wounded man is lying under the influence of chloroform [...] The surgeons are going about the repugnant but beneficial task of amputation' (pp. 47–8).[40] In the crowded hospital, 'you will witness fearsome sights that will shake you to the roots of your being; you will see war not as a beautiful, orderly, gleaming formation, with music and beaten drums [...] but war in its authentic expression – as blood, suffering and death' (p. 48).

It is striking that Tolstoy starts with the ghastly effects of war before he looks at the war itself. Yet he was also moved by the beauty and nobility which he saw alongside – even within – the horror. On the bastions, the men faced fearful explosions from the French artillery. He describes what it is like when a mortar hits the earth close by. Physically, it is terrifying, yet curiously exciting, too:

> you will hear this whistling sound [of the mortar] come nearer and nearer in an accelerating crescendo, and then you will see a black sphere and witness the shell's impact against the earth, its palpable, ringing explosion. Then shell-splinters will fly whistling and whining through the air, and you will be spattered with mud. You will experience a sensation that is a strange blend of fear and enjoyment. (p. 55)

Studying the faces of the Russian soldiers at work, Tolstoy feels that 'the danger, savagery and sufferings of the war' give the men 'marks of a conscious sense of dignity and the traces of lofty feelings and thoughts' (p. 54). The war elevates the men even as it degrades them.

By May 1855, many more people were dead and injured, and conditions inside Sebastopol had become worse.

> Hundreds of fresh, bloody corpses – the bodies of men who two hours earlier had been filled with all manner of hopes and desires, from the lofty to the trivial – lay with stiffened limbs on the floor of the dew-covered, flowering valley which separated the bastion from the trench, and on the smooth flagstones of the Mortuary Chapel in Sebastopol; hundreds of men, with curses and prayers on their parched lips, tossed and groaned, some among the corpses in the flowering valley, others on

stretchers, on camp beds, or on the bloody floorboards of the dressing station […].

Above all this horror, the beauty of nature still asserts itself; 'the white mist drifted in off the dark, thundering sea, the vermilion dawn flared in the east, the purple cloudlets trailed across the light blue horizon, and again, as on earlier days, promising joy, love and happiness to the whole of the quickening world, the sun's mighty, resplendent orb arose from the waves' (p. 102). But it is an empty promise.

The armies agree a brief truce to deal with the dead. Between the stinking corpses in the flowered valley and a 'resplendent' sunset over the dark sea, thousands of men from both sides come together, 'studying one another, speaking to one another, smiling at one another'. For Tolstoy, these soldiers have much in common; 'the fear of death, a love of the good and the beautiful'. Now they have seen one another at close quarters, surely they will recognize their common humanity and 'embrace one another with tears of joy and happiness, like brothers'. Surely, when they *see what they have done*, they will make peace. But of course this does not happen. As soon as the truce ends, 'once again the engines of death and suffering will start their whistling; once again the blood of the innocent will flow and the air will be filled with their groans and cursing' (p. 108).

In August 1855, just weeks before the city falls, Tolstoy writes of a young officer coming to Sebastopol who sees 'this terrible place' as 'a truly ravishing and unique spectacle' (p. 131). The city produces a powerful sense of ambivalence. As the Russians work desperately to save Sebastopol, they are moved by a deep and terrible love for the place. At the same time, they feel terrified, exhausted and betrayed as it falls slowly into ruin, and fails to protect them.

1855

By the end of February 1855, things began to improve for the allies. The weather was milder, though the nights were still cold; supplies were starting to reach them and more horses and troops arrived.

In January, Sardinia officially joined the war, with 15,000 troops arriving in May. In the spring, the allies comprised approximately 90,000 French troops, 20,000 British and 25,000 Turks, plus more Turkish troops at Eupatoria.[41] Food and shelter in the field had improved, and overall the allies felt considerably more optimistic. The British troops even started to have some entertainment, including horse races, foot races and games of cricket and football.[42] In March, Russell reported that 'The wreck we made of Balaklava is shovelled away'; the wreckage of the town was mixed with stones and other materials to form piers and roads. The filth was banished and a clean town emerged, with new wooden huts and barracks. Fresh food was now available and there were vegetables for the sick.[43]

A few months later, Mrs Duberly remarked how much the town has changed since the desperate winter. 'Balaklava was then filthy, naked, and starved. Balaklava is now washed, and dressed, and fed', improvements for which she credits *The Times*.[44]

On 2 March 1855, Tsar Nicholas died. News of his death reached London quickly, and some hoped that this would mean the end of the war. But his son, Alexander II, refused to accept any treaty that would humiliate Russia. On the other side, humiliation of Russia was precisely what some British political leaders hoped for. Alexander attempted to reach out to France, which seemed to be less enthusiastic about the war by now, but the British put Louis Napoleon under a lot of pressure to expand the war, and not to settle for peace. Peace talks opened in Vienna on 15 March, but, as Baumgart has shown, it is now known that France and Britain were secretly determined to make the peace talks fail, and to decide the matter on the battlefield. They pressed for a point which they knew Russia would not agree to, namely that Sebastopol no longer be a Russian naval base, that its docks be demolished and the Russian fleet be reduced to four ships of war. A further secret agreement was made between Russia and Austria (which was not known during the war). Austria promised not to accept any agreement that reduced Russia's sovereignty over the Crimea and the Black Sea; this further ensured that the talks would fail.[45] There is not space here to go into the secretive and complex diplomacy of the time, but one could argue that some of the secret negotiations helped to perpetuate the war unnecessarily and to delay a peace settlement, and with those involved never called to account for the suffering this caused. That said, diplomacy frequently averted war throughout the nineteenth century, especially when dealing with the Eastern Question.

The newspapers were full of the failings, real or otherwise, of the military and medical authorities. Much less was known at the time about the secretive political actions which went on, but there was perhaps a growing need to question how far the politicians and diplomats could be trusted with their powers over war and peace, a suspicion which became much deeper after the First World War.[46]

The allied campaign resumed in earnest in April. At last the allies were able to open out the eastern front inland from Sebastopol, making space for the growing numbers of troops.[47] They planned to weaken Sebastopol by very heavy bombardment, then to storm it with ground troops. This was not easily done. The allies worked hard: 'great exertions were made to complete platforms, mount guns, and get up ammunition' ready for the Second Bombardment which started on 9 April, in torrential rain.[48] The cannonade was severe, yet seemed oddly ineffective, as Dunscombe remarked: 'the bombardment goes on as usual and may go on to eternity without the artillery doing any good, as the Russians repair by night the injury that we do to the batteries by day'.[49] Russell wrote that the Russian big guns were made of excellent iron, 'enabling them to fire rapidly and continuously', and many Russian troops were well protected in 'caves, pits, and galleries at the back of the batteries'. Nonetheless, he wrote, 'the resolution, strength, indomitable perseverance and devotion of the allies give them the superiority in every kind of contest with the enemy' (p. 187), as if the war were, in the end, purely a moral struggle.

Like everyone in the British camp, Russell spent a lot of time looking at Sebastopol, remarking upon the Russians' activity. In his report dated 5 April, the scene seems curiously like a photograph, despite the movement he observes:

> It is exciting enough to look at the beleaguered city [...] and to watch the siege operations on a calm fine day [...] The soldiers are sauntering about in groups just below the cover of the parapets, and a deep greyish blue line denotes the artillerymen and covering parties, whose heads appear just above the trench. In front are the whitish mounds of the

> Russian intrenchments [sic], and batteries with the black muzzles of the
> guns peering through the embrasures. The grey-coated Russians stalk
> about on the inner slopes of the parapets, busily engaged in carrying up
> gabions and repairing the damaged works. (p. 180)

A telegraph cable was laid, and in December 1854 a railway
magnate, Samuel Morton Peto, made an unexpected offer to build
a short railway line inland from Balaklava harbour. Brimming
with confidence, Peto and his co-contractors offered to build the
line in three weeks, and to do it at cost price, on condition that the
army administration had no control over any aspect of the project.
The Duke of Newcastle, Secretary for War, gratefully accepted
the offer.[50] It was an enormous undertaking. All the materials –
rails, sleepers, stationary winding engines, plus the labour – had
to be brought in by a fleet of ships commissioned for the purpose.
The work was done by skilled navvies, notorious at home for
their drinking and brawling, and now represented as the unlikely
saviours of Britain's army.[51] They were not armed and were not
expected to fight; as Cooke remarks, 'they were too valuable to be
employed as soldiers' (p. 29). But the press enjoyed the fantasy of
Britain's industrial workers overcoming the Russians with picks
and spades. The first four miles of railway took longer than Peto's
original boast, but were completed in seven weeks.

The siege required a lot of heavy guns, with Raglan constantly
increasing the number of guns in the batteries. It was enormously
difficult to get the heavy guns into place, and many men and horses
died in the course of this work. The big 13-inch mortar shells
alone weighed close to 200 pounds. The railway was a great help,
carrying large quantities of ammunition to the British lines. On 9
April, the guns again began to pound Sebastopol mercilessly for
ten days. It was a terrible spectacle to see and to hear.

From a technical point of view, the building of the railway was
an extraordinary achievement. Yet many observed it with dismay. Is
this where industrialization – including the railways – has brought
us: to the heaviest bombardment in the history of the world? What
kind of achievement is this? (Such questions would seem all the
more pressing in 1914.) The Crimean War had a voracious appetite
for resources – human, animal, financial, industrial – which, it
seemed, could never be satisfied. And so the siege continued. But by

now the Russians were starting to feel demoralized, while the allies were more hopeful. The railway brought the British food, hay and fuel as well as ammunition. Early in April, the first hospital train was in operation, taking sick and injured soldiers into Balaklava. The Land Transport Corps was established, providing essential support to the army.[52]

By the end of April, Russell reported that the railway was carrying 240 tons a day, including 180 tons of ammunition (p. 195). 'If war is a great destroyer, it is also a great creator,' he remarked optimistically (p. 174). But the casualties continued, and rose again when the hot weather caused cholera to return. Like all major conflicts, the Crimean War created waste on a grand scale. The more advanced and industrialized the protagonists, the greater the capacity for waste. In the 1850s, Britain could send vast quantities of materials across the sea – as it did to build the railway. But huge amounts of the things sent were lost or wasted. Tons of goods which rotted on the docks in Balaklava through the winter had to be destroyed. Some warm clothing was sent to Constantinople to be cleaned, but a 'large number of sheepskins have been destroyed', which, Russell complained, 'had competent persons been consulted, might have been saved' (p. 195). Meanwhile, many more French troops arrived. Louis Napoleon was keen to secure a land victory to restore the glory of France, while the British were looking to take further naval action. The alliance, always somewhat strained, began to break down.

KERTCH

Early in May a joint expedition set off to the east for Kertch, on the Sea of Azov. An urgent telegram from Paris put Canrobert under such pressure that the French felt they had to turn back. (As a number of historians have noted, the telegraph opened up new possibilities for political leaders to interfere with military actions, a development which the generals did not welcome.) Now, Canrobert stepped down as French commander and was replaced by Pélissier. In late May, a new amphibious expedition was sent to Kertch, and had considerable success. Russell described how the Russians did not stay and fight, but destroyed their own forts, scuttled their warships and retreated. Allied troops moved in. Some sacked the local towns and attacked the Kertch museum of antiquities. Even Russell, hardened by all he had seen, was dismayed at the sight.

> It is impossible to convey an idea of the scene within this place [...] One might well wonder how the fury of a few men could effect such a prodigious amount of ruin in so short a time. The floor of the museum is covered for several inches in depth with the débris of broken glass, of vases, urns, statuary, the precious dust of the contents, and charred bits of wood and bone, mingled with the fresh splinters of the shelves, desks, and cases in which they had been preserved. Not a single bit of anything that could be broken or burnt any smaller had been exempt from reduction by hammer or fire [... The] glass was smashed to atoms, the statues pounded to pieces [...] the work of destruction was complete. (pp. 207–8)

Russell hoped that no British troops had been involved, and was inclined to blame the French and Turks, pointing out that Sir George Brown had attempted to stop the French from plundering local houses in Yenikale (pp. 208–9). But he was clearly worried that the 'civilised states' would be held to blame, and, indeed, that civilization itself might be resting uneasily upon a foundation of barbarism.

The Kertch expedition was seen as a 'signal' success (p. 210). One effect was a mass destruction of food. The British squadron in the Sea of Azov destroyed 245 Russian ships carrying provisions for the Russian army. 'Immense magazines of corn, flour, and breadstuffs were destroyed [...] comprising altogether more than 7,000,000 [...] rations.' The Russians themselves destroyed more: 'upwards of 4,000,000lbs. of corn and 500,000 of flour' (p. 210). The allies inflicted 'great ruin on the enemy', who demolished their own villages, and retreated (11 June, p. 211).

As Lambert and Badsey argue, these actions helped to turn the whole war strategy in favour of the allies. The Russians depended heavily on shipping to bring flour from Kertch, fish from the Azov, and so on, into the war zone. When the ships were destroyed and the links broken, 'the Russian position in the Crimea became untenable' (p. 211). There was no longer sufficient forage for the Russian cavalry's horses, which in turn forced the field army away from the allied right flank. This was the beginning of the end for Sebastopol. But the Russians would not give up easily.

***

On 6 June, another massive attack, the Third Bombardment, took place. This lasted less than 24 hours, but was even heavier than the cannonade of April, with yet more guns raining more ordnance upon Sebastopol. The British had an ample supply of heavy mortars, supplied by the railway, and could fire through the night.[53] On 7 June, allied troops advanced on two Russian defences, the Mamelon and the Quarries. Russell was impressed, at least at first:

> The French went up the steep to the Mamelon in most beautiful style and in loose order, and every straining eye was upon their movements [... Their] figures, like light shadows flitting across the dun barrier of earthworks, were seen to mount up unfailingly [...] scrambling like skirmishers up the slopes on to the body of the work, amid a plunging fire from the guns [...]. (p. 213)

Henry Clifford described how he found himself weeping as he watched the 'splendid' yet 'awful' sight of the French soldiers 'rushing up under such fire'. It took them just ten minutes to flourish the French flag over the Mamelon (Royle, p. 391). Dunscombe recorded:

> Fine night; [...] the French went in at the Mamelon tonight; and our Second and Light Divisions went in at the Quarry; both the Mamelon and Quarry were taken; the French afterwards went in at the Round Tower (Malakoff) but were repulsed; the whole army was out under arms; [...] the French now hold the Mamelon and we hold the Quarries. (p. 121)

Fired with success, the French then pressed on, unplanned, in an attempt to take the Malakov. But it was too ambitious. The Russians regrouped and forced them back. The French then had to re-fight for the Mamelon, which they did successfully. The British meanwhile forced the Russians from the Quarries and took possession of their naval guns. The Russians fought back; the allies held their ground, but at considerable cost: more than 5,400 French and 670 British casualties. Despite this, the event gave the allies a considerable boost in morale, and they hoped to attack the Malakov and the Great Redan again soon.[54]

Two days later, there was a few hours' truce to bury the dead. Dunscombe went to look at the scenes of the action. After two hot days, 'the stench from the dead bodies lying about was unbearable'. He noticed that the Russians were feeling the strain; they looked 'sulky, miserable, and quite down in the mouth', and hungry, too. But they managed to plant 'infernal machines' in the ground all around the Mamelon and Quarries. These machines were an early form of land mine, containing a glass fuze which broke when stepped upon, releasing an acid which fired an explosive powder.[55] Several men were killed in this way.

The French and British generals conferred and decided to continue the siege operations, with more heavy bombardment, followed by a French attack on the Malakov, then a British assault on the Redan. 'As the latter is commanded by the former,' explained Russell, 'it would not be possible to carry or hold it till the Malakov was taken' (p. 214). It was a high-risk plan. The Russians had proved themselves doughty defenders. Could they be weakened sufficiently to allow the allies to attack the fortifications? It would take considerable courage to try. On 17 June another massive bombardment began: 'such a storm of shot, grape, shell, and musketry as had never before annoyed the ears of Heaven', wrote Fanny Duberly, who watched from close by (pp. 192–3). More than 600 guns fired with 'great energy, weight, and destructiveness' upon the Russians, who were unable to keep up the rebuilding as they had done before.[56] It looked fairly promising, but then things went wrong.

The French decided to attack earlier, at 3 am. Then one French general was misled by a stray rocket, thinking this was the signal, and went into action earlier still.[57] The French advanced somewhat raggedly, into a hail of Russian shot and shell, over ground sown with landmines. It was a ghastly sight. Raglan knew he had to support his allies, against unattractive odds. There was no time for a detailed plan. The British were quickly given the command to advance. They had to cover a quarter of a mile. Two columns left the trenches and moved across the open ground under heavy fire, led by General Sir John Campbell and Colonel Lacy Yea. Seeing some French troops inside the Malakov, Campbell believed it must have been taken. He moved forward, ignoring information that the French were actually pulling out. Campbell was killed, along with many of his men. There were other problems. The British trenches were set in rocky ground, and had been painfully slow to dig, while the French trenches were located in much easier soil. Now, the British had to cross nearly 300 yards of open ground from their trenches, while the French faced only 30 yards. The British trenches were quite narrow. As they filled with wounded soldiers coming back, the reserve troops could not go forward.[58] It was a shambles.

Many of the men were young, inexperienced and had arrived quite recently. The original army which had landed the previous September was all but lost to death, injury and sickness. The new troops now faced a terrifying challenge, which many of them met with courage and dignity. But some were just too frightened to move, as Hamley described:

> In vain the officers stood up amid the iron shower and waved their swords; in vain the engineers returned to bring up the supports; the men could not be induced to quit the parapets in a body. Small bodies of half a dozen, or half a score, ran out only to add to the slaughter.[59]

Those who did venture out suffered severe losses.

Overall, the assault was not well planned; or plans were abandoned, leading to confusion. For Dallas, it was as 'nothing but mismanagement and frightful carnage'; 'a very sad thing' (pp. 146–7). This was a common view. The attack had failed, with 3,500 French and 1,500 British casualties.

The summer days were very hot. The cholera returned as many had feared, and after the failed attack, Lord Raglan got sick and died on 28 June, probably of cholera, but some felt he had died of a broken heart. Thousands of soldiers turned out to give him a dignified send-off from the Crimea. His body was transported back to Britain (preserved in a barrel of rum, according to Dunscombe), where he was given a huge state funeral. Having been much criticized while in command (unfairly, in certain respects), he was after death used as a scapegoat for all the incompetencies and the suffering of the war.[60] He was replaced by the chief of staff, Lieutenant-General James Simpson, who at 63 was not at all keen to become Commander-in-Chief. He did his duty and accepted the role, but, as General Codrington remarked, while Simpson was 'very kind, very gentlemanlike' and had been a good officer in India, he did not exhibit 'much decision, or originality or determination', nor have 'the energy of feeling and mind to enter into this business, which has plenty of difficulties now and to come'. He was seen as weak and uninspiring, not least in Russell's reports in *The Times*.[61]

In August, under considerable pressure from the Tsar, the Russians made one last attempt to attack the allies from outside Sebastopol, and to end the siege. A large Russian army made a flank attack, attempting to cross the River Tchernaya. French and Sardinian troops were ready, and attacked the Russians with rifles and artillery. For the Russians, it was a massacre; 'at least 10,000 Russian casualties for no gain'; 'complete defeat'.[62] Few British troops were involved, but it interested Russell, who published a long account of the battle in *The Times*. Another massive bombardment of Sebastopol followed, from 17 to 27 August. The mass of allied guns and mortars produced more than 1,000 casualties a day inside the city. The chief bastions of the Russian defences were pulverized into dust, yet somehow the Russians, though weakened, still managed to rally themselves to rebuild the defences overnight. But they were struggling without the guidance of Totleben, who had been wounded in June, and had gone away to recuperate.

Meanwhile, the allies had worked very hard to extend and enlarge their trenches, and were encouraged by rumours that the Russian troops were demoralized, disorganized and on the brink of revolt.[63] By mid-summer, Gorchakov was faced with a serious shortage of food, water and ammunition, along with problems of cholera, and in late June he began to plan the Russians' final evacuation of the city. Much of the civilian population had left by then, and military desertions were rising. Following the suggestion of a Russian engineer named Bukhmeier, Gorchakov approved a bold plan to build a massive pontoon bridge across the sea harbour, a distance of more than 900 metres. The task was difficult and risky, but the bridge was completed successfully by the end of August.[64]

As Sebastopol faced its final days of the siege, other parts of Russia were feeling the pressure of the allied blockade. The blockade hindered the war effort, and damaged the civilian economy, too, such as the cotton textile factories, which were unable to import cotton from America, or machinery from Britain.[65]

THE STORMING OF THE MALAKOV AND THE REDAN

On 5 and 6 September, Sebastopol was assailed yet again by some 52,000 rounds of heavy allied fire. The Russians returned 20,000 rounds, but suffered 2,500 casualties. By now, the French trenches were within about 20 metres of the Malakov redoubt. The British position before the Redan fortification faced hard rock, into which it had been impossible to dig trenches. The British had to cross several hundred metres of ground, under fire, to reach their target.[66] It was decided that on 8 September the French would attack the Malakov. As soon as the French took possession, the British were to assault the Redan, in much the same way as they had done, or rather failed to do, in the June attack.

Saturday, 8 September was a stormy day. There was 'a wintry searching wind bringing clouds of dust into one's face', reported Romaine in his journal (p. 206). The sea was very rough, making it impossible for the British fleet to provide support to the allies' planned attack. Further allied fire was followed by a bold dash by French troops from their trenches into the Malakov, at precisely the time the Russians changed their guard. 'At five minutes before twelve o'clock,' reported Russell, 'the French, like a swarm of bees, issued forth from their trenches close to the doomed Malakhoff, scrambled up its face, and were through the embrasures in the twinkling of an eye' (p. 237). At first the Russians were unable to respond, 'but they soon recovered themselves, and from twelve o'clock until past seven in the evening the French had to meet and repulse the repeated attempts of the enemy to regain the work' (p. 237). It was a desperate struggle.

Similarly, Dunscombe recorded in his diary:

> The French went in at the Malakoff at 12 noon, and the Russians were so completely taken by surprise, that they got into it with very little opposition; but when they got in there was a great scrimmage; however the French held it [...]. (p. 154)

This provided the cue for the British to attack the Redan:

> [...] after it was known that the French had taken the Malakoff, our
> storming parties went in at the Redan, but the Russians were fully
> prepared for them; the 3rd Buffs got into the Redan and spiked eight
> guns, but were obliged to quit it, as the supports were not sent up; a
> second attack was made, but they could not even cross the ditch; so the
> attempt was given up for this time; however it is a great to have the
> Malakoff [...].[67]

After eleven months of the siege, it was a huge relief to see the
Malakov taken. 'We are masters of Sebastopol!' wrote a French
soldier to his father.[68] It was the key to the defences; without it, the
Russians could no longer defend their city. Nor could they hold the
Redan. But the British attack had gone ahead anyway, more for
reasons of national pride and duty than out of military necessity.
It had not been an edifying sight. 'Against all the best opinion we
again tried to storm the Redan,' wrote Romaine on 11 September,
'and to do it with troops who had had all the fight taken out of
them –.' He saw it as a 'disgraceful defeat'. The British crossed the
ditch to the parapet

> [...] and then with few exceptions the men stuck, others remained
> stupified on our side of the ditch to be shot down by the cross fire of the
> Russians from the two flanks – the men having possession of the salient
> could not by any efforts of the officers be induced to advance and drive
> at the Russians [...] – The officers, boys as many of them were, behaved
> nobly. (p. 212)

An officer went to seek reinforcements, and in his absence Romaine
watched the men being driven out of the Redan:

> [I] shall never forget the bitter moment when I saw our men running
> back to the trenches from a work they had gained, pursued by volleys
> of stones from the Russians on the parapet.
> [...]
>
> The siege and the long course of dodging behind bad trenches has
> completely demoralized our men – Then, many in all regiments are
> mere boys who have never been disciplined to obey orders, and upon

whom neither the words nor the example of their officers had any effect. (Romaine, pp. 212–13; letter to Lord Mulgrave, 11 September 1855)

Sebastopol's defences were finally breached, but the British had a very muted sense of victory. Many observers felt that the French had won the glory of ending the siege, and looked at the British actions with considerable gloom. Some, like Dunscombe, reflected bitterly on the fact that the British assault on the Redan was actually unnecessary (p. 155). Once the Malakov was taken, the Russians could not hold the Redan; the British casualties suffered were yet another unnecessary waste of war.

Then events took a slightly unexpected turn. The Russians knew they could not hold the city any longer, and evacuated their troops throughout the night, across the pontoon bridge. An eerie quiet descended over much of Sebastopol. In the middle of the night, reported Russell, 'the men of the Highland division on duty in the trenches were surprised at the silence in the Redan, and some volunteers managed to creep into it. Nothing could they hear but the heavy breathing and groans of the wounded and dying, who, with the dead, were the sole occupants of the place' (p. 247). The Highlanders occupied the Redan during the night, though it no longer mattered as a point of defence.

Like other commentators, Russell had some sympathy with the departing Russians, who had defended their city so courageously. The Russians' own view of the evacuation is narrated very powerfully in the final pages of Tolstoy's *Sebastopol Sketches*.

Along the whole line of the Sebastopol bastions, which for so many months now had been seething with an unusually active life, had seen heroes released one by one into the arms of death, and had aroused the fear, hatred and, latterly, the admiration of the enemy forces, there was now not a soul to be seen. The whole place was dead, laid waste, uncanny – but not quiet; the destruction was still continuing. [pp. 182–3]

The enemy forces could see that something incomprehensible was taking place in grim Sebastopol [...They] did not yet dare believe that their unflinching antagonist had disappeared. (p. 183)

The Russians move slowly 'in a dense, impenetrable crush' across the pontoon bridge: 'Surging together and ebbing apart like the waves of the sea on this gloomy, swell-rocked night' (p. 183). They feel Sebastopol is 'entirely saturated in [their] blood', and do not understand why they have now been ordered to abandon the city 'without a struggle'.

> The first reaction of every Russian soldier on hearing this order was one of bitterness and incomprehension. This was succeeded by a fear of pursuit [... The] men felt exposed and unprotected, and crowded anxiously in the darkness by the entrance to the bridge, which was pitching in the high wind. (p. 183)

Soon everyone feels the same urgent need 'to escape from this terrible place of death as quickly as possible'. As each Russian crosses the bridge to safety, says Tolstoy, he makes the sign of the cross with visible relief. 'But this feeling concealed another – draining, agonizing, and infinitely more profound: a sense of something that was a blend of remorse, shame and violent hatred.' They feel 'bitterness that could find no words'; almost every man 'shook his fist at the enemy forces' (p. 184).

This futile gesture ends Tolstoy's account of Sebastopol. They left behind 10,000 allied and 13,000 Russian casualties.[69] After 11 months of increasingly desperate defence of the town, all the survivors could do now was shake their fists in wordless bitterness. What had it all been for?

4

SEBASTOPOL

THE FALLEN CITY

In the early hours of 9 September 1855, huge explosions shook the ground around Sebastopol.[1] 'The city was enveloped in fire and smoke, and torn asunder by the tremendous shocks of these volcanoes', wrote William Howard Russell in *The Times* (p. 248). By 9 am, 'The whole of Sebastopol was in flames; but nearly half of the burning city was hidden by the impenetrable cloud caused by the explosion.' Soon the city was 'a mass of flames, and the pillar of black, grey, and velvety fat smoke ascending from it seemed to support the very heavens.'[2] To some observers, it looked like a biblical apocalypse, but also 'beautiful', 'sublime and terrific', 'a magnificent sight'.[3] Civilian Mary Seacole recalled standing on Cathcart's Hill, watching 'the city blazing beneath us', feeling 'awe-struck at the terrible sight'. The air was cold and clear. 'The night was made a ruddy lurid day with the glare of the blazing town.'[4] As the siege ended, night became day, and nature itself seemed to be inverted. Observers found this uncanny, disturbing. This might have been the beginning of victory for the allies, but the feeling was not happy, triumphant nor even optimistic.

The military history of the 11-month siege of Sebastopol is well documented. In this chapter I will explore some of the cultural reverberations of this gruelling event, every day of which had been closely documented in the British newspapers, especially

The Times. What did the fall of Sebastopol *mean* to the British who were present, and how were those meanings expressed, both visually and in writing? Recent theoretical commentators, such as Susan Sontag, Judith Butler, Mary Favret and Paul Virilio, are very interested in the problems of how war is represented, and what place those representations have, or ought to have, in our political understandings of war.[5] These are complex questions whose roots lie very deep in our history. They are perhaps as old as warfare itself, but they take particular forms in relation to the Crimea, and deserve closer attention in current thinking about war and representation.

INTO SEBASTOPOL

Before evacuating the city, the Russians had mined it thoroughly. Explosions continued throughout the day on 9 September, and over the next few days as well. Some 30 to 40 booby traps were left behind. Frederic Dallas wrote that 'The Russians, outside all their works, have Machines, our men call them "Man traps", which explode when you touch, or rather tread upon them, and they are a frightful source of accidents.'[6] The *Illustrated London News'* war artist wrote a vivid account of such a trap, witnessed on 28 September:

> Yesterday, as I was sketching in the west of Sebastopol, an explosion shook the buildings around and reverberated through the roofless and untenanted edifices of the place. The Arsenal Creek was filled with a heavy black smoke, and showers of large stones fell into the water, lashing it for a moment into sheets of foam. The centre of the fire was a battery on the left flank of the Creek Battery. This was one of the works erected by the Russians to sweep the approaches of the Woronzoff road; it was built of stones taken from the houses around it, faced with earth externally, and without a ditch. The magazine was in the foundations of a house which had once stood there [...] The Russians had placed a *fougasse* over it, and an accidental tread upon a wooden peg driven into the earth broke a glass tube of inflammable matter which communicated with the powder below [...]

Three of the men in the work were blown to atoms; and a large number were buried in the ruins; whilst sad havoc was at the same time committed on parties of workmen leading mules along the road close by. Two soldiers of the guard in the Creek Battery were killed by stones projected with great violence into the air, and launched with fatal force upon them. Several mules and horses were killed in this same manner, and every point within 200 yards of the spot was visited by the terrible shower. The crater left by the explosion was about twenty feet deep and twenty wide; and in its crumbled sides were found some of the wounded, who were speedily conveyed to hospital.[7]

The men immediately searched for other traps, and discovered one in a nearby battery. They suspected that other Russian works were also mined and likely to explode at any time. These 'infernal machines' seemed to be everywhere, making it impossible for the British and French to occupy the city properly.

The victorious armies were in a state of limbo. What to do next? The British military authorities issued strict orders against entering Sebastopol, but a number of people made their way into the ruins.[8] 'For a few days all business seemed suspended in the camp,' wrote civilian chef Alexis Soyer, 'and the rage with every one was to visit the ruins of the far-famed city' (p. 385). Some immediately began looting and destroying. (Each nation had different rules about looting, which led to resentment between the troops.) Others went simply to look. Many observers were moved to represent the event – in letters, newspaper articles, diaries, drawings and paintings. Photographers came in to record the fallen city. By late autumn, remarked Mrs Seacole, visitors 'thronged the streets of Sebastopol, sketching its ruins and setting up photographic apparatus' (p. 178).

Sebastopol exercised a magnetizing fascination, despite, or perhaps because of, the danger. There were soldiers, sailors, war artists, journalists, war tourists, soldiers' wives and professional photographers all trying, in their different ways, to represent the inside of Sebastopol; to see what the war had done. Yet, like the war itself, Sebastopol remained elusive, an object which at once demanded and defied representation. It was a mesmerizing place, abandoned yet not empty; fallen yet dangerous; beautiful even in its damaged state, yet a disgusting site of mangled and decaying bodies; bereft, yet a treasure-house of abandoned objects, which some of the visitors immediately began to plunder. French officer Jean-Baptiste-Louis Berquin commented on 10 September, 'We took an immense amount of booty. I'm sitting as I write to you on a beautiful upholstered armchair covered in Morocco leather.' He observed thousands of French soldiers returning from Sebastopol 'with a chair, an arm chair, a piano, a mirror, a frame, a mattress, a Russian hat on the head, a coat on his back, a pair of chickens, a turkey, a cat, rabbits, all laughing like crazy'.[9]

According to her memoir, Mary Seacole was one of the first civilians to enter Sebastopol. 'For weeks past,' she reported, 'I had been offering bets to everyone that I would not only be the first woman to enter Sebastopol from the English lines, but that I would be the first to carry refreshments into the fallen city' (pp. 172–3). The day after Sebastopol was taken, she loaded up some mules with provisions and set off, only to discover that no unauthorized person was permitted to enter the city, because of mines. Undeterred, Mrs Seacole went to visit the general in charge. He immediately recognized her, and provided an official pass for herself and her 'attendants' to distribute food and drink. So many soldiers immediately joined her staff as temporary attendants that she could hardly get going, but eventually the large party managed to pass the sentries into Sebastopol, somewhat to the annoyance of the men left behind. Everyone, it seems, wanted to see the fallen city. The British and French had shelled it for months: what did it look like now? From a distance, it was hard to see any damage. As officer's wife Fanny Duberly remarked, Sebastopol seemed 'almost uninjured – so calm, and white, and fair did it look' (p. 282). What was going on; where did the firepower go? When they got inside, visitors realized that the city was in fact badly mauled; not a single building was untouched.

'Sebastopol must have been a beautiful town, quite a city of palaces,' wrote Lieutenant Robert Biddulph in a letter, 'but it is knocked about terribly by our shot; there is not a house that does not bear the marks of our bombardment. The interior of the Redan is like a ploughed field from our shells.'[10] Similarly, for Captain Nicholas Dunscombe, 'the barracks [in Sebastopol] must have been once magnificent buildings, but are gravely knocked about now [...] in fact there is not an entire house in the town standing'. He observed the effects of the shelling upon the population, as

Fig. 7: James Robertson, Interior of the Malakoff with Remains of the Tower, Looking Towards the Mamelon, 12 September 1855

hundreds of Russian bodies were taken for burial.[11] 'The more I see of the place the more I admire it,' wrote Lieutenant Colonel Dallas on 28 September. 'The Public Buildings are so beautifully situated, and are themselves so handsome.' But, 'I don't think that there is a single house that is not completely destroyed, excepting the mere outward shell' (p. 183).

'Sebastopol is finely situated, and laid out in broad spacious streets,' wrote Royal Engineer George Ranken. 'Some of the houses [...] must have been very handsome and elegant', though now little remains but 'blackened disfigured walls'. He looked 'with deepest interest at the remains of the famous city' (p. 75). There were buildings 'perforated in all parts, and a scene of desolation and ruin [...]. The whole of the civil portion of the city was still in a blaze; and as it was quite uncertain where the Russians might have secreted their mines, or what fort or buildings they might intend to blow up, it was by no means prudent to venture far into the town' (pp. 68–9). On 10 September, the city was still burning. Ranken observed 'the magnificent ranges of white barracks and public buildings all more or less injured; the barracks near the Redan perforated in all directions by cannon shot, or torn and smashed by shells; a number of smaller buildings, probably the poorer suburbs, literally a mere heap of ruins' (p. 69).

'I can give you no very clear description of Sebastopol,' wrote Mary Seacole. 'Many parts of it were still blazing furiously [on 9 September] – explosions were taking place in all directions – every step had a score of dangers; and yet curiosity and excitement carried us on and on' (p. 173). Lost for words to describe the city, Mrs Seacole turned her attention to the new inhabitants, hungry soldiers, to whom she passed out refreshments. Some had refreshed themselves already in the Sebastopol cellars. She observed one group of men, 'ingloriously drunk, and playing the wildest pranks. They were dancing, yelling, and singing – some of them with Russian women's dresses fastened around their waists, and old bonnets stuck upon their heads' (p. 174). Drunk or sober, the men plundered materials from the houses – furniture, crockery, every imaginable kind of domestic object. One inebriated soldier presented Mrs Seacole with a stolen parasol. He was dressed in a woman's silk skirt, with some torn lace around his wrists. He came 'mincingly' towards Mrs Seacole, 'holding the parasol above his head, and imitating the walk of an affected lady, to the vociferous delight of his comrades'. 'And all this, and much more,' noted Mrs Seacole, suddenly more serious, 'in that fearful charnel city, with death and suffering on every side' (p. 174). Mary Seacole's memoir is deliberately light, often amusing. She wrote it primarily as an entertainment, to save herself from bankruptcy, and she made no claim to offer a serious analysis of the war. Yet, like other witnesses, Mrs Seacole found this scene disturbing, even as she tried to make it comical.

Those who went inside Sebastopol were troubled by the sheer quantity of *things*, damaged and deranged, scattered among the dead and dying. So much human work went into making those things, and caring for them. So much human effort and courage went into the defence of the doomed city; and into attacking it. Where did all the labour end up? War produces a particular kind of *waste*, and at the Crimea it began to happen on an industrial scale. It was an early hint of what would come in 1914.

Fig. 8: Objects from Sebastopol, *Punch*, 13 October 1855

Looting and pillaging were the most immediate reactions. This is a familiar scenario at the end of a war – there were still vivid cultural memories of the Napoleonic armies in Moscow in 1812, looting while the city burns – and it was played out in a peculiarly intense form in Sebastopol.[12] Some intruders went in search of alcohol and ended up dancing in the streets, often dressed in bits of looted gear, and especially in women's clothing. Others gathered up vast quantities of domestic objects – china, cooking utensils, furniture, clothing, shoes, babies' carriages, cats and dogs, candlesticks, and so on. Some took weapons, ropes and other items which might be put to practical use. And much was simply destroyed; shredded, broken up, trampled, or burned by groups of soldiers moving randomly through the ruins.

Russell in *The Times* described the sight of the Russian barracks in Sebastopol as 'painful' after the victorious soldiers had passed through, creating 'as much havoc as lay in their power'.

> In the portions of the buildings underground vast quantities of new clothing and accoutrements were scattered about. Hundreds of helmets were being trodden down by the men, and bales of cloth lay on every side. Furniture of all kinds was being removed; pictures, lamps, dresses, and musical instruments were all there for those who went sufficiently early, and who cared to carry them home.

Russell noted that British sailors were quick to get in and plunder; he saw them 'staggering under chairs, tables, and lumbering old pictures, through every street, and making [their] way back to the trenches with vast accumulations of worthlessness' (p. 253). Many of the objects were of no value, except to their original owners; many were broken beyond repair. But the context made them newly desirable; any piece of rubbish might suddenly become saleable. The looters 'were laden with every conceivable article, I think, except "babies"', wrote Frederick Robinson on 10 September:

> [...] there were puppies and dogs, however, together with children's carriages, invalids' chairs, bedding, crockery ware, military and plain clothing, bales of cloth, and every kind of domestic utensil, looking glasses, richly gilt cornices, and chandeliers wrenched from their sockets, books, vegetables, and kegs of butter, – evidently prizes much valued; pictures, for the most part tawdry prints [...].[13]

The sheer jumble of objects was exciting, but also disturbing. The soldiers recognized the objects from their own domestic lives. The entire contents of houses were shaken up and tossed together, a sight which was at once familiar and unfamiliar – what Freud would later describe as uncanny. In response, the intruders were driven by two conflicting impulses: to preserve and to destroy. Many of the objects mentioned are associated with women, and this perhaps intensified the grief as well as the pleasure as the things were damaged, saved, mocked, destroyed or sold off. Either the objects were destroyed with the men's own hands in what looks like a kind of infantile rage (and pleasure); or they became commodities, carried about, exchanged, sold. A huge mobile market place sprang up out of the ruins, with a new kind of commerce, as *The Times* reported on 5 October 1855:

> The camps have consequently abounded with itinerant vendors of all
> kinds of goods, for every one of which fabulous prices were demanded.
> The variety of articles was astonishing, and from valuable silver plate to
> the most worthless of old books, which no one could read, everything
> seemed to meet with some purchaser. Pictures were most in demand,
> and some really valuable ones were taken. (p. 10)

People from all classes wanted war trophies. Military surgeon
Douglas Reid reported that he had taken a Russian book of poems
from Sebastopol and 'some doctor's prescriptions from the Hospital
in the town'; he also had 'a silver ring taken off a dead Russian in
the Redan'. His account does not seem at all embarrassed to take
possession of the spoils of war. Reid bought two photographs by
James Robertson: 'one of a Turkish, the other of a Circassian lady';
images not of the city, but of unknown women.[14] All these things
he sent back to England as souvenirs. Similarly, Major-General
William Allan noted tersely, 'I have picked up a few trashy things
from the town; they may, however, be prized in England some
day.'[15] As Sebastopol was rendered uninhabitable as a home for
its citizens, its objects, however useless, acquired a new monetary
value. The sense of what was valuable and what worthless became
inverted.

It is striking that pictures were often the most popular item. Mary
Seacole writes that she rarely accepted loot, but she was persuaded
to buy a painting stolen from above the altar of a Sebastopol
church (p. 176). She was moved by the face of the Madonna in
the painting: 'soft and beautiful', with a look of 'divine calmness
and heavenly love'. Mrs Seacole imagined people during the siege
kneeling before this image and finding some comfort 'in its soft
loving gaze' (p. 176). She expresses kindness and sympathy, at least
in fantasy, for the suffering Russians, even as she reports taking
away one of their precious possessions as a war trophy. The looters
took plenty of real objects to sell, but many of their customers, like
Mrs Seacole, preferred *representations* – pictures of things which,
we can be certain, were not scenes from the fallen city, nor images
of the reality in which they now lived.

Mrs Duberly, too, was consumed with curiosity about
Sebastopol, but she did not enter it immediately after it was
taken. Her first view of the fallen city was from the heights on

Sunday, 9 September, where she watched the south side burning. 'I counted ten separate fires', she wrote a few days later; 'a magnificent sight' (p. 239). Should the victors feel sympathy or regret after the long siege? For Mrs Duberly, the flaming vision produced 'greater satisfaction than pain', and effaced 'the destruction and desolation of war'.

> I could only remember that the long-coveted prize was ours at last, and I felt no more compunction for town or for Russian than the hound whose lips are red with blood does for the fox which he has chased through a hard run. It was a lawful prize, purchased, God knows! dearly enough, and I felt glad that we had got it. (p. 239)

To compare the siege of Sebastopol with chasing a fox is a particularly curious metaphor. A siege is static; the opposite, one would have thought, of a galloping hunt. The metaphor allows Mrs Duberly to imagine herself as an active participant in the war; a victor stained with the blood of battle. But it also has the effect of drawing attention to itself *as metaphor* precisely because it is so inappropriate. The moment of victory left her feeling rather troubled. She knew she ought to be delighted, self-righteous, triumphant; but when she tried to express these emotions, her imagination began to falter and her language seems forced.

A few days later, on 13 September, Mrs Duberly entered Sebastopol. If the city looked 'calm, and white, and fair' from a distance, inside was 'a very different tale': 'the ruined walls, the riddled roofs, the green cupola of the church, split and splintered to ribands' (p. 282). It was an ugly mess. Like other visitors, Mrs Duberly was troubled by the damaged buildings, the litter of objects, the waste and desolation. Despite this, she was calm and interested. Then she was struck by a 'pestilential' smell. 'Anything so putrid, so nauseating, so terrible, never assailed us before' (p. 284). Perhaps there were dead horses and cattle nearby, 'and yet they do not smell like this!'

> What is it? It cannot surely be – oh, horror! – a heap, a piled-up heap of human bodies in every stage of putrid decomposition, flung out into the street, and being carted away for burial. As soon as [the allies] gained possession of the town, a hospital was discovered in

the barracks, to which the attention of our men was first attracted by screams and cries. Entering, they found a large number of wounded and dying [...]. (p. 285)

This horrible discovery lay at the heart of Sebastopol: perhaps as many as 3,000 wounded Russians, festering, suffering and dying among the ruins of the city.

When one is exposed to such sights, writes Fanny Duberly, the mind protects itself, refusing to register the full horror (p. 286). But the vision returned with force later, and she knew she would never forget 'that foul heap of green and black, glazed and shrivelled flesh' (p. 285). Like Mary Seacole, Fanny Duberly found Sebastopol difficult to describe and impossible to forget. Where Mrs Seacole's book resorts, uneasily, to comedy, Mrs Duberly's account becomes self-righteous ('a lawful prize [...] I felt glad that we had got it'), even while admitting some sympathy. But neither writer's approach seems to answer the terrible sights of the battered city.

INSIDE THE CITY

The shelling in the last days of the siege took a heavy toll on the Russians inside Sebastopol, killing and injuring as many as 1,000 people every day. When the city was evacuated on 8 September, the Russians were faced with large numbers of wounded soldiers and civilians, many of them too sick or injured to make the journey across the pontoon bridge. So the worst cases were simply left behind in the hope that the invaders would take care of them. However, because the allies could not occupy the mined city, most of the injured Russians were not discovered for two days or more. By then, those who were still alive were in terrible condition, without food or water or medical care, as Ranken recorded:

I thought I had seen sufficient horrors on the 8th and the ensuing day; but on the morning of the 10th, I witnessed a spectacle more terrible than any I had yet seen. About a thousand or more poor wounded Russian soldiers and officers were found in a large building near the ruins of Fort Paul, on the morning of the 10th. They had passed nearly two days in agony and misery, without food or any assistance. Many dead were there, and the stench in the vast charnel-house of horror so dreadful, that it is a marvel how any had supported existence. (p. 72)

Russell wrote in *The Times*:

Of all the pictures of the horrors of war which have ever been presented to the world, the hospital of Sebastopol presents the most horrible, heart-rending, and revolting. It cannot be described, and the imagination of a Fuseli could not conceive anything at all like unto it. How the poor human body can be mutilated and yet hold its soul within it when every limb is shattered, and every vein and artery is pouring out the life stream, one might study here at every step, and at the same time wonder how little will kill! (pp. 256–7)

The scenes in the hospital were shocking:

Entering one of these doors I beheld such a sight as few men, thank God, have ever witnessed! In a long low room [...] lay the wounded Russians, who had been abandoned to our mercies by their General. The wounded, did I say? No, but the dead – the rotten and festering corpses of the soldiers, who were left to die in their extreme agony, untended, uncared for, packed as close as they could be stowed, some on the floor, others on wretched trestles and bedsteads, or pallets of straw, sopped and saturated with blood, which oozed and trickled through upon the floor, mingling with the droppings of corruption.

Russians who had served their nation loyally throughout the siege, writes Russell, were simply abandoned.

Many might have been saved by ordinary care. Many lay, yet alive, with maggots crawling about in their wounds. Many, nearly mad by the scene around them, or seeking escape from it in their extremest agony, had rolled away under the beds, and glared out on the heart-stricken spectator – oh! with such looks! Many with legs and arms broken and twisted [...] implored aid, water, food, or pity [...].

Russell's powerful account was widely read in Britain, and became known around the world. Many other people wrote private accounts in diaries or letters. For many observers, this was surely the most pitiful event of the war.[16] According to Figes, the Russian doctor in charge of the evacuation of the hospitals, Dr Guibbenet, had left the wounded behind deliberately, in the full expectation they would be found and cared for in a short time.[17] He was 'mortified', writes Figes, to learn afterwards that help took so long to arrive (p. 394).

Visual images of the hospital also appeared in some of the illustrated papers. The *Illustrated London News*, for example, printed a drawing on 6 October 1855 which is much less disturbing than the written accounts. Some things could be said in words but not in pictures.

The ambivalence expressed by observers such as Mary Seacole and Fanny Duberly is typical of writings about the Crimean War, and is especially true of representations of the siege of Sebastopol. These works are some of the most powerful cultural legacies of the war, expressing both hatred and love for the city and its brave defenders; joy and sorrow (and possibly some guilt) at the outcome of the siege. More than this, the writings, photographs and other representations of the fall of Sebastopol open up new ways of seeing

Fig. 9: Hospital in Sebastopol, *Illustrated London News*, 6 October 1855

modern warfare. They raise questions of looking and witnessing which remain both important and perplexing to us today.

These matters are explored by recent theorists such as Sontag in *Regarding the Pain of Others* and Favret in *War at a Distance* (among others). Both books are concerned with the question of how wars are represented, particularly to those far away. Neither engages closely with the Crimean War, even though it occupies such a crucial place in the history of war and representation. Sontag argues convincingly that while war photographs are often deeply disturbing, their meaning can be quite ambiguous, and that they can be mobilized for different, even opposing, political purposes (pp. 9–10, 35). She pays little attention to the Crimea, the first war to be photographed, apart from a very short discussion of Fenton's photographs (pp. 43–4).[18] Mary Favret argues that the modern 'structure of feeling' in relation to warfare was created by the Romantic poets, imagining events of distant conflicts, inspired by contemporary words and pictures. Favret's argument is suggestive, yet it is oddly indifferent to the actual conflicts and the experiences of millions of people, both soldiers and civilians, who were directly affected by the Napoleonic Wars. Favret has almost nothing to say about the Crimean War or the significant changes in representation which took place in the 1850s. Both writers suggest that, in Sontag's words, 'Being a spectator of calamities taking place in another country is a quintessential modern experience' (p. 16), as if those who were present in 'another country', actually in the war, being killed, hurt or displaced by the conflict, were somehow not modern, or not part of history. The representations, and the feelings of those who see those representations far away, become more important, in this approach, than those who are affected directly by war. But this is not what we learn from the representations of the Crimean War. The poetry, newspaper reports and photographs of the Crimea raise questions of proximity and distance, but they do not privilege the distant civilian, sitting by his fireside, reading the newspaper or writing a poem.[19] These representations are intensely aware of events and experiences of the war itself – the hard labour, the violence, the suffering, the boredom and also the pleasures – even as they find 'the war itself' difficult to describe. Favret is of course right that people far away from the war zone rely on these representations in their attempts to make sense of the conflict, but it seems to me we need to pay closer attention to those who were present, and who did so much to represent the experience to others.

For more than 11 months in 1854–5, Sebastopol was a very powerful *idea*. The siege was observed by the British and French from a distance. That distance might be just 25 yards (as for the French soldiers in the trenches in front of the Malakov fortification), or it might be several miles, from one of the camps or settlements outside the city. Near or far, those besieging Sebastopol watched and wondered as it was battered with the heaviest shelling in the history of warfare, yet appeared, miraculously (and falsely), hardly touched by it all. Many other British people followed the siege from thousands of miles away, in the newspapers. People felt very strongly that they were witnessing an important (and possibly barbaric) historical event. This raised complex new questions. How is one placed as a witness to war? The literate middle class had access to a huge amount of information from the newspapers and magazines, art and photography exhibitions, panoramas and other representations of the war. The representations in the press, especially, included a large amount of accurate, or near-accurate, information: much more accurate, indeed, than most news sources today.[20] So the civilian witnesses were, on the one hand, very well informed. On the other hand, apart from a few war tourists in the Crimea, civilians actually saw nothing at all first hand. All they had were representations. What did the representations mean? How should they be interpreted; and how did they position the civilian citizens, making them complicit in the war, paying for it through raised taxes, witnessing it daily, indirectly, in the press? This question of witnessing versus seeing was to become quite pressing during the First World War, as I have argued elsewhere.[21] This modern paradox has important roots in the Russian War, and especially in the fall of Sebastopol.[22]

VISUALIZING SEBASTOPOL

Watching from above the ruins as Sebastopol burns was at once 'sublime and terrific', writes Alexis Soyer. How can one describe this? Soyer looked to the visual arts to express what he had seen: 'A

Martin or a Danby alone could trace on canvas, with their vigorous tints and their wild genius, the stupendous scene which my eyes are now beholding' (p. 379). Only the apocalyptic paintings of artists John Martin (1789–1854) or Francis Danby (1793–1861) – who produced huge, violent canvases, often on biblical or classical themes – could do justice to the sight of the fallen city. Soyer looked to a particular kind of art – extreme, fantasmatic, hysterical paintings, mainly from the 1820s and 1830s – to bring the experience of 1855 into history and cultural memory. Yet most of the visual art of the Russian War is *not* in fact in this style. There are a few such works (such as William Simpson's *Fall of Sebastopol*, 1856), but these are unusual.[23]

Most of the paintings and sketches of Sebastopol are quite modest and factual in style. There are works by soldiers as well as by civilian artists, both amateur and professional, including William Simpson and Henry Clifford. These works are often a kind of reportage, depicting the scene as straightforwardly as possible. They avoid the biblical analogies and hyperbole imagined by Soyer. Others attempt an epic, heroic interpretation of the end of the siege, especially of the French storming of the Malakov. But such dramatic scenes are less common, it seems to me, than the images of everyday life through the months of the siege.

A few commentators liken the ruins of Sebastopol, somewhat bizarrely, to ancient catastrophes: the destruction of Pompeii, or a biblical disaster.[24] But the siege was not high drama; it was grinding, dismal, relentless fear and hard work, together with periods of great suffering from cold, disease and hunger. As Colin Robins points out, boredom, fear, cold were the typical experiences of the war, and the art often presents precisely this.[25]

Indeed, the images of Sebastopol that speak most powerfully are almost the opposite of what Soyer imagined. The most haunting pictures of the war are the curious, quiet photographs by James Robertson and Felice Beato; works which are all the more powerful for their understatement.

James Robertson (1813/14–1888) was a British engraver who had a long career at the imperial mint in Constantinople. For about 15 years he was also active as a photographer, working with his brother-in-law, Felice Beato. They photographed in the Crimea in the autumn of 1855 and spring of 1856.[26] Their photographs are, I

Fig. 10: James Robertson, Interior of Redan, 1855

suggest, some of the most important cultural documents of the fall of Sebastopol.

Robertson's photograph of the interior of the Redan fortification, taken not long after it had been abandoned by the Russians, is a masterpiece of understatement. Contemporary viewers would have had quite a detailed knowledge of the siege, from the newspaper reports, and might have had a fairly good idea of what the image meant. ('What wonderful engineering!' wrote Mrs Duberly on first seeing the Redan (p. 243)). But even if one has little military knowledge, the photograph has tremendous power. Robertson merely documented places, landscapes, things. The fact that photography was fairly primitive, in technical terms, gave it a kind of honest simplicity which, one might argue, got lost as cameras and techniques became more sophisticated. Ulrich Keller goes so far as to say that Robertson's 'sparse' photos 'come close to that

119

Fig. 11: James Robertson, Barrack Battery, 1855

impossibility: the image without a rhetoric' (p. 165). His pictures of Sebastopol convey a real sense of anguish and loss, which one can feel even now, across the years.

How is this achieved? I think through stillness and the absence of things that can move: people, animals, even plants. Nothing living is present. All here is solid, hard to move. It is nearly all damaged; wrecked. It cannot move itself; but it has been moved. Which things have been thrown about by explosions and which by human hands? Where are those human hands now?

The scene suggests both protection and exposure. There are sandbags and gabions, some still in protective formation. But the place is also frighteningly open. And much of the protective material is broken and has fallen, or has been shoved roughly, into a hole in the middle. The scene is quite desolate; empty, yet filled. It is filled with things that had been useful until very recently but are now just rubbish; it is filled with despair and failure. Robertson is British, but this is not an image of allied triumph. The point of view is from the inside; not a Russian perspective, exactly; more the view of a neutral, sad observer.

In the photo of the Barracks Battery, there is a stronger sense of protection. The stone wall looks solid. The cannons seem in about the right place; one can imagine the Russians defending themselves. The woven rope mantlets look strong and more or less in one piece. One can see the work and skill that went into making the objects, whether by hand or in a factory. Here they are still reasonably intact; in the photo of the Redan more things are broken and useless. In both, there is a sense of what Keller calls Robertson's 'stubborn austerity'. The images are at once simple – simply composed – and complex, full of *stuff* and of powerful, unspoken, unimaginable emotions. 'Small things are made great by events,' remarked the *Illustrated London News*.[27] Thirty years later, English readers would get a vivid sense of the experience of being *inside* those batteries, when Tolstoy's *Sebastopol Sketches* were translated.[28]

At the time, the fall of Sebastopol was marked in English by a considerable amount of poetry, much of it published in the press. The city was the prize of the Russian War, at least in theory. The phrase 'Sebastopol has fallen!', or variations on it, appears triumphantly in many newspaper reports, as well as in patriotic poems and songs about the event. For example, 'Sebastopol is Won!' by Irish lawyer and poet Joseph Michael Barry, opens confidently:

'Tis won! – three cheers of triumph – hurrah, hurrah, hurrah!
And yet another cheer, boys – we *may* exult to-day!
[...]
How many gallant hearts, this hour, are throbbing high, with pride,
Behind those broken ramparts, that shot and shell defied: (I, ll. 1–2,
    5–6)

The very debris of Sebastopol itself supposedly celebrates the victory of its enemies:

The shattered roofs – the blackened walls – attest the ruin done,
And every desert street proclaims – Sebastopol is won! (II, ll. 11–12)[29]

Fig. 12: Ruins in Sebastopol, *Illustrated London News*, 20 October 1855

Similarly, Canadian poet Augusta Baldwyn writes in 'The Victory':

> Shine, brilliant lights, and tell the story
> Of England's joy and France's glory;
> Their flags o'er Russian tow'rs are shown, –
> The work, the mighty work, is done. [ll. 1–4]
> [...]
> Sebastopol! the Russians' pride,
> England and France its spoil divide;
> And loud the Black Sea's moaning wave
> Echoes above the war-ships' grave. (ll. 21–24)[30]

That was the rhetoric, far away. But, as we have seen, for many of those present it was a strangely muted occasion. As Mrs Duberly notes, in the British camp, there was 'no elation, no cheers, no drunkenness, no bonfires, except the vast bonfire of the smoking blazing city' (p. 238).

Few of the poems about Sebastopol are of great literary or even historical worth. Poetry somehow did not answer this particular event, unlike the charge of the Light Brigade, so powerfully memorialized by Tennyson. The end of the siege was most memorably represented not by poetry, nor by the apocalyptic paintings imagined by Soyer, but by the simple yet profound photographs of Robertson and Beato. The new medium of photography offered new ways of memorializing war. Its technical clumsiness made it, paradoxically, a most nuanced medium. As Keller notes, it did not yet have the claim to mimetic truth that it gained later, but it seems to offer some other kind of truth; the truth about our ambivalent relationship to war, perhaps, that the Russian War so profoundly revealed.[31]

As we have seen, many commentators found it difficult to describe the interior of Sebastopol; they faltered at the sight of 'that charnel city'. Why? The sheer horror was difficult to describe, and mitigated the relief that the war would soon be over. And there was perhaps some element of disappointment; the allies had won the city, but they could not really occupy it and they didn't know what to do next. It took some time to establish that the war was finished; the peace treaty was not signed until March 1856. More than a century later, we came to realize that the sad fate of Sebastopol made little if any difference to the outcome of the war. As Lambert has shown, the war was won not in the Crimea, but in the Baltic, not least by an economic blockade that was a key element in convincing the Tsar to agree peace terms (pp. 4–6, 341).

What remained was the *fantasy* investment in Sebastopol. British visitors were fascinated to see the effects of their bombardment up close. Look at what we have done! But at the same time they were rather frightened: *look at what we have done*. The industrial age had brought an astonishing ability to create and build: Brunel's bridges, steam power, the railways, all kinds of manufacturing; and a vast range of commodities and objects, great and small. Britain was filling up and expanding through machines, things, power – all much celebrated a few years earlier, in the Great Exhibition of 1851. But industry has a huge capacity to destroy, too, and this came into focus in new ways at the Crimea. Some 60 years later, the First World War was perceived as the first industrial war. Men faced machines, with the machines always winning. Killing was organized on an industrial scale.[32] This is the great trauma of the First World War, and it retains its ability to shock, even today. But there were early intimations of industrial warfare, of industry put

Fig. 13: James Robertson, Sebastopol Docks before Destruction, 1855

at the disposal of warfare, at the Crimea, and this was one of the many things that troubled writers about Sebastopol. On the other hand, observers were excited and delighted by the destruction around them. The Russians had excellent fuses, good explosions; they showed great technical competence. All over Sebastopol, the British were impressed by the 'extreme strength and solidity' of the Russian works: the huge defences; the massive docks (Ranken, p. 78).

For engineer Nicholas Dunscombe, the Russian batteries were 'all perfect'; 'the Malakoff is a perfect work'.[33] Major-General William Allan admired the 'indefatigable labour' of the Russian soldiers in constructing 'such formidable bomb proof earthworks within their bastions', under the direction of their 'great and renowned Engineer', General Totleben.[34] On 12 September, William Howard Russell noted that, 'The wonder of all visitors to the ruins of Sebastopol is divided – they are astonished at the strength of the works, and that they were ever taken; they are amazed that men could have defended them so long with such ruin around them' (p. 251). Once they had looked at the fallen city, most

Fig. 14: James Robertson, Sebastopol Docks in Ruins, 1856

visitors to Sebastopol, both military and civilian, then studied the great docks; marvellous works of engineering. For military surgeon Frederick Robinson, the docks were 'the lion of Sebastopol'; 'beautiful structures' produced by an enormous investment of labour, time and money (p. 404). 'They seem the works of giants,' commented engineer Ranken. 'It is impossible not to be astonished at the vastness of the undertaking' (p. 78). 'Prodigious' declared Russell (p. 252); 'splendid' wrote Douglas Reid. 'It seems a pity to destroy them' (p. 112).

The British continued to admire the docks, even as they prepared to blow them up, a painstaking job which took several months. Viewers were excited all over again by the sublime beauty of the docks in a state of ruin. Robertson's photographs document the docks before and after; from a mighty feat of engineering to a mighty pile of rubble (see Figs 13 and 14).

Responses to Sebastopol were among the most profoundly ambivalent representations of the Crimean War. The desolate city generated pleasure and terror; admiration and horror. Wars have always stirred such emotions, of course, but as weapons became more powerful and more dreadful, war became increasingly horrible as well as more exciting, even, perversely, in some respects more beautiful. British representations of the fall of Sebastopol in 1855 record these paradoxes. On the other hand, there was hope that the horrible fate of the city might bring about the end of this terrible war. But how much difference did it make? Not very much at all. As Andrew Lambert has shown us, the immense courage and suffering on all sides at Sebastopol had very little effect upon the outcome of the war (pp. 31–3). This knowledge surely casts a further shadow of sadness over the conflict, and should give us even greater pause today.

5

THE BALTIC CAMPAIGN

On Saturday, 11 March 1854, after weeks of urgent preparation, a large fleet was assembled at Spithead. Huge crowds came from all over Britain to witness the rare spectacle of British ships departing for war. It was an astonishing sight, all the more so after 40 years of peace. War had not yet been officially declared. The fleet was greeted with great enthusiasm by the press. *The Times* reported that, 'The first Division of the Baltic fleet has departed on its warlike mission, amid the cheers of thousands of spectators, in the presence of the Queen and the Royal family, and attended by the best wishes of the whole nation.'[1] There had been considerable problems in fitting out and manning the ships, and they were even now far from ready for war. The newspapers suppressed any news of difficulties, however; for now, their reports were highly – and unrealistically – optimistic. One reason for their excitement was the use of new steam technology, with many of the ships partly or fully powered by steam.[2] For *The Times,* the fleet is 'an armament such as the world has never seen equalled, and not unworthy of that supremacy which we claim to hold upon the ocean'.[3] This was the first war fleet of the industrial age.

This chapter tells the neglected story of the war in the Baltic, where the British and French navies fought together in an awkward alliance. France was also in the process of converting to steam, but sent mainly sailing ships to the Baltic in 1854. I will focus on

Britain's part of the story, tracing the history alongside some of the representations in the press. While the papers devoted much more space and interest to events in the Crimea (not least because that is where most of the journalists and artists were based), there were also frequent, if briefer, reports from the Baltic. The campaign received quite a lot of coverage in the *Illustrated London News*, which sent artists with the Baltic fleets: Oswald Brierly from March to October 1854, and J. W. Carmichael from May to August 1855.[4] The *ILN* regularly published reports and pictures from the Baltic campaign, and reached a wide audience: by 1855 it had a circulation of 130,000.[5]

The *Illustrated London News* was fascinated by the fleet, devoting an entire supplement to the subject on 18 March 1854.

> The Departure of the Baltic Fleet, on Saturday last, grand and inspiriting as it may have been, was not intended for a show. It was the commencement of serious business. Though a beautiful sight, the many thousands of people who witnessed it were no doubt impressed with emotions of a deeper character than those which would have been excited by any merely holiday performance.[6]

The *ILN* remembered the 'holiday performance' of a naval review some months earlier, in the summer of 1853. This event had generated considerable interest, but few imagined then that the fleet would soon be setting off to war. Now, the paper argued, people were newly conscious that they had lived through a long period of peace.

> The assemblage of such an armament is happily a new thing to the present generation; and pride in the resources and energies of the country, that could in a few months equip and prepare for sea, so magnificent a fleet must have been the predominant sentiment in the mind of every spectator.[7]

Like *The Times*, the *Illustrated London News* made no reference to the many difficulties which 1had attended the fleet's preparations and which remained unresolved. It claimed that the departure is not merely 'a show', but, like most of the press, the *ILN* could not get much beyond the exciting spectacle of the event.

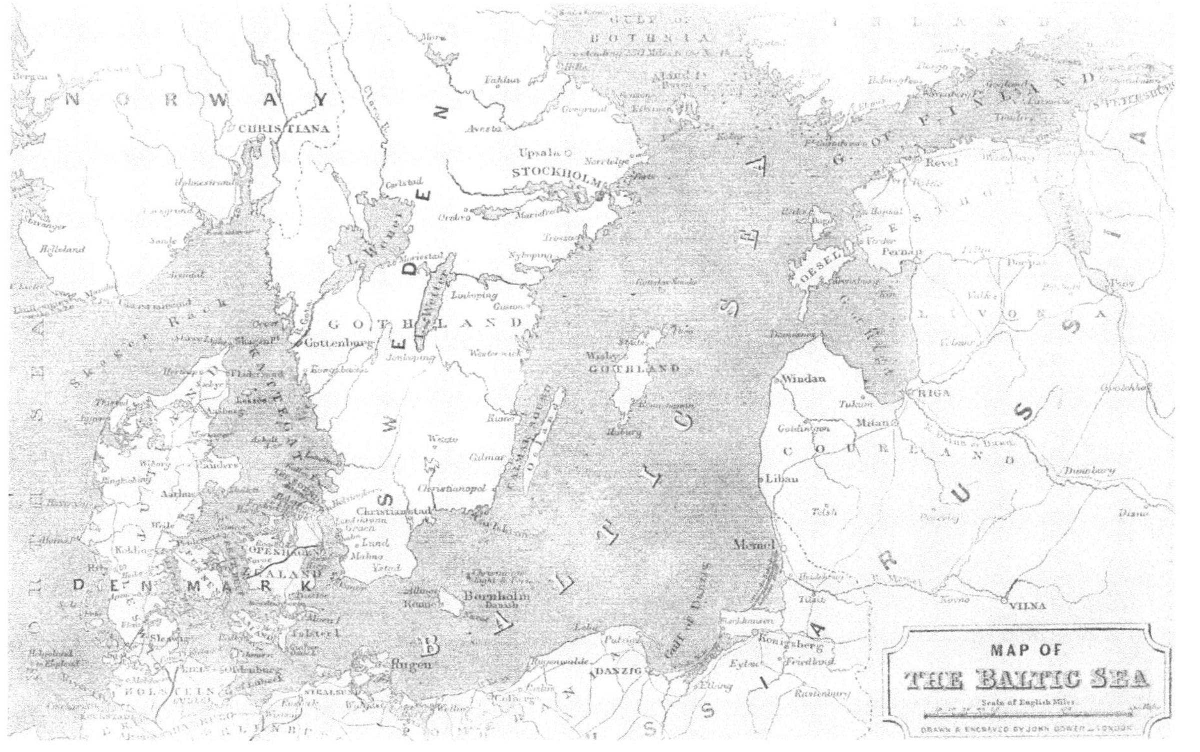

Fig. 15: Map of the Baltic, *Illustrated London News*, 18 March 1854

Fig. 16: Baltic Supplement, *Illustrated London News*, 18 March 1854

The Times went further, placing little value on the idea of peace, except as preparation for war. 'It is this extraordinary productive energy of the country, husbanded and matured to the highest pitch during 40 years of peace, with which our enemies will have to reckon.'[8] The *Daily News* took a more sober view. Like the *Illustrated London News*, it set the spectacle alongside the memory of the naval review the previous summer, 'a great national holiday'. But this was no holiday: it was a serious undertaking; it was work. Even the crowds who came to see the ships depart had 'an earnest and thoughtful expression of countenance'; they seemed 'fully alive to the importance of the coming struggle in which Admiral Napier and his brave sailors are expected to play so conspicuous a part.'[9] Similarly, for the *ILN*, the mere sight of the ships and men represented 'the stern reality of war'.[10]

The departure of the Baltic fleet signalled a return to the 'serious business' of war, even before war was officially declared, and many people wondered where it might lead. The idea of challenging and weakening Russian power seems to have been widely supported. But the use of military force to achieve that aim was regarded with less certainty. The newspapers emphasized the excitement and hope, but there was anxiety and fear, too, as the fleet departed for the Baltic.

The newspapers were also excited by the presence of Queen Victoria in her little boat, the *Fairy*, which moved to the head of the fleet, as the *Daily News* enthused,

> [...] her Majesty literally leading them out to sea, standing on deck all the time, and watching every movement with an interest which never tired. When did ever British sailors have such incentives to deeds of daring, led thus almost into action by the foremost lady in the world, to be the defenders at once of her woman's helplessness and her royal honour?[11]

The image is somewhat bizarre; even the most geographically naive reader would know that the sea off Portsmouth was hardly 'almost into action' in the Baltic. The archaic chivalry ('her woman's helplessness and her royal honour') also sits awkwardly as the nation moves towards industrialized war. War was officially declared 16 days later, on 27 March, and news of this reached the fleet on 4 April.[12]

VICE-ADMIRAL CHARLES NAPIER

The leader of the 1854 Baltic fleet was Vice-Admiral Charles Napier. After early service in the Napoleonic Wars, Napier had a brilliant if unorthodox naval career serving British interests against the Americans in 1814, in Portugal in the 1830s (under the *nom de guerre* Dom Carlos de Ponza) and in Syria in 1840–1. He was recognized as highly effective at sea, able to take risks and seize opportunities. He was not an easy character, however, and was perceived as quite a nuisance on land.[13] He was appointed to lead the fleet against Russia by Sir James Graham, the First Lord of the Admiralty, who had known Napier for 40 years.[14] While he supported Napier's appointment, he did not entirely trust him, and frequently withheld crucial information, or gave Napier incomplete or misleading news and orders. The awkwardness and mistrust between the two men created further difficulties in the course of the campaign. And the fleet itself was in many respects in a parlous state, despite the exciting new steam technology. As Lambert remarks, Napier had been appointed 'to command a Baltic fleet that existed largely on paper, being short of ships, seamen, officers, intelligence, and even basic geographical knowledge'.[15]

Now in his late 60s, Napier was something of a controversial figure, but his appointment was much celebrated in the press. A dinner chaired by Lord Palmerston was held in his honour at the Reform Club on 7 March and reported with approval: 'a splendid entertainment', demonstrating 'an enthusiasm truly English'.[16]

On the morning of the fleet's departure, on 11 March, Napier was keen to catch the wind and set off promptly, but the municipal leaders of Portsmouth were determined to mark the occasion with fine speeches. A brief Dickensian comedy followed, its absurdity rather enjoyed by the press despite their fawning upon the fleet. Napier waited impatiently through two convoluted discourses praising him as 'one of the greatest men of our age' and wishing him success.[17] His response was brief, sounding a sensible warning. 'I beg to thank you for this very kind and handsome address [...] I know a great deal is expected from the fleet, but, gentlemen, you must not expect too much. (Cheers.)' The Russians are 'no common enemy', but 'an enemy well prepared'. Napier was sure that the officers and men will do their duty 'gloriously'; 'but, at the same time, I warn you again that you must not expect too much. (Cheers.)' 'The fleet is a new one;' he reminded his audience; 'the system of warfare is new'. Officers and crew all need to learn how to manage ships powered by steam. 'The system of warfare is entirely different now to what it was formerly.'[18] Napier knew well that the newspapers had raised absurd expectations which the fleet could only fail to meet.[19] His warnings, though widely quoted, were widely ignored.

Alongside his naval career, Napier had been elected to Parliament in 1841, where he took a close interest in naval matters and argued for the abolition of physical punishment and impressment. To encourage experienced seamen into the navy, it was now possible to offer a bounty. Skilled, enthusiastic volunteers could replace the old press-ganged crews. This was a good idea in theory, but in practice James Graham refused to provide the funding to attract experienced seamen.[20] Those who volunteered for the Baltic fleet included sailors who were old and no longer fit. Some had no previous experience at sea. It was hugely frustrating to Napier that he could not offer the bounty to attract experienced young seamen into the navy. The shortage of competent crews created a huge problem; tackling that problem was one of Napier's most urgent tasks.

The fleet of 16 battleships leaving Spithead on 11 March was an impressive sight. Further ships departed over the following weeks. But behind the surface glory lay serious difficulties. Too little time had been allowed to equip the fleet adequately. As Lambert explains, 'Napier had been sent to sea with a hastily collected agglomeration of ships, more or less badly manned, forcing him to spend the first three months of the campaign working them up into a combat-ready fleet. Nothing could be done until they were efficient.'[21] The fleet arrived at Wingo Sound in Sweden on 17 March. Napier immediately started a rigorous programme of drilling and training. This did not provide an interesting story for the press – to untrained eyes it looked as if the fleet were doing nothing at all. Worse, the press frequently claimed that the ships were well staffed; that Graham had brilliantly (and cheaply) managed to find all the men needed. *The Times*, for example, praised 'the speed with which this force has been raised'.[22] The custom of impressment had ended, the men were all volunteers, and *The Times* was optimistic that there would be no problems manning the ships. This was quite a misleading view.

To complicate matters, the naval orders coming from London were often contradictory. At Wingo, Napier had orders from the Admiralty to stay put, while a later dispatch from the Foreign Office directed him to stop Russian ships from leaving the Baltic. The latter order required him to leave Wingo, which he did, only to be reprimanded by the Admiralty, much to Napier's irritation. Similar confusions occurred throughout the campaign. Furthermore, the Admiralty refused to admit that the crews were inadequate, and refused to help put the matter right. To be effective in the shallow coasts of the Baltic, Napier needed small gunboats and mortar vessels. For months, Graham flatly refused to provide these, on grounds of cost, arguing that Sweden would join the war effort and provide these boats as well as extra men. Sweden did not join in, however, and without the small boats, the job of blockading Russia was all the more difficult. The newspapers were not much interested in these problems, and were soon criticizing Napier for his apparent lack of action.

The French arrived in the summer, but the two navies' commanders did not cooperate very easily. Cholera broke out on some of the ships, and there were a few potentially serious collisions between vessels.[23] Napier's relationship with several of his captains was often difficult, and he struggled with a shortage of ammunition, warm clothing and even food for the men. Nonetheless, the blockade gradually took hold, and by late May the *Illustrated London News* could report the 'Capture of a Russian Prize Before Riga'.[24] It described how, a month earlier, several Russian merchant ships were observed in the ice outside the Riga Roads. Some British ships, powered by steam, were able to break through the ice and tow away a large Russian barque, a merchant ship which had been drifting in the ice for four weeks. The crew of the ship did not mind being captured, reported the *ILN*; on the contrary, they were pleased to be rescued from possible starvation. The British towed the Russian barque safely to open water. Two British ships then moved to the entrance of a river near Riga. There they found very little ice, but 'no shipping of any kind'. The mouth of the river was defended by three forts, and thousands of Russian soldiers were observed on the shore.

Fig. 17: Weather in the Baltic, *Illustrated London News*, 23 December 1854

The story is modest, but telling: it shows 'the superiority of the screw, in a practical sense', and it shows that the blockade is taking hold, slowly but effectively.[25] And it signals that the Russians were on the defensive, forced to put a lot of resources into defending the Baltic, and unable to do much there. At no point did the Russian fleet emerge to engage with the allies, much to the frustration of the press, so longing for direct conflict. This quiet yet sustained pressure would, eventually, win Britain the war. But no one could see that yet.

Other incidents took place in late May and early June. A squadron of ships went to Brahestad in Finland under the command of Rear-Admiral Plumridge. His orders were to seek out and destroy any gunboats being built. Plumridge and his officers interpreted the order quite broadly, taking the view that all shipbuilding materials were fair game. They burned shipyards, warehouses, tar and other materials in Brahestad and in nearby Uleaborg worth some £365,000, assuming that they were all connected with the Russians. In fact, much of the material had been bought by British merchants (some of whom then spent years trying to recover these losses, as the *Illustrated London News* reported after the war, in

January 1857). Some in the navy disapproved of these actions. To the Scandinavians, they were outrageous attacks on neutral nations. Overall, they can be seen as a blunder: they did not harm Russia, and they did considerable damage to Britain's reputation in the very area in which Britain wanted support.[26] The burning of Brahestad and Uleaborg were minor but contentious events in the war. The *ILN* gave two conflicting accounts of the incidents. They could be seen as successful attacks on military targets (alleged gunboats for the Russians), or pointless assaults on the private property of non-belligerents, including British civilians.[27]

By the end of June, the blockade of Russia was complete. This was an important achievement, but it was not fully recognized at the time. Some in government felt the need to answer the demand from 'public opinion' for more spectacular action at sea. How far this affected naval policy is hard to be certain.[28] Meanwhile, important work was going on, much of it out of sight of the press, in a new area of operation, at Bomarsund.[29]

BOMARSUND

Bomarsund lies at the heart of the Åland Islands, an archipelago of about 600 islands at the mouth of the Gulf of Bothnia, not far from the entrance to the Gulf of Finland. In 1809, control of Finland, including the Ålands, passed from Sweden to Russia. The Russians soon decided to build a new naval base at Bomarsund. The other fortified places in the Gulf of Finland at that time, Reval (Tallinn) and Sveaborg, were frozen for many months of the year.[30] At Bomarsund the sea froze for a shorter period. A strong base there could help to protect St Petersburg and would strengthen the power of the Russian fleet in the Baltic. It took some years for planning and approval to be finalized and work did not begin in earnest until 1832. It was a huge project. There was to be a large fortress with a circular system of walls, nearly 1 kilometre in diameter, supported by 14 heavily-armed towers. Building continued for the next 20 years, but by 1854 the fort was unfinished and only three of the towers had been built, one of which was incomplete. Constructed out of brick and rather beautifully faced with hexagonal blocks of pink granite, the Bomarsund fortress in 1854 housed about 2,300 troops and 120 guns.[31] It looked impressive and incredibly strong, but in its incomplete state it was weak, and vulnerable to attack.

The Russians had surveyed the sea in this area, but with uneven results, and some of their charts were unreliable. The British fleet was fortunate in having the services of brilliant hydrographer Captain Bartholomew Sulivan (1810–90), perhaps best known for his work as surveyor on Darwin's voyages on the *Beagle* in the 1830s.[32] In 1854, Sulivan was appointed fleet surveying officer, and commanded a small steamship called *Lightning* in the Baltic fleet. He worked closely with Napier, resurveying the sea, especially in the area around the Ålands. His work provided accurate charts which made the allied attack on Bomarsund possible.

In late July a British squadron of paddle steamers moved to the north of the Åland Islands, cutting them off from the rest of Finland and from Russian relief. In the very early hours of 8 August, other ships brought approximately 10,000 troops to the shore on the other side, near the fort of Bomarsund. Most of the troops were French, but there were also British marines and engineers. At 3 am, the *Edinburgh* attacked the woods on the shore, to clear out any defenders. Several heavy guns and horses were landed. At 4 am, reported *The Times*, one British and one French ship 'steamed through an intricate passage, and moored themselves to the west of the earthwork battery, where no guns could be brought to bear upon them. They then opened a terrific fire with shot and shell, which fell with beautiful precision, the trees which partly masked it cracking and falling in all directions.' The men landed, and discovered that the Russians had deserted the battery 'upon finding their guns useless in the unforeseen position which the ships had taken up'.[33] The towers were attacked and soon fell, though one tower, Notvik, managed to hold out against severe bombardment. The Russians inside Notvik struggled on, short of food, water and medicines, but after 15 hours they were forced to surrender.

The allies attacked the Bomarsund fort from both sea and land. It was soon defeated, with few allied casualties. The Russians defended it bravely, but the bombardment was overwhelming and the massive fortification disintegrated around them. The Russian commander, General Bodisco, officially surrendered and was taken prisoner by the French. A few weeks later, on 30 September, the *Illustrated London News* published a picture of the ceremony of surrender.

Fig. 18: Surrender of Bomarsund, *Illustrated London News*, 30 September 1854

Soon after the fort was taken, British Rear-Admiral Henry Byam Martin went to look at the ruins. Even in their damaged state, the fortifications were impressive.

> We walked then to the batteries in course of construction, and half-finished. These works are of prodigious magnitude, towers and a long line of casemented battery, which would have commanded all the points from which an enemy could have made his approaches. [...] The large semi-circular fort on the sea has eighty guns mounted. It is faced with large masses of granite, rubbish and brick within.

The works were wrecked both by the allies and by the Russians' efforts to defend themselves. 'It seemed to me,' wrote Martin, 'that the principal damage which this building had received was from its own fire. The guns had been elevated so much for distant firing that the concussion had shaken down the upper part of all the embrasures that were much engaged.' The interior was a sorry sight:

A pretty scene of confusion we found [...] there are heaps of loose powder, which one cannot help treading on as one walks along [...] Large quantities of straw, which formed the bedding of the Russian soldiers; thousands of live shells, musket cartridges, priming tubes – clothing, accoutrements – books – bottles of medicine – spirits of wine all lying higgledy piggledy [...].[34]

Once Bomarsund was taken, the allies offered to return the Åland Islands to Sweden, but the King of Sweden declined, not wishing to enter into the conflict. He knew that the French and British were keen to leave the Baltic and he had no desire to face the Russians alone over the winter.

As the Swedes would not take them, the Bomarsund fortifications, to deny them to the Russians, were systematically destroyed. This did not prove easy. The towers of Prästö and Notvik were blown up with powder charges in the casements and in the centre. The structure of the main fort was first weakened by lighting large bonfires along the walls. A complicated pattern of powder charges was then laid which were fired on 2 September 1854 at 7 o'clock in the evening, and there followed a massive and spectacular firework display which left the place in total ruin.[35]

These spectacles of destruction were described with some interest in the press. The *Daily News*, for example, reported:

The fortresses that stood upon the Aland islands are amongst the things that were. Mines were sprung beneath them [...] Three explosions took place in quick succession; on the third the entire fort seemed to open out and then went upwards amidst a thick volume of smoke. All the hewn granite which formed the outer casing of its walls slipped over the tongue of land upon which it was built into the sea, leaving a heap of bricks and rubble on its site. Nottick [Notvick tower] was destroyed on the following day. The first explosion was like a clap of the loudest thunder [...] Its walls visibly started on the first report, and these shot upwards, enveloped in a cloud of the heaviest and densest smoke, which floated heavily away over the ruins of Prasto.[36]

'Stones and splinters came down in a shower upon the surrounding rocks.' As the smoke clears, one could see 'two shaken portions of the circular tower were still standing, like solitary sentinels, over the fallen fort, [which] served only to render the picture of the ruin more striking and impressive'. The whole scene was 'a melancholy picture of desolation'. Like many of the eyewitness accounts of Sebastopol a year later, the *Daily News* correspondent was thoughtful, even saddened, by the destruction wrought by victory.

False reports that Bomarsund had fallen appeared in the press for several days early in August, before news of the actual attack had arrived in England. For example, the *Daily News* noted on 2 August that 'A report was current in Copenhagen [on 31 July] that Bomarsund had been taken with great loss on both sides.' On 5 August the same paper commented that most of the recent Baltic reports were unconfirmed or incorrect. The editorial in the *Illustrated London News* on 12 August remarked that, 'The telegraphic news from the Baltic, the Danube, and the Black Sea continues to be as untrustworthy as usual.' Another article in the same issue of the *ILN* observed that 'the telegraphic announcements of the taking of Bomarsund prove to have been entirely apocryphal' (p. 127). But it remained optimistic that 'a severe blow against Russia in the Baltic is imminent' (p. 130). An article in the *Daily News* on 14 August (dated 5 August) attempted to give an account of what was going on at Bomarsund, but lacking any hard information, most of the article was speculation. (In fact, there was little visible action to report until 8 August.)

On 21 August the editorial in the *Daily News* announced the fall of Bomarsund, declaring that the importance of the event 'far transcends the mere capture of an important fortified position. It marks the commencement of a real earnest effort to turn back the irruption of Russian conquest in the north of Europe.' Like most of the papers, it took a long historical view: 'When Peter the Great transferred the metropolitan seat of his empire from Moscow to Petersburg [in 1712] he commenced an invasion of civilised Europe.'[37]

On 26 August, the *Illustrated London News* confirmed that 'The first blow has been struck at Bomarsund.' It regarded the action as 'serious business', an event 'of the highest interest and importance'. 'Bomarsund was a strongly-fortified place,' it declared, 'but it fell an easy victory to the skill which planned and the bravery which directed and supported the assault.' It took a stand against harsh critics of the fleet. 'There is no longer room for cavil at the inaction of the Baltic expedition. The long and skilful preparations that have brought the war to its present issues, have reached majority.'[38] Fleets and armies, it remarked, are 'mighty machines to construct and put in motion': they were massive undertakings; they were hard work. It was all too easy for 'indolent' critics in the press to find fault.

The victory at Bomarsund involved some remarkable achievements, but they were not the stuff of heroic reporting. Sulivan's skilful surveying, for example, was not something exciting for the press, though it ensured the success of the attack. Or, to take just one of many examples of the ordinary labour of war, a group of seamen took six large guns ashore and had to drag them by sledge more than 4 miles, to General Jones' battery. The guns weighed more than 2 tons each. As Greenhill and Giffard note, 'This feat was performed over ploughed earth, over rocks, and through forest areas by men with bare feet, up to 200 on each sledge [...] in seven hours.'[39] Sheer hard work helped to win the day. This humble yet demanding task is set against what turns out to be more than 20 years of wasted work by the Russians – much of it undertaken under harsh conditions by convict labour – constructing the massive fortifications in the first place. In this great age of engineering and building, the return to warfare on a significant scale brought new spectacles of destruction, some of which were newly visible in the press. Warfare has always provided vast spectacles, both real and imagined, and these have long been memorialized in words and images. But such representations entered British civilian culture more widely and deeply in the 1850s, and had a profound effect upon people's *imaginary* relationship with war.

In the end, Bomarsund was defeated by the allies, as Greenhill and Giffard argue, 'because the artillery of industrial Britain and relatively industrialized France were superior to that of non-industrialized Russia' (p. 248). The technologies of naval warfare were in the process of dramatic changes. Within a few years, even the most formidable of fortresses would be obsolete, unable to withstand modern artillery. And the fleets which took Bomarsund would also be obsolete, due to technological and industrial advances, and also as a result of lessons learned from the Russian war.

***

After the humiliation at Bomarsund, reported the *Illustrated London News*, 'such was the new and sudden mistrust which the Russians conceived of their boasted defences, that they themselves blew up, a few days afterwards, the fortifications of Hango'.[40] This action was witnessed by some of the French and British generals, who were out checking the fortifications at Reval and Sveaborg in late August 1854.

Autumn sets in early in the Baltic, and after Bomarsund there was not enough time to take on another serious military target before the seas began to freeze. Both the French and British fleets prepared to return. The British press demanded more action, and turned against Napier, claiming that he did not do enough in the summer months. Behind the scenes, a campaign to discredit Napier went on, emanating mainly from James Graham, who went to some lengths to blame Napier for all the shortcomings of the campaign, not least those of the government and Graham himself. Some of Napier's close political allies, such as Delane of *The Times*, no longer supported him. Having been, in reality, quite successful, Napier was unjustly disgraced. As Lambert remarks, 'Napier was universally damned for a failure that no-one could actually describe' (*The Crimean War*, pp. 187–9).

Even the *Illustrated London News*, one of the fleet's most enthusiastic supporters, was by October 1854 much more subdued. It reported on 21 October that the British and French fleets had now finished their operations for the year, as the Baltic iced up. 'But,' it remarked, 'though the return of the fleets may be accepted as a necessity, the public may be excused for the expression of a natural disappointment that some enterprise worthy of the strength and splendour of the armament was not sooner attempted.' Who was responsible? The *ILN* said it would hold back from blaming either the admirals or the governments of Britain and France, until more facts were known. 'But in the meantime [...] there is a strong belief that there has been mismanagement somewhere.' It looked back somewhat nostalgically at the first days of the campaign:

The Fleet sailed amid a popular ovation. It was the most magnificent armament the world had ever seen. Never before were so many splendid vessels assembled together for a warlike, or a peaceful purpose [...] never was power so great displayed for a grander purpose, or supported by a more majestic weight of moral sentiment, and of national energy and hope. The very name of its commander [Napier] was looked upon as a prognostic of victory; and the annihilation of the Russian power in the Baltic, and the destruction or seizure of Cronstadt, were at once the greatest and the least of the achievements that were anticipated.

'Perhaps the people expected too much,' it admitted, 'and perhaps the Admirals in command have done all that was possible with the means at their disposal, and with the difficulties – perhaps unknown to the public – against which they have had to contend. But it cannot be denied that the country is disappointed.' The fleet was certainly struggling with difficulties which were perhaps not well known to the public – the lack of gunboats and trained seamen, especially. But having raised the question, the *ILN* went on to complain that the fleet seemed have been inactive throughout most of its time in the Baltic, wasting the good summer weather. However, if the British people felt 'regret that so fine an armament was not more vigorously employed', how much more disappointed the commanders must feel. Both Napier and French Admiral Duchesne, it argued (not necessarily with much accuracy), were keen to attack Helsingfors (Helsinki and the fortress of Sveaborg – modern day Suomenlinna) and Cronstadt. 'They had stomach for both achievements, and feel something not unlike shame or disgust that the comparatively small affair of Bomarsund is all that they have to boast of.'[41] Whether the admirals or the navy generally felt 'shame or disgust' is doubtful – frustration seems more likely – but such terms are typical of the harsh view taken of the fleet by the press at the end of 1854. As it turned out, Napier had done a lot that would win the allies the war. But for now, he was dismissed in disgrace, his achievements unrecognized.

THE BALTIC CAMPAIGN OF 1855

Napier did not take his dismissal passively, but campaigned publicly and aggressively to clear his name. He never really succeeded in this, but his attacks on Graham (including the publication of letters which revealed Graham's duplicity during the 1854 Baltic campaign) seriously damaged Graham's reputation.[42] In February 1855, Graham left the Admiralty and was replaced by Sir Charles Wood. Meanwhile, the British fleet prepared to return to the Baltic in the spring. A fleet of ships set off on 4 April 1855, led by Admiral Sir Richard Dundas (1802–61). With all the ships now powered by steam, the sight might have been even more impressive than the departure of the fleet a year earlier. But where the 1854 fleet set off in glorious sunshine, the new fleet departed on choppy seas, surrounded by thick fog. Big crowds turned up, as they had done the previous year, but no one could see very much.

On 14 April 1855, the *Illustrated London News* produced another special supplement to mark the departure of the fleet. The cover article begins with another wistful recollection of the previous fleet, 'the noblest fleet that ever left the shores of this country'; its departure on 11 March 1854 under Napier's command a 'glorious spectacle'; most 'memorable – at least as a show'. 'But the performance of that great fleet fell sadly short of its promise'; it 'did little more than perform a minatory promenade in the Baltic Sea'. It did manage to 'imprison the Russian fleet', but the paper does not value this action very highly. As the new fleet sets off in dismal fog, the paper hopes it will have more to show for its actions.

And indeed, provided with the gunboats and mortar vessels that Napier had been denied, Dundas was able to re-establish a complete blockade of the Gulf of Finland by July 1855. He inspected the large Russian naval bases and in August 1855 he and his French allies turned their attention to Sveaborg.

SVEABORG

Sveaborg is the Swedish name for a chain of forts constructed across several islands, now known as Suomenlinna, just off

Helsinki on the Gulf of Finland.[43] Sweden started this huge project in the mid-eighteenth century, in response to Russia's great fortification at Cronstadt. This was Sweden's most ambitious building project of the period, and its construction took more than 50 years. Like Bomarsund, Sveaborg was taken over by Russia in 1809. The Russians did not develop the fortifications, nor even look after them, and by the 1850s, Sveaborg was in a very poor state. The Russians hastily attempted to make some improvements in 1854 and 1855, but too much needed to be done after decades of neglect, and the Russian administration was too disorganized and corrupt to mend things effectively. Russian naval leaders were worried about Sveaborg, not least when they tested the fortress's guns, and a long section of wall immediately fell down. In 1854, Russian Admiral Matyushkin had warned the Commander of the Russian fleet that 'Materially and in the art of using our artillery we belong to the last century.' If the allies knew the parlous state of the Russian guns and defences, they could 'destroy everything'. Sveaborg was saved in 1854 by its 'undeserved reputation' and poor allied intelligence.[44] In 1855, this was to change.

Before the British navy went into action, the area around Sveaborg was surveyed by Captain Bartholomew Sulivan, who had done so much to contribute to the success at Bomarsund. With his unique skills in hydrography and naval strategy, Sulivan provided detailed and accurate information about the area, and also put together the entire plan of attack. The allies launched a joint attack on Sveaborg on 9 August. According to the *Illustrated London News*, the British had 17 man-of-war ships, 15 gunboats and 16 mortar vessels, while the French had two men-of-war, six gunboats and five mortar vessels. The French also built a battery on the island of Langörn, approximately 2,000 yards north of the main fortress.[45] Between them, the small boats and the battery bombarded the fortress constantly on 9 and 10 August. Sulivan's plan ingeniously kept the gunboats moving. *The Times* reported how the gunboats took the mortar boats in tow. They formed 'a half-moon shaped line before the fortress, from which they [hauled] into or out of range by means of a hawser about 800 yards long, fastened to a small anchor placed by the boats during the night'. The Russians' fire was 'very good once they get the range; to prevent their doing this, the gun-boats kept moving in circles' (p. 300). Similarly, the *Illustrated London News* described how

> [...] the mortar-vessels were towed into position, about 3700 yards from the fortress, with 400 fathoms each of cable to 'haul and veer on', as circumstances might require. This arrangement proved of the greatest advantage, and much credit is due to the originator of it.[46]

The larger ships stayed to the rear of the mortar vessels, ready to assist as needed.

> At 7.30 am the first mortar was fired, and taken up along the whole line, the gun-boats running in to within 3000 yards, and getting their range. The enemy returned our fire very briskly with red-hot shot and shell; but, although their range was good, the damage inflicted was comparatively trifling, owing principally to the excellent handling of the gun boats and mortar-vessels – the former being continually on the move, and the latter hauling or veering on their 400-fathom cable as soon as they found the Russian shot falling too close to be pleasant.[47]

By mid-morning, the bombardment was having its effect. The first Russian magazine exploded. Then 'at 12.15 a most terrific explosion took place, followed by a succession of minor ones'. A battery of guns was 'literally blown to pieces'. More magazines exploded. By now, 'the dockyards, arsenal, barracks, all the Government buildings, storehouses, &c., were burning furiously' (*ILN*, p. 235). *The Times* likened this to 'a volcano in a state of eruption, vomiting forth light, shells, roofs of houses, and beams of timber'.[48] For the *ILN*, 'The sight was most grandly imposing', even more so at night:

> The scene during the night was grand beyond description: the whole of Sveaborg appeared one mass of flame, the rockets and shells adding not a little to the awful splendour of the fiery landscape.

The *Illustrated London News* estimated that around 160 gunboat sheds, barracks, storehouses, dockyards and other property to the value of around £2 million had been destroyed. It quoted with some satisfaction a dispatch from French Admiral Penaud, who says that for two days and two nights, Sveaborg looked like 'a vast fiery furnace'. It then offered a more florid version of the same events, written by its war artist, J. W. Carmichael, who described the biggest explosion:

> At 12.15 the grandest of all the explosions took place, shaking the earth. It was a long succession of explosions, with a heavy black inky smoke, and as another explosion went into it, it looked like transparent vermilion endeavouring to displace clouds of black velvet. This scene was terrific: it seemed as if hell had burst open to destroy. (p. 235)

A raging fire engulfed the citadel and the town: 'The sight was grand.' The next day, Carmichael reported, the fire spread, 'and where the town was not on fire there issued a deep yellow-brown dense smoke, which contrasted beautifully with the other smoke and flames in all their freshness. The burning continued all day; at night it was beautiful.' These oddly aestheticized celebrations of the sight of destruction were not unusual, and would be repeated, though with greater ambivalence, soon afterwards, on the other

Fig. 19: Sveaborg, *Illustrated London News*, 8 September 1855

side of the Russian Empire, at the fall of Sebastopol. Here, in the Baltic, there was the curious sight of massive fortifications, until recently regarded as indestructible, falling within a couple of days to allied attack. The complicated histories of the forts at Bomarsund and Sveaborg added a certain piquancy to their destruction now, as writers reflected upon the long struggle of Russian convict labour to build Bomarsund, or the grandeur of the Swedish project which created Sveaborg. Both were heroic undertakings; both near worthless now.

***

Why is the Baltic campaign so little remembered now? Perhaps because we have comparatively little in the press about the Baltic, compared to the many powerful representations of the Crimea in the newspapers, photographs, paintings and literature. Over time, these Crimean representations have come to stand for the entire war itself. Without such a wealth of pictures and newspaper reports, the Baltic campaign was gradually forgotten. It is a sobering lesson in historiography. As modern representations of war are developed, they have a profound effect upon the ways histories are written. In some ways, the newspaper reports, photographs, and so on, make history writing possible – or at least one version of it. But they also make that history *impossible*.

Andrew Lambert argues convincingly that the Baltic campaign was crucial in the outcome of the war. But in Britain, most eyes were looking elsewhere, on Sebastopol. After it was taken in September 1855, what would happen next?

6

THE END OF THE WAR

The siege had ended, but the Russians were still present on the northern side of Sebastopol and could shell the southern part of the city. Russian field troops were close by. Having won the city, the allies had to get their troops out again; it was a strange, unsatisfactory victory. As autumn approached, conditions improved for the British troops. A railway had been built at Balaklava and the roads were better, so they were better supplied with food, shelter and other essentials. Medical care had also improved. This second winter was harder for the French, and the British were able to offer some medical support. Now that they were not actually fighting, the allied officers and men outside Sebastopol found other things to do. Some were already busy with archaeological excavations (and some looting), exploring the real and imaginary classical histories of the Crimea.[1] Others organized race meetings, drag hunts, cricket matches, drama, lectures and sightseeing. And there was a considerable amount of drinking among the troops. Indeed, drunkenness became a serious problem at this time. In an attempt to attract more men into the army, pay for British troops had been increased during the war. Men received a sum of back pay and a higher regular payment, much of which was spent on alcohol.

British Captain Arthur Earle complained in November 1855 that the men's pay was now 'ridiculous':

The extra 6d a day field allowance and 8d a day whenever they are on fatigue duty increases their pay to nearly 3/-, half a crown too much for any soldier. It only serves to fill the pockets of all the scoundrels who keep canteens in the Camp.[2]

Massie comments:

Attempts were made to try and persuade the soldiers to send money home to their families, but to little avail. Nor was the threat of punishment sufficient to deter drunkenness, Earle lamenting the fact that in the years before the outbreak of the war the maximum number of blows which could be inflicted in a flogging had been restricted to fifty: 'A man cares nothing for 50 lashes, but 500 will certainly stop his drinking for a month or two.' (p. 236)

British politicians and the press felt frustrated at the state of the war and pressed for more action. Commander-in-Chief General Simpson was much criticized and on 29 September 1855 he resigned. He was replaced by General Codrington in November.

KINBURN AND KARS

In October 1855, a joint French–British expedition set off for Kinburn, a fortress on the Bay of Kherson on the Black Sea. There were 6,000 French and 4,000 British troops and dozens of ships. Kinburn was taken but it did not amount to much and the British still felt frustrated. A garrison was left at Kinburn but this was later withdrawn. Meanwhile, at Kars in Armenia, Turkish forces, supported by British Military Commissioner General William Williams, were defending their heavily fortified citadel against a Russian siege. The Russians made an unsuccessful attack in September, with heavy loss of troops. They renewed the blockade of Kars, cutting off all food supplies. Hundreds of people in Kars were dying weekly. British medical officer Humphrey Sandwith kept a diary of the siege:

The hospitals are fast overflowing with patients. All the mosques, khans, and large houses are full of invalids [...] Women are seen gathering the dust from before the flour-depots to eat, mixed as it is with flour. I observe people lying at the corners of the streets, groaning and crying out that they are dying of hunger.

The streets present a soul-harrowing appearance. Old women are moaning and crying out that they are dying of starvation; the children have a gaunt and famished look. Numerous donkeys are lying dead in the streets, others wandering around eating dung, old rags, &c. [...] Our hospitals are daily more difficult to manage, since all our water-carrying horses are dead [...]

Some of the citizens exhume the carcases of horses, which they devour [...] We now have about 2000 men in hospital, and more than 100 deaths per diem: we have only seven days' provision left. [... The] nights are intensely cold [...] A heavy fall of snow during the night [...] We have almost reached the limits of human endurance; our soldiers lie dead and dying in every part of the camp [...] Several naked corpses are found in the camp, since the threadbare clothes of the dead soldier are seized by his shivering comrades.[3]

After immense suffering, the fortress with its 30,000 troops and civilians surrendered to the Russians on 26 November 1855.[4]

***

'Diplomacy has settled the affairs of Europe, or fondly hopes so,' commented the *Illustrated London News* on 3 May 1856. 'The war is over' (p. 465). Peace talks took place secretly in Vienna intermittently throughout 1855; late that year more secret talks began between France and Russia, without Britain. After the fall of Sebastopol, Louis Napoleon was no longer interested in pursuing the war, but was looking to negotiate a peace advantageous to France. In December 1855, an Austrian mission went to St Petersburg to negotiate peace with the following conditions: confirmation of autonomy for Moldovia and Wallachia; freedom of navigation for all nations on the Danube; neutralization of the Black Sea, with abolition of installations on its shores; and a guarantee of the rights of all Christian subjects in Turkey.[5]

If Russia did not accept the peace terms, Austria threatened to declare war. Russia felt under considerable pressure, with Austria, Prussia and Sweden likely to join the allied forces, and the risk that parts of its empire – Poland, Finland, the Crimea and the Caucasus

– might secede if the war continued into 1856. The war had put the Russian economy under enormous strain: the deficit was rapidly growing and trade was hugely reduced, due to the blockade. The Russian army was low on guns, ammunition and food supplies; military transport was poor and the army was struggling to recruit more men. After several intensive consultations with his advisors, the Tsar felt he had no option but to agree to peace.

On 16 January 1856 Russia agreed to Austria's terms, and a formal peace conference opened in Paris on 25 February 1856. Negotiations moved quickly; an armistice was agreed on 28 February and the Treaty of Paris was signed on 30 March and ratified on 27 April 1856.

The British press had plenty to say about the coming of peace, not always with much enthusiasm. The *Illustrated London News*, for example, was keen to pursue the war for another year, in the hope of further restraining Russian power. Its argument was presented mainly in terms of domestic politics. For the *ILN*, 'the people' had 'forced an unwilling Government to undertake [the war], because they believed it to be just and necessary'; it claims they even paid for it 'cheerfully'. Now, it complained, having made the war, the British people had no say in the terms of the peace. The *ILN* regarded the settlement as unpopular; this was not an unusual view. As I argued in the Introduction, the newspapers had no way of really knowing 'public opinion', but frequently claimed their own views as representing those of the population.

Moreover, the idea that the war was somehow determined by the British people is a myth. In reality, the international issues were enormously complex, the morality far from clear, the diplomacy secretive, and the power politics among the interested nations difficult for even the most experienced diplomat to comprehend fully. But all this was reduced to a few simplistic ideas of right and wrong in the name of 'the people', who, with few exceptions, had little knowledge of the issues and no actual say in the decisions taken.

The idea of war as democratic and a force for good because it is supposedly the will of the people is a powerful myth which gained traction in the Crimean War and has been used in war propaganda ever since. It's an early example of the modern manufacture of consent.[6] Even in limited democracies, governments need a degree of consent to go to war, and to stay there. Consent needs to be constantly renewed and dissent stifled.[7] On 30 April 1856, *The Times* declared that 'By this time the people have well-nigh forgotten the sores that were rankling even two short months ago, – the Redan, the hope of revenge, the open field, the one more campaign.' These were in fact all opinions expressed by the newspaper itself. Now, however, people 'have reason to be satisfied with the terms which our diplomatists have battled for and won'.

THE GREAT ARMAMENT

Complex diplomatic negotiations produced the peace treaty. At the same time, the nations were assessing their own military capabilities. In Britain, a huge amount of naval building had been going on throughout the war. To a large extent, this was done in anticipation of future naval conflict with France, even as the present war was fought in alliance with the French. It was decided to create a 'Great Armament': a huge flotilla of steam ships, gunboats, floating batteries and much else, which could return to the Baltic, destroy all Russian defences and seriously threaten the Russian capital, St Petersburg. Even as the war wound down, construction continued at a rapid pace, with one eye on the Russians and the other on France, America and any other potential future threat to British naval dominance.

The Great Armament was not a secret; quite the opposite. It was exhibited in all its glory at the peace celebrations held at Spithead on St George's Day, 23 April 1856. It was a remarkable spectacle: 24 battleships, 37 cruisers, 4 floating batteries, 120 gunboats, 50 mortar vessels and 5 auxiliaries: a total of 240 vessels with more than 30,000 seamen.[8] For *The Times*, this was unique:

> Nowhere in the world can be paralleled that scene which will be witnessed this morning on the waters of the Solent [... N]o other country except England can afford an exhibition at once so impressive by its magnitude, so imposing by its character, so fascinating by the sympathies which it excites, as the spectacle which this morning's sun will reveal at Spithead.[9]

Similarly, the *Illustrated London News* praised this 'exhibition of our unimpaired strength'; a 'mighty gathering'. This was the most

Fig. 20: Grand Naval Review, *Illustrated London News*, 26 April 1856

powerful fleet ever assembled, in peace or war. Queen Victoria presided over 'the greatest and most splendid armament that ever floated' that even Cleopatra would envy.[10]

As Lambert argues, the celebration was much more than merely a victory parade; it was 'a demonstration of Britain's industrial, economic and naval power'. And while it attracted huge crowds, its real target was not 'the Queen, the assembled parliamentarians or the taxpayers':

> It was directed at a foreign audience: France, the real naval rival, the truculent Americans and the bitter Russians. The fleet at Spithead was a restatement of overwhelming naval power, with the addition of a fully prepared coastal flotilla, purpose-built to carry the war into the shallowest waters and destroy the most powerful forts. America and Russia were wide open to such attacks.[11]

PEACE CELEBRATIONS

Some weeks after the naval review, peace was officially celebrated on 29 May with an extravagant display of fireworks and illuminations in Hyde Park. The *Illustrated London News* reported this with some disapproval, arguing that, while the war had been unpopular in 'official circles', the peace was unpopular with the nation at large. To mark the peace, the government put on an extravagant display of fireworks and illuminations to try to win round the population:

> The Government, having made up its mind for the celebration, managed the business with much tact and skill. It was necessary that the people should share, or appear to share, in the joy felt by the official mind that diplomacy had put an end to that very inconvenient and very troublesome war in which Great Britain was incurring such large expense, and reaping such small satisfaction.[12]

The *ILN* grumbled at the cost of the fireworks, which it estimated at between £10,000 and £20,000. At the same time, the newspaper declared itself content with the addition of £100,000,000 to the national debt, insisting that the people were happy to sacrifice this and more for the 'noble and disinterested purpose' of war. But this war was over; the press turned its attention elsewhere, and soon had new conflicts to report: Britain in India and China; France in Indochina and Syria – part of what Eric Hobsbawm describes as the 'general victimization of the non-European world' (p. 95). Then four significant if short wars took place between European powers in the period 1858–70 (p. 97).

The system of the balance of power had been kept in place since 1815 through diplomacy. Many disputes were resolved without war. But after the revolutions of 1848, the system was less stable. The emergence of Louis Napoleon increased the instability. As Hobsbawm points out, the Crimean War was a consequence and also a further cause of major changes in the power system in the following decades. These changes led to the unification of Italy in 1870 and Germany in 1871. Louis Napoleon's Second Empire collapsed in 1870–1. 'Austria was excluded from Germany and profoundly restructured.' All the major powers apart from Britain underwent important changes from 1856 to 1871. After the Crimean War, the Concert of Europe had broken down and the era of *Realpolitik* began.[13]

The Crimean War affected all the European powers, redrew parts of the map of Europe, strengthened Britain and France, weakened Russia and forced the Tsar to reform the system and liberate the serfs. Russia withdrew from foreign affairs, to some extent, which in turn made possible the unification of Germany. The war produced new instabilities, yet one of its main effects, paradoxically, was to artificially preserve the crumbling Ottoman Empire for a few more decades.

DEPARTURE

William Howard Russell left the Crimea in December 1855. He was replaced by Thomas Chenery, who reported for *The Times* in January 1856; then Russell returned in March 1856. News of the peace treaty signed in Paris on 30 March 1856 reached the Crimea within two days, but it took several months to complete the withdrawal of the allied troops. One of the last tasks the British undertook was to mark the graves of the dead. In June, Russell reported the sad sight of 'those stark-white stones, singly or in groups', covering a vast area from Balaklava to the edge of Sebastopol (pp. 269, 272–3). Stone memorials were built at Inkerman and Balaklava to mark the battles there. The last British troops left with General Codrington on 12 July 1856.[14]

The troops' return was noted in the newspapers and magazines in stories, images and poetry. There was new interest in the fate of soldiers injured in war; what did the nation owe them? Some writings reflected upon those who would not return, expressing pious hopes that the suffering caused by 'inglorious war' would somehow bring about permanent peace.

Guns of Peace
    Sunday Night, March 30th.

Ghosts of dead soldiers in mid-battle slain;
    Ghosts of dead heroes, dying, nobler far,
    In long slow travail of inglorious war,
Of famine, sickness, weariness, and pain; –
All ye whose loss makes our victorious gain; –
    This quiet night, thrilled with the cannon's tongue,
    Do ye look down the quivering stars among,
And view our peace, our war, with like disdain?

> Or, wiser grown in your celestial spheres,
>   Smile ye on those poor bones ye sowed as seed
>   For earth's peace-harvest, nor regret the deed?
> Oh lift this cry with ours to heavenly ears, –
> 'Strike with Thy bolt the next red flag unfurled,
> And make all wars to cease throughout the world![15]

The international effects of the war were far-reaching. Five years after the Crimean War ended, the American Civil War (1861–5) began. American commanders learned a lot from the Crimea. The American government had sent military observers to the conflict, and published a report, *The Art of War in Europe*, in 1860. The Americans observed keenly and made use of their findings about developments in weapons, fortifications, sea mines, warships and many other aspects of the war, including photography and war reporting. The Crimean War is not always given much weight by Civil War historians, but it was an important influence on weapons, tactics and equipment, as well as on war photography. Civil War photographs were in some cases more explicit, and more explicitly a commodity, but the very idea of using photography to record, memorialize or rewrite the experience of war has its roots in the Crimea. As Ulrich Keller argues, there was a kind of honesty in the Crimean War photographs (particularly by Robertson) which Civil War photographers soon abandoned.[16]

For Britain, the war brought about, or facilitated, some social benefits. The work of Florence Nightingale established modern nursing and hygiene and developed the field of statistics. The status, pay and conditions of ordinary soldiers were much improved. Important army and administrative reforms were achieved.

WOMEN

The war also shaped Victorian ideas of gender, sometimes in rather surprising ways. The enormous fame of Florence Nightingale brought the ideal of heroic womanhood into the fabric of everyday life for anyone who read the newspapers.[17] And many who could not read had newspaper and magazine stories read to them. Nightingale's reputation was very widely known. Many papers and magazines published images of Nightingale and poems about her. She was also the subject of a poem by Lewis Carroll, 'The Path of Roses' (1856). Very different from Carroll's clever nonsense poems, this work imagines Nightingale thinking about the war, yearning to serve, but limited by the constraints placed upon women:

> 'Alas!' she sighed, 'for what can woman do?
> Her life is aimless, and her death unknown;
> Hemmed in by social forms she pines in vain:
> Man has his work, but what can woman do?'[18]

A voice answers her:

> 'Peace, for thy lot is other than a man's:
> His is a path of thorns; he beats them down –
> He faces death – he wrestles with despair:
> Thine is of roses, to adopt and cheer
> His barren lot, and hide the thorn in flowers.'

In the poem, Nightingale is not very impressed with the advice that women should be like flowers, but Carroll goes on to transform the metaphor into an image of Nightingale as a light and a lamp. She is then imagined in the war zone, comforting sick and wounded men. Her mere presence is imagined as redeeming men's suffering. The anonymous voice advises her:

> 'So in the darkest path of man's despair,
> Where War and Terror shake the troubled earth,
> Lies woman's mission; with unblenching brow
> To pass through scenes of anguish and affright
> Where men grow sick and tremble; unto her
> All things are sanctified, for all are good.
> Nothing so mean, but shall deserve her care;
> Nothing so great, but she may bear her part.
> No life is vain: each hath his place assigned:
> Do thou thy task, and leave the rest to heaven.' (p. 179)

It's an odd poem, apparently steeped in sentimental ideas about women, yet respectful of Nightingale's moral strength and heroism. What the poem doesn't see is Nightingale's hard work, though this was what she did most of all. She worked long hours on administration, statistics, logistics, procurement, as well as lobbying for better support and for administrative reform. But here, as in many representations, she is simply a presence who does nothing except soothe and inspire. The reality of her work is brushed aside in Carroll's poem even as it appears to be most admired. Even so, female heroism was a powerful idea, still taught and still inspiring to school children a century and more later.[19]

In recent years the achievements of Jamaican Mary Seacole (1805–81), 'doctoress', herbalist, chef and caterer, have been rediscovered. Seacole did not have the long-term institutional influence of Nightingale, who was heard at the highest levels of government. But Seacole made a valuable contribution to the healing and comfort of individual soldiers and officers at the front. Her good-humoured challenges to authority, and her determination to be involved in defiance of officialdom, were it seems much appreciated by those she helped. Her British Hotel, which sold food and supplies, was well known among the British troops outside Sebastopol. After the war she tried to open a business in England, but went bankrupt. Several warm letters of support for her were published in *The Times*, and she was highly praised by William Howard Russell for her 'courage, devotion, goodness of heart, public services':

> I have seen her go down under fire with her little store of creature comforts for our wounded men, and a more tender or skilful hand about a wound or a broken limb could not be found among our best surgeons.[20]

Seacole's memoir, *The Wonderful Adventures of Mrs Seacole in Many Lands*, was published in 1857.[21] As public figures, both Seacole and Nightingale showed in their different ways that women could be strong and resourceful in a time of conflict. Nightingale's years of reform work after the war showed the enormous amount that women could contribute to the public good. Other women at the war, such as Nightingale's nurses, showed tremendous courage and endurance. Some, such as Fanny Duberly, were feisty adventurers.[22] A few soldiers' wives were permitted to accompany the troops and did what they could to help look after the men. Some women came illegally, in disguise, to be with their husbands. Some of these women had babies in the most difficult of circumstances, and many of them died. The exact numbers are unknown, but Helen Rappaport estimates that between 750 and 1,200 women travelled out with the army in March 1854; of these some 75 per cent died.[23]

MASCULINITY AND THE WAR

In assessing masculinity in the Crimean War, Holly Furneaux has shown us that thinking and writing about manhood in the nineteenth century could be complex and nuanced. Crude ideas of male heroism were to be found, but writings by and about Crimean soldiers showed a number of different views of masculinity, including gentleness, sensitivity, nurturing and domestic creativity.

On 19 June 1855, Queen Victoria paid a visit to several English hospitals to meet men wounded in the war. One of the veterans who moved her most was Private Thomas Walker, who had suffered a terrible injury from a shell bursting on his head. He was making a remarkable recovery after a year in hospital, where a surgeon had removed 13 pieces of his skull. *The Times* reported that the Queen saw him every time she visited, and gave him a present of ten pounds. He recovered fully and went on to live an active life.[24] While he was in hospital, Walker learned a new skill: how to make patchwork. In July 1856, *Cassell's Illustrated Family Paper* reported:

> He has employed much of his time whilst in hospital, and relieved the tedium of his confinement, in making patchwork rugs and table covers from the scarlet cloth and facings of soldiers' jackets.[25]

Cassell's noted that one of the rugs was bought by the Queen for ten pounds (this might be the 'present' mentioned by *The Times*) and praised the 'taste and ingenuity' of his handiwork. Walker was also the subject of a painting by Thomas Wood; in it he is 'propped up in bed [his head bandaged] making a vibrantly coloured quilt using the red, black, white, and gold of army uniforms' (Furneaux, p. 182). The painting is now at the Royal College of Surgeons. It's an intriguing image. As Furneaux argues, the portrait shows Walker seriously injured but recovering and able to undertake meaningful, skilled, even beautiful work. The image suggests that the veteran is recovering, the hospital is exceptionally clean and hygienic, and the patient is usefully employed. The scraps of military uniform from the war, some from dead men, are turned into a quilt, something which warms and comforts. It is a comforting image, yet, says Furneaux, it is also uncomfortable. The look on Walker's face is inscrutable. How has he suffered; how does he experience his own body; how does he feel about being an object of scrutiny for the Queen and the press? The Queen wrote in her journal that Walker did not suffer (so the doctors claimed), but the painting questions this, and subtly conveys the ambivalence of creative work which transforms military items into domestic objects. It is a version of the idea of turning swords into ploughshares, and it is rather unsettling.[26]

The Queen was very interested in the wounded veterans, and visited them several times in hospital. In 1856 she commissioned a series of photographs by Joseph Cundall, some of which were exhibited the following year at the Royal Photographic Society in London. The exhibition was announced in *The Athenaeum*:

Mr Cundall's portraits of *Crimean Heroes* [...] have been executed for the Queen. What king or queen ever before thought of the bravery of a private soldier? – not 'the perfect gentleman' or Farmer George, verily. These are the men who had not to order but to do, – men who did not fuss, and brag, and quarrel, and lament, or ask for leave of absence on particular family business, but sweated, and bled, and well earned their shillings and their tardy food. There is an order and obedience, a calm, Spartan, thoughtful courage in their faces that makes us long to shake them by the hand. They are of various types. There is the broad brow and strong grave features, calm, stern, and accustomed to command. There is the suffering, wrinkled forehead, fierce mouth, and strained staring eyes, still dazzled by the blaze of mines and spattering burst of shells. There is the Highlander, with the protruding eyebrow and comical, twisted mouth. It is singular what a common character there is in the old tried solider of all ages and countries. Many of these with a slight change of dress would pass for Caesar's legionaries or Napoleon's

Grenadiers. Clenched lips, full, glaring eyes, and strong, shelving brows
are common to man as the fighter, whether he be Gladiator or bruiser,
Greek Hoplite or English drummer.[27]

Fig. 21: Joseph
Cundall, Three
Soldiers of the
Coldstream
Guards, 1856

One photograph depicts three veterans who had lost limbs in
the war and were recuperating at Chatham Hospital.

The three men's faces are unreadable, like the painting of
Thomas Walker discussed by Furneaux. Is the interest in the
wounded veteran compassionate, or prurient – or could it be both?
Does the photo press the viewer to recognize the humanity and
courage of the disabled veteran; or does it turn the veteran into an
object of compassion or pity, or even indifference?

A photograph can be read in many different ways, but it seems
to me that Cundall's photograph conveys both compassion and
respect for its subjects. Though the veterans might appear passive,
looking down, they have a dignity and integrity which seem

Fig. 22: Joseph Cundall, Amputees at Chatham Military Hospital, 1856

removed from, or beyond, the gaze of the viewer. The wounded veterans impressed and moved Queen Victoria very deeply. Her visit to the military hospitals in July 1855 left her 'Full of what I had seen, which so brought home to my mind & heart, the horrors and sufferings as well as the gallantry, heroism, and resignation of these brave, noble men.'[28] Perhaps she wondered what the war meant to those men, who would live with their injuries for the rest of their lives. What had they gained from the conflict?[29]

***

Was the Crimean War the last old-fashioned war with its cavalry charges and Napoleonic weapons and infantry tactics; or was it the first modern war, with its use of the Minié rifle, iron-clad warships and the telegraph? Arguably it was both. For Lambert, the Crimea 'operated in a transitional phase. Many of the ideas, hardware and practices that held sway in March 1854 were out of date by March 1856.' The war was both static and subject to rapid and often confusing changes which made the commanders' task particularly difficult.[30] In the end, trying to decide whether the Crimea was modern or not seems a fruitless exercise. It drew upon modern technology of its day, out of which further technology was developed for later conflicts. It both used and misused modern thinking about democracy and the will of the people. And, like all wars, its effects were complex, far-reaching, often unexpected, and in some respects the opposite of what had been intended. It succeeded in checking Russian power, but only temporarily. It kept the Ottoman Empire intact for a little longer, but at considerable cost. Was it worth it?

For Lambert, keeping Russia within its borders was a valuable outcome. For other historians, the enormous cost might have been avoided by effective diplomacy early in the dispute. And did Britain back the right side? This might seem a strange question, but some argued at the time that Britain had supported the wrong cause. The long slow disintegration of the Ottoman Empire was periodically halted by outside forces, but it was too weak to survive much longer. By supporting Turkey against Russia in 1854, Britain and France inadvertently contributed to the chaotic break-up of the Ottoman Empire in the Balkans, which in turn was a major factor in the outbreak of the First World War in 1914. An orderly dismantling of the Ottoman Empire in Europe in the nineteenth century might have led to a very different history in the twentieth century. Perhaps some of the warfare and suffering of the past 100 years might have been avoided.

CODA: WAR REPORTING

What do we learn from the representations of the Crimean War in Britain? The birth of modern war reporting, of war brought in words and images to a mass readership, does not prevent war, or stop war. It is questionable how much the representations even inspire opposition to war. On the contrary, even if many felt dismayed when they read about the war, or saw images of its damage, there is no evidence, it seems to me, that these representations did anything to limit the war. Governments and military leaders did not like the representations of the war, but they were not particularly swayed by them. The government did take steps to ensure that reporting would never again be uncensored. The liberal idea of free reporting was soon quashed. But the fiction of free and fair reporting has persisted, despite a host of factors rendering it unfree, and far from disinterested, right up to the present day.

The Crimean War started what was to become an immense flood of representations of warfare; first in the American Civil War, in which photographs of death and mutilation quickly became popular souvenirs of the war, sold on city streets. By the time of the First World War, strict censorship was in place, but there was a wealth of newspaper reports, paintings, photographs and even film (much of it wholly or partly fake), all forming quite an important part of civilians' war experience. (In Robert Graves' memoir, *Goodbye to All That* (1929), he complains that civilians talked 'a foreign language', and it was 'newspaper language'.)

Throughout the twentieth century and into the twenty-first, representations of war – again, many of them half-true, or completely false, or compromised in various ways – are increasingly part of daily life, especially for those living outside war zones. As I write in the 2010s, people are potentially exposed to large numbers of war images every day, through the press, television and especially the internet. Images of war, often unreliable, misleading or wholly false, circulate across millions of social media accounts. As Susan Sontag has argued, the mass media (and now the internet) has over the past century turned war images into mass entertainment.

We might think that the rise in representation signals a rise in awareness, and potentially greater pressure against war. This is often argued about the American–Vietnamese war (1965–73), for example, which was covered intensively in newspapers and magazines and on television. But did the reporting really curtail the long American involvement in Vietnam? Indeed, it can be argued that critical news reports actually strengthened the determination of the American leaders (notably Nixon) to defy public opinion, defeat the peace movement and continue the conflict on their own terms. And much of the reporting was not critical; much of it was lies and pro-war propaganda reproduced uncritically in some sections of the media. In some conflicts, at least, it might be the case that the more representation there is, the *less* the effective opposition to war. The many images of war make us feel well informed, when we are lamentably ill informed. Tennyson or Dickens or George Eliot reading *The Times* in 1854 had a much more accurate knowledge about the Crimean conflict than any of us has today about wars in our own time.

There are many reasons for this paradox, ranging from the economics of the mass media to lies and propaganda from government and military sources. There isn't space here to explore this question further, but it seems to me an important lesson we learn when studying the Crimean War is that, with all its problems and bungling, it was accurately reported (at least from the Crimean theatre), but that it paved the way for mass representations of war which soon became unreliable, inaccurate and not particularly useful for anyone wanting to think critically or intelligently about a conflict.

In other words, representations of warfare might be overrated in terms of their political and ethical value; they do not always help us to understand the complexities of war. Of course representations can be hugely important as acts of memorial, mourning, nationalism or propaganda for the next war. And some images do have a profound moral effect when they are published: British representations of the liberation of Bergen-Belsen concentration camp in April 1945, for example, or the newspaper photograph of Kim Phuc, aged nine, hit by napalm in Vietnam in 1972.[31] Many people who saw those images at the time say that they formed their political consciousness, their conscience, for a lifetime. I believe this is true, and at the same time, it seems to me that the increasing mass of war images over the past 150 years might have precisely the opposite effect. This is another lesson of the Crimea for us today.

Further Reading

Adkin, Mark, *The Charge: Why the Light Brigade Was Lost* (London: Leo Cooper, 1996).

Anderson, Edgar, 'The Crimean War in the Baltic Area', *Journal of Baltic Studies* 5, no. 4 (1974): 339–61.

Anderson, Olive, *A Liberal State at War: English Politics and Economics during the Crimean War* (London: Macmillan, 1967).

Arnold, Guy, *Historical Dictionary of the Crimean War* (Lanham, MD: Scarecrow Press, 2002).

Auerbach, Jeffrey, *The Great Exhibition of 1851: A Nation on Display* (New Haven, CT: Yale University Press, 1999).

Bates, Rachel, '"All touched my hand": Queenly Sentiment and Royal Prerogative', *19: Interdisciplinary Studies in the Long Nineteenth Century* 20 (2015): 1–25.

——, 'Negotiating a "Tangled Web of Pride and Shame": A Crimean Case-Study', *Museum and Society* 13, no. 4 (2015): 503–21.

Bates, Rachel, Holly Furneaux and Alastair Massie (eds), *Charting the Crimean War*, special issue of *19: Interdisciplinary Studies in the Long Nineteenth Century* 20 (2015).

Baumgart, Winfried, *The Crimean War, 1853–1856* (London: Arnold, 1999).

——, (ed.), *Englische Akten zur Geschichte des Krimkriegs*, 4 vols (Munich: R. Oldenbourg, 1988–2006).

Bolloch, Joëlle, *War Photography: From The Crimean War to World War I* (Milan: Five Continents Editions, 2004).

Brackenbury, George, *The Campaign in the Crimea: An Historical Sketch, illustrated ... from drawings taken on the Spot by William Simpson* (London: Paul & Dominic Colnaghi & Co. and Longman, 1855–6).

Bright, John, *The Letters of John Bright, Esq., MP., on the War, Verified and Illustrated by Extracts from the Parliamentary Documents, &c.* (London: W. & F. G. Cash, [1854]).

Butler, Judith, *Frames of War: When is Life Grievable?* (London: Verso, 2009).

Calthorpe, Somerset J. Gough, *Cadogan's Crimea* (London: Hamish Hamilton, 1979).

Ceadel, Martin, *Semi-Detached Idealists: The British Peace Movement and International Relations, 1854–1945* (Oxford: Oxford University Press, 2000).

Chodasiewicz, Robert Adolf, *A Voice From Within the Walls of Sebastopol: A Narrative of the Campaign in the Crimea, and of the Events of the Siege, by Captain R. Hodasevich* (London: John Murray, 1856).

Clifford, Henry, *Henry Clifford V.C: His Letters and Sketches from the Crimea* (London: Joseph, 1956).

Cooke, Brian, *The Grand Crimean Central Railway: The Railway that Won a War* (Knutsford: Cavalier House, 1990).

Crimean War Research Society, http://cwrs.russianwar.co.uk/ (accessed 17 March 2018).

Dallas, George Frederic, *Eyewitness in the Crimea: The Crimean War Letters (1854–56) of Lt. Col. George Frederic Dallas*, ed. Michael Hargreave Mawson (London: Greenhill Books, 2001).

Dereli, Cynthia, *A War Culture in Action: A Study of the Literature of the Crimean War Period* (Oxford: P. Lang, 2003).

Duberly, Fanny, *Journal Kept During the Russian War: From the Departure of the Army from England in April, 1854, to the Fall of Sebastopol* (London: Longmans, 1855).

——, *Mrs Duberly's War: Journal and Letters from the Crimea*, ed. Christine Kelly (Oxford: Oxford University Press, 2007).

Duckers, Peter, *The Crimean War at Sea: The Naval Campaigns against Russia, 1854–6* (Barnsley: Pen and Sword Maritime, 2011).

Dunscombe, Nicholas, *Captain Dunscombe's Diary: The Real Crimean War that the British Infantry Knew*, ed. Colin Robins (Bowdon: Withycut House, 2003).

Elton, Arthur Hallam, *An Inquiry into the Alleged Justice and Necessity of the War with Russia: By an English Landowner* (London: Hamilton, Adams, and Co., 1855).

Emig, Rainer, 'Bringing War Home: The Crimean War, the Telegraph, and Florence Nightingale', in Claudia Glunz and Thomas Schneider (eds), *Wahrheitsmaschinen: Der Einfluss technischer Innovationen auf die Darstellung und das Bild des Krieges in den Medien und Künsten* (Göttingen: Vandenhoeck and Ruprecht, 2010).

Favret, Mary, *War at a Distance: Romanticism and the Making of Modern Wartime* (Princeton, NJ: Princeton University Press, 2010).

Figes, Orlando, *Crimea: The Last Crusade* (London: Allen Lane, 2010).

Finnin, Rory, 'Forgetting Nothing, Forgetting No One: Boris Chichibabin, Viktor Nekipelov, and the Deportation of the Crimean Tatars', *Modern Language Review* 106, no. 4 (2011): 1091–124.

Fisher, Alan, *The Crimean Tatars* (Stanford, CA: Hoover Institution Press, 1978).

Fletcher, Alison, '"To Us the War is a Spectacle": Domestic Consumption of the Crimean War in Britain', *Cahiers Victoriens et Edouardiens* 66 (2007): 153–76.

Florence Nightingale Museum, http://www.florence-nightingale.co.uk/ (accessed 17 March 2018).

Furneaux, Holly, *Military Men of Feeling: Emotion, Touch, and Masculinity in the Crimean War* (Oxford: Oxford University Press, 2016).

Gordon, Sophie, *Roger Fenton, Julia Margaret Cameron: Early British Photographs from the Royal Collection* (London: Royal Collection, 2010).

——, *Shadows of War: Roger Fenton's Photographs of the Crimea, 1855* (London: Royal Collection, 2017).

Gowing, Timothy, *Voice from the Ranks; A Personal Narrative of the Crimean Campaign by a Sergeant of the Royal Fusiliers* (1885), ed. Kenneth Fenwick (London: Folio Society, 1954).

Grainger, John, *The First Pacific War: Britain and Russia, 1854–56* (Woodbridge: Boydell Press, 2008).

Greenhill, Basil and Ann Giffard, *The British Assault on Finland, 1854–1855: A Forgotten Naval War* (London: Conway Maritime, 1988).

Grieg, David, *Letters from the Crimea: Writing Home, a Dundee Doctor*, ed. Douglas Hill (Dundee: Dundee University Press, 2010).

Henisch, B. A. and H. K., 'James Robertson of Constantinople: A Chronology', *History of Photography* 14, no. 1 (1990): 23–32.

——, 'James Robertson and his Crimean War Campaign', *History of Photography* 26, no. 4 (2002): 258–68.

Herbert, Sidney, MP, *The Conduct of the War: A Speech delivered in the House of Commons on Tuesday, 12th of December, 1854* (London: John Murray, 1854).

Hopkins, John Baker, *Words on the War* (London: George Newbold, 1855).

Howard, Michael, *The Invention of Peace and the Reinvention of War*, rev. edn (London: Profile, 2001/2002).

James, Lawrence, *Crimea 1854–56: The War with Russia from Contemporary Photographs* (Thame: Hayes Kennedy, 1981).

Keller, Ulrich, *The Ultimate Spectacle: A Visual History of the Crimean War* (Amsterdam: Gordon and Breach, 2001).

——, 'Photography, History, (Dis)belief', *Visual Resources: An International Journal of Documentation* 26, no. 2 (2010): 95–111.

Kia, Mehrdad, *The Ottoman Empire: A Historical Encyclopedia* (Santa Barbara, CA: ABC-CLIO, 2017).

Kinglake, Alexander William, *The Invasion of the Crimea: Its Origin and an Account of its Progress down to the Death of Lord Raglan* (Edinburgh: Blackwood, 1863–87).

Lalumia, Matthew Paul, *Realism and Politics in Victorian Art of the Crimean War* (Epping: Bowker, 1984).

Lambert, Andrew, *Battleships in Transition: The Creation of the Steam Battlefleet 1815–1860* (Annapolis, MD: Naval Institute Press, 1984).

——, 'Looking for gunboats: British naval operations in the Gulf of Bothnia, 1854–55', *Journal for Maritime Research* 6, no. 1 (2004): 65–86, https://www.tandfonline.com/doi/abs/10.1080/21533369.2004.9668337 (accessed 16 June 2018).

——, *The Crimean War: British Grand Strategy against Russia 1853–1856*, rev. edn (Farnham: Ashgate, 2011).

Lambert, Andrew and Stephen Badsey (eds), *The War Correspondents: The Crimean War* (London: Bramley Books, 1994/1997).

Layton, Susan, 'The Maude Translations of the Sevastopol Stories', *Tolstoy Studies Journal* 20 (2008): 14–26.

Leary, Patrick, 'A Brief History of the *Illustrated London News*', ILN database, http://gale.cengage.co.uk//images/PatrickLeary.pdf (accessed 17 March 2018).

Liddle, Dallas, *The Dynamics of Genre: Journalism and the Practice of Literature in Mid-Victorian Britain* (Charlottesville: University of Virginia Press, 2009).

Maag, Georg, Wolfram Pyta and Martin Windisch (eds), *Der Krimkrieg als erster europäischer Medienkrieg* (Berlin: Lit Verlag, 2010).

Markovits, Stefanie, *The Crimean War in the British Imagination* (Cambridge: Cambridge University Press, 2009).

Martin, Kingsley, *The Triumph of Lord Palmerston: A Study of Public Opinion in England Before the Crimean War* (London: Hutchinson, 1924/1963).

Massie, Alastair (ed.), *A Most Desperate Undertaking: The British Army in the Crimea, 1854–56* (London: National Army Museum, 2003).

——, *The National Army Museum Book of the Crimean War: The Untold Stories* (London: Sidgwick and Jackson, 2004).

Mieszkowski, Jan, *Watching War* (Stanford, CA: Stanford University Press, 2012).

Moore, David and Geoffrey Salter, *Mallet's Great Mortars* (Fareham: Palmerston Forts Society, 1996).

Nightingale, Florence, *Letters from the Crimea 1854–1856*, ed. Sue Goldie (Manchester: Mandolin, 1987/1997).

Orwin, Donna Tussing (ed.), *The Cambridge Companion to Tolstoy* (Cambridge: Cambridge University Press, 2006).

Palmer, Alan, *The Banner of Battle: The Story of the Crimean War* (London: Weidenfeld and Nicolson, 1987).

Paroissien, David (ed.), *A Companion to Charles Dickens* (Oxford: Blackwell, 2008).

Porter, Whitworth, *Life in the Trenches before Sebastopol* (London: Longman, Brown, Green, and Longmans, 1856).

Purbrick, Louise (ed.), *The Great Exhibition of 1851: New Interdisciplinary Essays* (Manchester: Manchester University Press, 2001).

Ranken, George, *Six Months at Sebastopol: Being Selections from the Journal and Correspondence of the Late Major George Ranken, Royal Engineers*, ed. W. Bayne Ranken (London: Charles Westerton, 1857).

Rappaport, Helen, *No Place for Ladies: The Untold Story of Women in the Crimean War* (London: Arum Press, 2007).

Reed, John, 'Fighting Words: Two Proletarian Military Novels of the Crimean Period', *Victorian Literature and Culture* 36, no. 2 (2008): 331–42.

Reid, Douglas, *Soldier-Surgeon: The Crimean War Letters of Dr Douglas A. Reid 1855–1856*, ed. Joseph Baylen and Alan Conway (Knoxville: University of Tennessee Press, 1968).

Richardson, Edmund, *Classical Victorians: Scholars, Scoundrels and Generals in Pursuit of Antiquity* (Cambridge: Cambridge University Press, 2013).

——, 'Of Doubtful Antiquity: Fighting for the Past in the Crimean War', in Astrid Swenson and Peter Mandler (eds), *From Plunder to Preservation: Britain and the Heritage of Empire, c.1800–1940*, pp. 31–48 (Oxford: Oxford University Press for the British Academy, 2013).

Robinson, Frederick, *Diary of the Crimean War* (London: R. Bentlely, 1856).

Rogers, Kathleen Béres, 'Embodied Sympathy and Divine Detachment in Crimean War Medical Poetry', *War, Literature, and the Arts* 25 (2013).

Romaine, William Govett, *Romaine's Crimean War: The Letters and Journals of William Govett Romaine, Deputy Judge-Advocate to the Army of the East 1854–6*, ed. Colin Robins (Stroud: Sutton, 2005).

Royle, Trevor, *Crimea: The Great Crimean War, 1854–1856* (London: Little, Brown, 1999).

Rubery, Matthew, *The Novelty of Newspapers: Victorian Fiction After the Invention of the News* (Oxford: Oxford University Press, 2009).

Russell, William Howard, *General Todleben's History of the Defence of Sebastopol, 1854–5: A Review* (London: Tinsley Brothers, 1865; rpt Cambridge University Press, 2012).

Samuels, Maurice, 'Regarding the Crimean War: History, Spectacle, Modernity', *Dix-Neuf* 6 (2006): 26–41.

Sandwith, Humphrey, *A Narrative of the Siege of Kars: And of the Six Months' Resistance by the Turkish Garrison Under General Williams to the Turkish Army* (London: John Murray, 1856).

Schramm, Jan-Melissa, *Atonement and Self-Sacrifice in Nineteenth-Century Narrative* (Cambridge: Cambridge University Press, 2012).

Seacole, Mary, *Wonderful Adventures of Mrs Seacole in Many Lands* (1857; New York: Oxford University Press, 1988).

Sevastopol, by Two Brothers (London: Richard Bentley, 1856).

Shelston, Alan, 'Elizabeth Gaskell and the Crimean War', *Gaskell Journal* 23 (2009): 54–63.

Shepherd, John, *Crimean Doctors: A History of the British Medical Services in the Crimean War* (Liverpool: Liverpool University Press, 1991).

Silver, Christopher, *Renkioi: Brunel's Forgotten Crimean War Hospital* (Sevenoaks: Valonia Press, 2007).

Simpson, William, *The Seat of War in the East* (London: Paul and Dominic Colnaghi and Co., 1855–6).

Smith, Karen W., *Constantin Guys: Crimean War Drawings, 1854–1856* (Cleveland, OH: The Museum, 1978).

Sontag, Susan, *Regarding the Pain of Others* (London: Penguin, 2003).

Soyer, Alexis, *Soyer's Culinary Campaign: Being Historical Reminiscences of the Late War* (London: G. Routledge, 1857).

Sweetman, John, *War and Administration: The Significance of the Crimean War for the British Army* (Edinburgh: Scottish Academic Press, 1984).

——, *The Crimean War* (Oxford: Osprey, 2001).

Tate, Trudi, *Modernism, History and the First World War* (Penrith: HeB, 1998/2013).

——, 'On Not Knowing Why: Memorializing the Light Brigade', in Helen Small and Trudi Tate (eds), *Literature, Science, Psychoanalysis: Essays in Honour of Gillian Beer*, pp. 16–80 (Oxford: Clarendon Press, 2003).

——, 'Sebastopol: On the Fall of a City', *19: Interdisciplinary Studies in the Long Nineteenth Century* 20, special issue on the Crimean War, ed. Rachel Bates, Holly Furneaux and Alistair Massey (2015).

Tolstoy, Leo, *The Sebastopol Sketches* (1855–6), trans. David McDuff (London: Penguin, 1986).

Tran, Tri, 'Behind the Myth: The Representation of the Crimean War in Nineteenth Century British Newspapers, Government Archives and Contemporary Records', *Cahiers Victoriens et Edouardiens* 66 (2007): 53–82.

Victorian Web, http://www.victorianweb.org/ (accessed 16 June 2018).

Voice from Westminster, A, *Is the War Just? A Letter to the Right Honorable the Viscount Palmerston, M.P.* (London: W. H. Dalton, 1855).

Waddington, Patrick, *'Theirs But to Do and Die': The Poetry of the Charge of the Light Brigade at Balaklava, 25 October 1854* (Nottingham: Astra, 1995).

War Correspondent, Journal of the Crimean War Research Society.

War Office, *Siege of Sebastopol*, 3 vols (London: Eyre and Spottiswoode, 1859).

Williams, William, *The Siege of Kars, 1855: Defence and Capitulation* (London: Stationery Office, 2000).

Youngblood, Norman, *The Development of Mine Warfare: A Most Murderous and Barbarous Conduct* (Westport, CT: Praegar Security International, 2006).

Notes

1   *Social Life and Manners in Australia: Being the Notes of Eight Years'
    Experience* (London: Longman, Green, Longman and Roberts, 1861), pp.
    127–8. Published anonymously. Some attribute this to Isabel Massary,
    pseud. of Elizabeth Ramsay-Laye, but the authorship is not certain. Kay
    Walsh, 'Ramsay-Laye, Elizabeth', in William Wilde, Joy Hooten and
    Barry Andrews (eds), *Oxford Companion to Australian Literature*, 2nd
    edn (Oxford: Oxford University Press, 2005).
2   See, for example, 'Threatened Invasion of Australia', *Punch*, 18 February
    1854, p. 63, which mocks the Australian settlers' nervousness.
3   Hew Strachan, Preface to Winfried Baumgart, *The Crimean War, 1853–56*
    (London: Arnold, 1999), p. vi. Here and throughout this book, historical
    material is drawn from Olive Anderson, *A Liberal State at War: English
    Politics and Economics during the Crimean War* (London: Macmillan,
    1967); John Barham, *A Journey through the Crimean War*, Crimean
    War Research Society website, 2000–18, http://cwrs.russianwar.co.uk/
    (accessed 17 March 2018); Baumgart, *The Crimean War*; Orlando Figes,
    Crimea: The Last Crusade (London: Allen Lane, 2010); Andrew Lambert,
    The Crimean War: British Grand Strategy against Russia 1853–1856, rev.
    edn (Farnham: Ashgate, 2011); Andrew Lambert and Stephen Badsey
    (eds), *The War Correspondents: The Crimean War* (London: Bramley
    Books, 1994/1997); Alastair Massie (ed.), *The National Army Museum
    Book of the Crimean War: The Untold Stories* (London: Sidgwick and
    Jackson, 2004); Alan Palmer, *The Banner of Battle: The Story of the
    Crimean War* (London: Weidenfeld and Nicolson, 1987); Colin Robins,
    Introduction to William Govett Romaine, *Romaine's Crimean War:*

The Letters and Journals of William Govett Romaine, Deputy Judge-Advocate to the Army of the East 1854–6, ed. Colin Robins (Stroud: Sutton, 2005); Trevor Royle, *Crimea: The Great Crimean War, 1854–1856* (London: Little, Brown, 1999); John Sweetman, *The Crimean War* (Oxford: Osprey, 2001); and original sources as indicated.

4 Estimates of the numbers of dead range from 300,000 to more than 1 million. Lambert, *The Crimean War*, p. 31; Sweetman, *The Crimean War*, p. 89; BBC website: *Crimean War*, 2011, http://www.bbc.co.uk/history/british/victorians/crimea (accessed 17 March 2018). Baumgart estimates 640,000 dead in total, *The Crimean War*, pp. 215–16. Rachel Bates et al. put the number of combatants killed at around three-quarters of a million, alongside many civilian deaths. Rachel Bates, Holly Furneaux and Alastair Massie (eds), *Charting the Crimean War*, in *19: Interdisciplinary Studies in the Long Nineteenth Century* 20, special issue (2015): 1. See also Eric Hobsbawm, *The Age of Capital 1848–1875* (London: Abacus, 1975), p. 96.

5 Lambert and Badsey, introduction, *The War Correspondents*, p. 2.

6 Lambert, *The Crimean War*.

7 Mary Favret's *War at a Distance* is interesting on the question of witnessing war from afar, but has little to say about the Crimean War, and does not engage with its eyewitness reports, which seem to me very important in the history of representations of warfare. Mary Favret, *War at a Distance: Romanticism and the Making of Modern Wartime* (Princeton NJ: Princeton University Press, 2010).

8 Royle, *Crimea*, 'Prologue: 1851'; Louise Purbrick (ed.), *The Great Exhibition of 1851* (Manchester: Manchester University Press, 2001).

9 Anderson, *A Liberal State at War*, p. 15.

10 Edmund Richardson, *Classical Victorians: Scholars, Scoundrels and Generals in Pursuit of Antiquity* (Cambridge: Cambridge University Press, 2013), pp. 76–7.

11 On the war artists, see Matthew Paul Lalumia, *Realism and Politics in Victorian Art of the Crimean War* (Epping: Bowker, 1984).

12 Stefanie Markovits, *The Crimean War in the British Imagination* (Cambridge: Cambridge University Press, 2009).

13 His reports may sometimes have provided useful information to the enemy inside Sebastopol: *The Times* was read avidly there as soon as it arrived, and in St Petersburg, too. George Frederic Dallas, *Eyewitness in the Crimea: The Crimean War Letters (1854–56) of Lt. Col. George Frederic Dallas*, ed. Michael Hargreave Mawson (London: Greenhill Books, 2001), pp. 161–2.

14 By mid-1855, a British telegraph line extended to Balaklava. Lambert and Badsey, *War Correspondents*, p. 272.

15 Romaine, *Romaine's Crimean War*, p. 32.

16 Sweetman, *The Crimean War*, pp. 15–16; Sweetman notes there were in effect two armies, and Raglan commanded only one of them. He did not control the Commissariat, which was a Treasury department. See also John Sweetman, *War and Administration: The Significance of the Crimean War for the British Army* (Edinburgh: Scottish Academic Press, 1984).

17 A note on spelling. I am using the standard nineteeth-century spelling 'Sebastopol', as used in nearly all the sources quoted. Today the correct spelling in English is 'Sevastopol'.

18 Baumgart, *The Crimean War*, pp. vi, ix–x.

19 Charles Baudelaire, *The Painter of Modern Life and Other Essays*, trans. and ed. Jonathan Mayne, 2nd edn (London: Phaidon, 1995), p. 18.

20 For a detailed discussion, see Trudi Tate, 'On Not Knowing Why: Memorializing the Light Brigade', in Helen Small and Trudi Tate (eds), *Literature, Science, Psychoanalysis: Essays in Honour of Gillian Beer* (Oxford: Clarendon Press, 2003); and Markovits, *The Crimean War*, ch. 3.

21 Hobsbawm, *The Age of Capital*, 94–8.

22 Baumgart, *The Crimean War*, ch. 1; David Goldfrank, *The Origins of the Crimean War* (London: Routlege, 1994), ch. 3.

23 Sweetman, *The Crimean War*, p. 17. The material here on the Eastern question is based on Baumgart, *The Crimean War*, pp. 3–4. Mehrdad Kia, *The Ottoman Empire: A Historical Encyclopedia* (Santa Barbara, CA: ABC-CLIO, 2017), p. 22. Turkey conquered Gallipoli in 1354.

24 Baumgart, *The Crimean War*, pp. 3–4.

25 Richardson, *Classical Victorians*.

26 Sweetman, *Crimean War*, p. 16. On the complexities of military administration and reform, see Sweetman, *War and Administration*.

27 Sweetman argues that for many people, victory over Russia 'embodied the spirit of the mid-Victorian age' (*The Crimean War*, p. 14), but it seems to me the attitude is rather more ambivalent.

28 See, for example, Favret, *War at a Distance*; Susan Sontag, *Regarding the Pain of Others* (London: Penguin, 2003); Jan Mieszkowski, *Watching War* (Stanford, CA: Stanford University Press, 2012). There are many examples of false representations on social media being widely circulated, including atrocities from one part of the world being published as if it were from somewhere completely different. Occasionally this is exposed

– for example, the BBC revealed that film of a fight between drug gangs in Mexico was circulated on social media with the claim that it was a war atrocity from Syria. False news items were much in circulation on social media during the US presidential election and the EU referendum vote in Britain in 2016, though this was not really exposed until afterwards. The discourse moves so rapidly, and there is so much material, that there is little chance to pause and really understand where and how events have been misrepresented.

CHAPTER 1: THE DRIFT TO WAR AND THE BATTLE OF THE ALMA

1 Miles Taylor, 'Urquhart, David (1805–1877)', *Oxford Dictionary of National Biography* (Oxford: Oxford University Press, 2004), http://www.oxforddnb.com/view/article/28017 (accessed 17 March 2018). Urquhart was dismissed by some as eccentric, but he was a well-informed influence on foreign policy reform after the Crimean War.

2 *Punch*, 30 July 1853, p. 50; 27 August 1853, p. 90; 16 July 1853, p. 27.

3 *Punch*, 3 December 1853, p. 233; 28 January 1854, p. 37.

4 For example, 'A Bare Probability', *Punch*, 4 August 1849, p. 44.

5 *Illustrated London News* (hereafter *ILN*), 21 January 1854, p. 62.

6 'Church of the Holy Sepulchre', *ILN*, 2 April 1853, p. 249.

7 *Punch*, 9 July 1853, p. 17.

8 For detailed discussion of the religious disputes, see Orlando Figes, *Crimea: The Last Crusade* (London: Allen Lane, 2010), ch. 1; David Goldfrank, *The Origins of the Crimean War* (London: Routlege, 1994), ch. 5.

9 Letter to Clarendon, quoted in Winfried Baumgart, *Crimean War 1853–56* (London: Arnold, 1999), 29.

10 Andrew Lambert, *The Crimean War: British Grand Strategy against Russia 1853–1856*, rev. edn (Farnham: Ashgate, 2011), p. 94; Baumgart, *Crimean War*, p. 15; Colin Robins, Introduction to William Govett Romaine, *Romaine's Crimean War: The Letters and Journals of William Govett Romaine, Deputy Judge-Advocate to the Army of the East 1854–6*, ed. Colin Robins (Stroud: Sutton, 2005), p. 2; John Barham, *A Journey through the Crimean War* (Crimean War Research Society website, 2000–18, http://cwrs.russianwar.co.uk/, last accessed 17 March 2018), ch. 1.

11 Report reprinted from *Morning Chronicle*, *ILN*, 31 December 1853, p. 590.

12 Editorial, *ILN*, 31 December 1853, p. 606.

13 'Wanted: A Casus Belli', *Punch*, 4 February 1854, p. 47; 'Latin Lesson for Nicholas', *Punch*, 1 April 1854, p. 128.

14 *The Lady's Newspaper* (London), 24 December 1853, p. 383.

15 Editorial, *The Times*, 20 December 1853, p. 8.

16 *ILN*, 4 March 1854.

17 Andrew Lambert and Stephen Badsey (eds), *The War Correspondents: The Crimean War* (London: Bramley Books, 1994/1997), pp. 5–6.

18 Baumgart, *Crimean War*, pp. 17–18, p. 28. Baumgart provides a detailed summary of the complex of different interests.

19 *John Bull*, 2 January 1854, p. 840.

20 John Bright, speech given to Peace Society Conference, Edinburgh, October 1853.

21 *Hansard* 3, 136, 23 February 1855, col. 1761. See also A. J. P. Taylor, 'John Bright and the Crimean War', *Bulletin of the John Rylands Library* 36, no. 2 (1954): 501–22; Miles Taylor, 'Bright, John (1811–1889)', *Oxford Dictionary of National Biography* (Oxford: Oxford University Press, 2004), online edn, September 2013, http://www.oxforddnb.com/ view/article/3421 (accessed 17 March 2017).

22 See further E. M. Lloyd, 'Somerset, FitzRoy James Henry, first Baron Raglan (1788–1855)', rev. John Sweetman, *Oxford Dictionary of National Biography* (Oxford: Oxford University Press, 2004), online edn, September 2014, http://www.oxforddnb.com/view/article/26007 (accessed 17 March 2018); John Sweetman, *Raglan: From the Peninsula to the Crimea* (Barnsley: Pen and Sword, 1960/2010).

23 Fanny Duberly, *Journal*, 5 September 1854.

24 Lieutenant-Colonel S. J. G. Calthorpe, *Letters from Head-quarters; or, the Realities of War in the Crimea, by an Officer on the Staff* (1856), 3rd edn (London: John Murray, 1858), p. 57.

25 William Howard Russell, rpt Lambert and Badsey, *The War Correspondents*, p. 43. Page references for Russell's reports are from this edition.

26 Figes, *Crimea*, p. 202.

27 Mara Kozelsky, 'Casualties of Conflict: Crimean Tatars during the Crimean War', *Slavic Review* 67, no. 4 (2008): 852–91.

28 Captain R. [Robert] Hodasevich [Chodasiewicz], *A Voice From Within the Walls of Sebastopol: A Narrative of the Campaign in the Crimea, and of the Events of the Siege, by Captain R. Hodasevich* (London: J. Murray, 1856), pp. 37, 47.

29 Lt-Col. Calthorpe reports that the British paid for the things they used.

He writes that when the French Zouaves stripped bare a local village, the British tried to stop further plundering. Looting was a serious offence for British troops. Calthorpe, *Letters from Head-quarters*, p. 57.

30 Duberly, *Journal*, 15 September 1854.

31 Kingscote, Letter to Mapleton, 16 September 1854; rpt on Crimean War Research Society website. Ernest Clarke, 'Kingscote, Sir Robert Nigel Fitzhardinge (1830–1908)', rev. K. D. Reynolds, *Oxford Dictionary of National Biography* (Oxford: Oxford University Press, 2004).

32 Timothy Gowing, *Voice from the Ranks; A Personal Narrative of the Crimean Campaign by a Sergeant of the Royal Fusiliers* (1885), ed. Kenneth Fenwick (London: Folio Society, 1954), p. 12. Gowing's lively personal narrative is not always seen as a reliable historical source.

33 John Fisher, First Battalion Rifle Brigade, in Alastair Massie (ed.), *The National Army Museum Book of the Crimean War: The Untold Stories* (London: Sidgwick and Jackson, 2004), p. 30.

34 Colin Robins, personal communication.

35 Richard Chenevix Trench, 'Alma', *Alma, and Other Poems* (London: John W. Parker and Son, 1855). Rpt on Victorian Web, http://www. victorianweb.org/authors/trench/alma.html (accessed 3 June 2018).

36 Calthorpe, *Letters from Head-quarters*, pp. 64–5.

37 Ibid., p. 65.

38 Trevor Royle, *Crimea: The Great Crimean War, 1854–1856* (London: Little, Brown, 1999), p. 219; Massie, *NAM Book*, p. 34.

39 John Sweetman, The *Crimean War* (Oxford: Osprey, 2001), p. 41.

40 *ILN*, 14 October 1854, p. 374. The Zouaves were an elite force within the French army. Originally tribal soldiers serving in the French army in Algeria, by the 1850s, most Zouaves were of French origin. They wore a distinctive uniform of voluminous red trousers, short jacket, long sash and tasselled cap, and were renowed for being courageous, resourceful and rather wild. Baumgart, *Crimean War*, p. 69; Guy Arnold, *Historical Dictionary of the Crimean War* (Lanham, MD: Scarecrow Press, 2002), pp. 152–3.

41 *Recollections of a Zouave before Sebastopol*, ed. Dr Felix Maynard, trans. Mrs M. Harrison Robinson (Philadelphia: Hayes and Zell, 1856); first published in French in Paris, 1856.

42 De Lacy Evans, battle report, rpt in Massie, *NAM Book*, p. 35.

43 Massie, *NAM Book*, p. 37.

44 'Arrival of the Wounded in the Bosphorus', *The Times*, 9 October 1854, p. 8.

45 'From Our Own Correspondent, Constantinople', *The Times*, 12 October

1854, p. 7.

46 See further John Sweetman, *War and Administration: The Significance of the Crimean War for the British Army* (Edinburgh: Scottish Academic Press, 1984).

47 *The Times*, 9 October 1854, p. 8.

48 [John Delane], Editorial, *The Times*, 12 October 1854, p. 6.

49 *The Times*, 13 October 1854, p. 6.

50 Captain W. P. Richards, Letter from camp outside Sevastopol, 12 January 1855; rpt Victorian Web, http://www.victorianweb.org/history/crimea/richards/richards10.html (accessed 3 June 2018).

51 Florence Nightingale, letters to Sidney Herbert, 5 February 1855 and 18 March 1855, in Sue Goldie (ed.), *Florence Nightingale: Letters from the Crimea 1854–1856* (Manchester: Manchester University Press, 1997), pp. 85, 109.

52 Tim Coates, *Delane's War* (London: Biteback Publishing, 2009), pp. 93–4.

53 Ibid.

54 Monica E. Baly and H. C. G. Matthew, 'Nightingale, Florence (1820–1910)', *Oxford Dictionary of National Biography* (Oxford: Oxford University Press, 2004); online edn, January 2011, http://www.oxforddnb.com/view/article/35241 (accessed 17 March 2018).

55 Her letters are now available online, http://archives.bu.edu/web/florence-nightingale (accessed 17 March 2018).

56 Stefanie Markovits, *The Crimean War in the British Imagination* (Cambridge: Cambridge University Press, 2009), pp. 68–9.

57 Report dated 25 September, *The Times*, 12 October 1854, p. 8.

58 Paget, entry for 21 September 1854, *The Light Cavalry Brigade in the Crimea: Extracts from the Letters and Journal of General Lord George Paget* (London: John Murray, 1881); rpt Victorian Web, http://www.historyhome.co.uk/forpol/crimea/paget/paget1.htm (accessed 3 June 2018).

59 Barham, *A Journey*, ch. 8.

60 For example in *The Times*, 2 October 1854, p. 6. This report notes that the alleged fall of Sebastopol has not been verified.

61 C. M., 'The Heroes of the Alma', *ILN*, 14 October 1854, p. 359.

62 Mrs T. K. Hervey, 'Alma', *ILN*, 21 October 1854.

63 D.M.M. [Dinah Mulock Craik], 'By the Alma River', *ILN*, 28 October 1854.

64 Arnold, *Historical Dictionary of the Crimean War*, p. 120.

CHAPTER 2: THE SIEGE ESTABLISHED AND THE BATTLE OF BALAKLAVA

1   Winfried Baumgart, *Crimean War 1853–56* (London: Arnold, 1999), p. 115. Serhii Plokhy, 'The City of Glory: Sevastopol in Russian Historical Mythology', *Journal of Contemporary History* 35, no. 3 (2000): 369–83. An earlier version of part of this chapter is published as 'On Not Knowing Why: Memorializing the Light Brigade', in Helen Small and Trudi Tate (eds), *Literature, Science, Psychoanalysis: Essays in Honour of Gillian Beer* (Oxford: Clarendon Press, 2003), pp. 16–80.

2   Aleksey Zaytsev, 'The Three Earliest Charts of Akhtiar (Sevastopol) Harbour', *Imago Mundi* 53 (2000): 119.

3   'The Fortifier of Sebastopol', *The Times*, 9 October 1854, p. 5.

4   Nolan in Alastair Massie (ed.), *The National Army Museum Book of the Crimean War: The Untold Stories* (London: Sidgwick and Jackson, 2004), p. 60.

5   Russell, preface, *General Todleben's History of the Siege of Sebastopol 1854–5: A Review* (London: Tinsley Brothers, 1865; rpt Cambridge University Press, 2012).

6   'Eduard Totleben', National Army Museum website, 2014, https://www.nam.ac.uk/ (accessed 17 March 2018).

7   Leader, *The Times*, 6 October 1854, p. 6.

8   'A Peep at Sebastopol', by an Occasional Correspondent, *The Times*, 21 October 1854, p. 8.

9   Brigadier-General Richard Airey, Letter, 8 October CUL Add.9554/1/5. Rpt Crimean War Research Society website, http://cwrs.russianwar.co.uk/ (accessed 17 March 2018). From September 1854 Airey was Quartermaster General at Raglan's headquarters.

10 Colin Robins, Introduction to William Govett Romaine, *Romaine's Crimean War: The Letters and Journals of William Govett Romaine, Deputy Judge-Advocate to the Army of the East 1854–6*, ed. Colin Robins (Stroud: Sutton, 2005), p. 5; Nicholas Dunscombe, *Captain Dunscombe's Diary: The Real Crimean War that the British Infantry Knew*, ed. Colin Robins (Bowdon: Withycut House, 2003), pp. 226–7. See Robins' map of the trenches in *Romaine*, pp. xviii–xix.

11 William Radcliffe, 20th Regiment, letter rpt in Massie, *NAM Book*, pp. 66–7.

12 Airey, Letter, 8 October 1854. CUL Add.9554/1/5. Rpt Crimean War Research Society website, http://cwrs.russianwar.co.uk/ (accessed 17 March 2018).

13 Fanny Duberly, *Journal*, 17 October 1854, p. 85.

14 Mundy, letter, 21 October 1854, rpt in Massie, *NAM Book*, p. 73.

15 Major William Forrest, letter, rpt Massie, *NAM Book*, p. 80.

16 Russell, report written 25 October. Russell's wonderful phrase *'thin red streak tipped with a line of steel'* was misremembered over the years as 'thin red line'.

17 Kingscote rpt in Massie, *NAM Book*, p. 81.

18 Alfred, Lord Tennyson, 'The Charge of the Heavy Brigade at Balaclava', *Macmillan's Magazine* 45 (March 1882).

19 George Paget, *The Light Cavalry Brigade in the Crimea: Extracts from the Letters and Journal of General Lord George Paget* (1875; London: John Murray, 1881); rpt Victorian Web, http://www.historyhome.co.uk/forpol/crimea/paget/heavy.htm (accessed 7 June 2018). Paget (1818–80) was next senior officer to Cardigan in the Light Brigade (*Dictionary of National Biography*).

20 Mark Adkin, *The Charge: Why the Light Brigade Was Lost* (London: Leo Cooper, 1996), pp. 125–7; Alan Palmer, *The Banner of Battle: The Story of the Crimean War* (London: Weidenfeld and Nicolson, 1987), p. 128. For a more detailed discussion of the charge in cultural history, see Trudi Tate, 'On Not Knowing Why: Memorializing the Light Brigade', in Helen Small and Trudi Tate (eds), *Literature, Science, Psychoanalysis: Essays in Honour of Gillian Beer* (Oxford: Oxford University Press, 2003).

21 Adkin, *The Charge*, pp. 132–4. Nolan was killed in the charge.

22 Colin Robins et al., 'Artillery', *The War Correspondent* 23, no. 1 (April 2005): 14. A half-pood is approx. 18 lbs.

23 Colin Robins, 'Lucan, Cardigan and Raglan's Order', *Journal of Society for Army Historical Research* 75 (1997): 89; rpt Crimean War Research Society website, http://cwrs.russianwar.co.uk/cwrs-crimtexts-topics-crobins01.html (accessed 7 June 2018).

24 Adkin notes that the 11th Hussars' cavalry division was reduced from 2,000 to 200 horses by December 1854; *The Charge*, p. 216.

25 Robins calls the order 'military lunacy'; 'Lucan'. Robins also points out that for more than a century, historians failed to look at the relevant contour maps of the area.

26 Alfred, Lord Tennyson, 'The Charge of the Light Brigade' (1854), rpt in *Tennyson, A Selected Edition*, ed. Christopher Ricks (Harlow: Longman, 1989), pp. 508–11. The punctuation varies across editions; I follow the punctuation of this edition.

27 B. L. Chapman, Letter to Tennyson, 3 August 1855, in *Letters of Tennyson*, ed. Cecil Lang and Edgar Shannon, 3 vols (Oxford: Clarendon Press, 1987), vol. 2, pp. 117.

28 *The Times*, editorial, 13 November 1854, p. 6.

29 'What is the meaning of a spectacle so strange, so terrific, so disastrous, and yet so grand?', editorial, *The Times*, 14 November 1854, p. 6. *Morning Chronicle*, 14 November 1854, p. 4.

30 David Cannadine, *Aspects of Aristocracy: Grandeur and Decline in Modern Britain* (New Haven, CT: Yale University Press, 1994), p. 10; David Cannadine, *The Decline and Fall of the British Aristocracy* (New Haven, CT: Yale University Press, 1990).

31 Dominic Lieven, *The Aristocracy in Europe, 1815–1914* (Basingstoke: Macmillan, 1992), p. 181; C. B. Otley, 'The Social Origins of British Army Officers', *Sociological Review* 18, no. 2 (1970): 213–40.

32 'The Voice of the Omnibus', *Punch*, May 1855, p. 179; G. R. Searle, *Entrepreneurial Politics in Mid-Victorian Britain* (Oxford: Oxford University Press, 1993), pp. 90–4.

33 John Sweetman, The *Crimean War* (Oxford: Osprey, 2001), pp. 15–16; for a more detailed account see John Sweetman, *War and Administration: The Significance of the Crimean War for the British Army* (Edinburgh: Scottish Academic Press, 1984).

34 Olive Anderson, *A Liberal State at War: English Politics and Economics during the Crimean War* (London: Macmillan, 1967).

35 Richard Trench, 'Balaklava', in *Alma: And Other Poems*, 2nd edn (London: John W. Parker & Son, 1855), p. 19. Trench suggests that the sacrifice is not in vain; the rest of the nation is learning about duty from the heroes and martyrs of the Light Brigade.

36 Adkin, *The Charge*, p. 87.

CHAPTER 3: SCUTARI, INKERMAN AND THE SIEGE

1 Florence Nightingale, Letter, 4 November 1854, in *Florence Nightingale, Letters from the Crimea*, ed. Sue Goldie (Manchester: Mandolin, 1997), pp. 32–3. Letters quoted here are from this edition.

2 Nightingale, Letter, 14 November 1854, p. 36.

3 Nightingale, Letter, 5 February 1855, p. 83.

4 Ibid., p. 85.

5 John Downham, *Heroes of Inkerman 1854*, Lancaster Infantry Museum website, http://www.lancashireinfantrymuseum.org.uk/heroes-of-inkerman-2/ (accessed 7 June 2018). Historical material in this chapter is taken from this source and from Patrick Mercer, *Inkerman 1854: The Soldiers' Battle* (London: Osprey, 1998); John Barham, *A Journey through the Crimean War*, Crimean War Research Society website, 2000–18, http://

cwrs.russianwar.co.uk/ (accessed 17 March 2018); and original sources as cited.

6 Russell estimates 4,000; Downham estimates 6,000.

7 [Edward Hamley], 'The Story of the Campaign', Part III, *Blackwood's Edinburgh Magazine* 77 (February 1855): 238. Sir Edward Hamley was a serving officer, later a military historian, who wrote regularly for *Blackwood's* from his tent outside Sebastopol. E. M. Lloyd, 'Hamley, Sir Edward Bruce (1824–1893)', rev. Roger Stearn, *Oxford Dictionary of National Biography* (Oxford: Oxford University Press, 2004).

8 George Frederic Dallas, *Eyewitness in the Crimea: The Crimean War Letters (1854–56) of Lt. Col. George Frederic Dallas*, ed. Michael Hargreave Mawson (London: Greenhill Books, 2001), p. 44.

9 Hamley, 'The Story of the Campaign', 238.

10 'The Battle of Inkerman', *ILN*, 25 November 1854, p. 526.

11 Downham, 'Heroes of Inkerman'.

12 Hamley, 'The Story of the Campaign', p. 242.

13 Mercer, *Inkerman*, p. 59; Andrew Lambert and Stephen Badsey (eds), *The War Correspondents: The Crimean War* (London: Bramley Books, 1994/1997), p. 130.

14 *ILN*, 25 November 1854, p. 526.

15 Mercer, *Inkerman*, p. 78. Some earlier reports put the Russian figures higher.

16 Hamley, 'The Story of the Campaign', p. 243.

17 Editorial, *ILN*, 25 November 1854, p. 526.

18 Editorial, *Daily News*, 23 November 1854.

19 Downham, *Heroes of Inkerman 1854*.

20 William Romaine, Letter, 1 December 1854, *Romaine's Crimean War: The Letters and Journal of William Govett Romaine*, ed. Colin Robins (Phoenix Mill: Sutton, 2005), p. 38.

21 Robins, introduction to *Romaine's Crimean War*, p. 6.

22 Lambert and Badsey, *War Correspondents*, p. 134. John Sweetman, *The Crimean War* (Oxford: Osprey, 2001), p. 60.

23 Lambert and Badsey, *War Correspondents*, p. 134.

24 John Sweetman, *War and Administration: The Significance of the Crimean War for the British Army* (Edinburgh: Scottish Academic Press, 1984).

25 Airey, letter to Hardinge, 18 November 1854. CUL Add.9554/1/8. Rpt Crimean War Society website, http://cwrs.russianwar.co.uk (accessed 17 March 2018).

26 Dallas, *Eyewitness*, p. 50.

27 Ibid., p. 49.

28 Russell in *War Correspondents*, pp. 136–7.

29 Fanny Duberly, *Mrs Duberly's War: Journal and Letters from the Crimea*, ed. Christine Kelly (Oxford: Oxford University Press, 2007), p. 104.

30 Hamley, 'The Story of the Campaign', p. 246.

31 Introduction to Nicholas Dunscombe, *Captain Dunscombe's Diary: The Real Crimean War that the British Infantry Knew*, ed. Colin Robins (Bowdon: Withycut House, 2003), p. 7.

32 Robins, introduction to Dunscombe, *Diary*, p. 9.

33 Dunscombe, *Diary*, pp. 43–4.

34 Romaine, *Romaine's Crimean War*, p. 39.

35 Brian Cooke, *The Grand Crimean Central Railway: The Railway that Won a War* (Knutsford: Cavalier House, 1990), p. 13.

36 R. Hodasevich [Robert Chodasiewicz], *A Voice from Within the Walls of Sebastopol: A Narrative of the Campaign in the Crimea, and of the Events of the Siege* (London: John Murray, 1856). The firm John Murray (est. 1768) was a well-respected London publisher whose authors included Coleridge, Austen, Faraday, Lyell and Darwin, *Oxford Dictionary of National Biography* (Oxford: Oxford University Press, 2004).

37 Andrew Wachtel, 'History and Autobiography in Tolstoy', in *The Cambridge Companion to Tolstoy* (Cambridge: Cambridge University Press, 2006), p. 176.

38 Susan Layton, 'The Maude Translations of the Sevastopol Stories', *Tolstoy Studies Journal* 20 (2008): 14–26. Different English translations appeared in 1887 and 1901.

39 Leo Tolstoy, *The Sebastopol Sketches* (1855–6), trans. David McDuff (London: Penguin, 1986), p. 39.

40 As Figes points out, Russian surgeon Nikolai Pirogov was a pioneer in the use of anaesthetics in field surgery. Orlando Figes, *Crimea: The Last Crusade* (London: Allen Lane, 2010), p. 295.

41 Sweetman, *The Crimean War*, p. 66; Trevor Royle, *Crimea: The Great Crimean War, 1854–1856* (London: Little, Brown, 1999), p. 360.

42 Dunscombe, *Diary*, pp. 88, 105.

43 Lambert and Badsey, *War Correspondents*, p. 174.

44 Duberly, *Journal*, p. 249.

45 Winfried Baumgart, *Crimean War 1853–56* (London: Arnold, 1999), p. 19. On the diplomatic history, see Winfried Baumgart (ed.), *Englische Akten zur Geschichte des Krimkriegs*, 4 vols (Munich: R. Oldenbourg, 1988–2006).

46 See E. H. Carr, *The Twenty Years' Crisis 1919–1939: An Introduction*

to the *Study of International Relations* (1939; Basingstoke: Palgrave Macmillan, 2001).

47 Lambert and Badsey, *War Correspondents*, p. 168.

48 William Russell, *Times*, 9 April 1855; Lambert and Badsey, *War Correspondents*, pp. 182–3.

49 Dunscombe, *Diary*, 15 April 1855, p. 99.

50 Cooke, *The Grand Crimean Central Railway*, pp. 18–21.

51 Ibid., p. 31.

52 Ibid., pp. 73–5.

53 Sweetman, *The Crimean War*, p. 67; Cooke, *The Grand Crimean Central Railway*, pp. 86–7.

54 Royle, *Crimea*, pp. 391–2.

55 Robins in Dunscombe, *Diary*, p. 122, n. 170.

56 Russell in Lambert and Badsey, *War Correspondents*, p. 214.

57 Robins, *Romaine's Crimean War*, p. 166; Royle, *Crimea*, p. 394.

58 Robins, *Romaine's Crimean War*, p. 166.

59 Hamley, quoted in Royle, *Crimea*, p. 396.

60 Lambert and Badsey, *War Correspondents*, p. 211.

61 Quoted in Alastair Massie (ed.), *The National Army Museum Book of the Crimean War: The Untold Stories* (London: Sidgwick and Jackson, 2004), p. 213. Lambert and Badsey, *War Correspondents*, p. 221; Alan Palmer, *The Banner of Battle: The Story of the Crimean War* (London: Weidenfeld and Nicolson, 1987), p. 208.

62 Lambert and Badsey, *War Correspondents*, p. 220; Figes, *Crimea*, p. 380.

63 1 September, Lambert and Badsey, *War Correspondents*, p. 233.

64 Figes, *Crimea*, pp. 378–9, p. 385.

65 Royle, *Crimea*, p. 406. For a discussion of the complexities of the blockade, see Andrew Lambert, *The Crimean War: British Grand Strategy against Russia 1853–1856*, rev. edn (Farnham: Ashgate, 2011), pp. 110–11.

66 Robins, *Romaine's Crimean War*, p. 169.

67 Dunscombe, *Diary*, p. 154.

68 Sous-Lieutenant Jean-Baptiste-Louis Berquin, 3ᵉ Batterie, 13ᵉ Régiment d'Artillerie, letter to his father. J. Colnat, *Lettres d'un Combattant de Sebastopol (1855–1856)* (Metz: Editions de Lorraine, 1965), p. 4; trans. Anthony Dawson.

69 Lambert, *The Crimean War*, p. 262.

CHAPTER 4: SEBASTOPOL

1   An earlier version of this chapter was published in the journal *19: Interdisciplinary Studies in the Long Nineteenth Century* 20, special issue on the Crimean War, ed. Rachel Bates, Holly Furneaux and Alistair Massey (2015), https://www.19.bbk.ac.uk/88/volume/2015/issue/20/ (accessed 17 March 2018).

2   George Ranken, *Six Months at Sebastopol: Being Selections from the Journal and Correspondence of the Late Major George Ranken, Royal Engineers*, ed. W. Bayne Ranken (London: Charles Westerton, 1857), p. 63; Russell, p. 248.

3   Nicholas Dunscombe, *Captain Dunscombe's Diary: The Real Crimean War that the British Infantry Knew*, ed. Colin Robins (Bowdon: Withycut House, 2003), 8 September 1855, p. 154; Alexis Soyer, *Soyer's Culinary Campaign: Being Historical Reminiscences of the Late War* (London: G. Routledge, 1857), ch. 30; Fanny Duberly, *Mrs Duberly's War: Journal and Letters from the Crimea*, ed. Christine Kelly (Oxford: Oxford University Press, 2007), p. 239. Page references are from this edition. Mrs Duberly's original *Journal* was published in 1855.

4   Mary Seacole, *Wonderful Adventures of Mrs Seacole in Many Lands* (1857; New York: Oxford University Press, 1988), p. 172. Page references are from this edition.

5   For example, Susan Sontag, *Regarding the Pain of Others* (London: Penguin, 2003); Judith Butler, *Frames of War: When is Life Grievable?* (London: Verso, 2009); Mary Favret, *War at a Distance: Romanticism and the Making of Modern Wartime* (Princeton, NJ: Princeton University Press, 2010); Paul Virilio, *War and Cinema: The Logistics of Perception*, trans. Patrick Camiller (London: Verso, 1989); Paul Virilio, *Desert Screen: War at the Speed of Light*, trans. Michael Degener (London: Continuum, 2002).

6   George Dallas, *Eyewitness in the Crimea: The Crimean War Letters (1854–56) of Lt. Col. George Frederic Dallas*, ed. Michael Hargreave Mawson (London: Greenhill Books, 2001), Letter, 30 September 1855, pp. 185–6.

7   'The War in the Crimea: From our Artist and Special Correspondent', *Illustrated London News*, 13 October 1855, p. 434.

8   The French troops were given more freedom to enter and plunder the city, somewhat to the irritation of the British soldiers. A number of French looters were killed by explosions.

9   Sous-Lieutenant Jean-Baptiste-Louis Berquin, letter to his father, 10 September 1855, trans. Anthony Dawson.

10 Robert Biddulph, Letter, 'The Fall of Sebastopol: A Contemporary Account by Lieutenant Robert Biddulph, RA', ed. H. Biddulph, *Journal of the Society for Army Historical Research* 19 (1940): 197–9.

11 Dunscombe, *Diary*, 13 September 1855, p. 157.

12 Paul Britten Austin, *1812: Napoleon in Moscow* (London: Greenhill Books, 1995). A number of writers in 1855 draw precisely this comparison. French Sous-Lieutenant Jean-Baptiste-Louis Berquin wrote to his father, 'for two days we saw a terrible fire, this fire was the fleet and the city burning, which recalls the burning of Moscow'. Letter, 10 September 1855; trans. Anthony Dawson. See also Anthony Dawson, *French Infantry of the Crimean War* (Leigh-on-Sea: Partizan Press, 2011).

13 Frederick Robinson, *Diary of the Crimean War* (London: Richard Bentley, 1856), pp. 393–4. Similarly, an anonymous medical officer, writing in *The Times* about the battle of Alma, looks forward to some 'grand "looting" at Sebastopol'. 'This is a horrible way to talk, and, no doubt, will shock you much; but it is one of the concomitants of grim war, and, perhaps, one of the most agreeable.' *The Times*, 12 October 1854, p. 8.

14 Douglas A. Reid, *Soldier-Surgeon: The Crimean War Letters of Douglas A. Reid, 1855–1856*, ed. Joseph O. Baylen and Alan Conway (Knoxville: University of Tennessee Press, 1968), 20–22 September 1855, p. 111.

15 William Allan, *Crimean Letters from the 41st (The Welch) Regiment, 1854–56*, ed. W. Alister Williams (Wrexham: Bridge Books, 2011), letter 17 September 1855, p. 125.

16 For Trevor Royle, witnessing the plight of the wounded Russians left behind in Sebastopol 'was living proof of the old military adage that next to a battle lost there is nothing so pitiable as "a battle won"'. Trevor Royle, *Crimea: The Great Crimean War, 1854–1856* (London: Little, Brown, 1999), p. 415.

17 Prince Gorchakov admitted in his dispatch that wounded Russians were left behind, but he estimated the numbers to be around 500. The precise history of this aspect of the siege remains to some extent unknown. Why the Russians expected the allies to save the wounded immediately, given that the city was so heavily mined, is yet to be fully researched. Some Russian historians argue that the British accounts of finding the Russian wounded are exaggerated, perhaps as a kind of propaganda, to discredit the Russians in defeat. Dr N. Yulia, personal communication at *Charting the Crimean War: Contexts, Nationhood, Afterlives* conference, July 2013, National Army Museum, London.

18 Sontag's discussion of the Crimea contains a number of factual errors. For example, she argues that Fenton was 'under instruction from the War Office not to photograph the dead, the maimed, or the ill'. This is incorrect. Fenton was not under direction from the War Office; it was his own decision not to photograph dead bodies, probably as a matter of decorum, respect or good taste. Sontag states that Fenton was sent to war by the British government (p. 48), but this is also incorrect. See Ulrich Keller, *The Ultimate Spectacle: A Visual History of the Crimean War* (Amsterdam: Gordon and Breach, 2001), ch. 4; Jan Mieszkowski, *Watching War* (Stanford, CA: Stanford University Press, 2012), pp. 113–17.

19 Favret, 'Prelude', *War at a Distance*.

20 Phillip Knightley, *The First Casualty: The War Correspondent as Hero and Myth-maker from the Crimea to Kosovo*, rev. edn (London: Prion, 2000), ch. 1.

21 Trudi Tate, *Modernism, History and the First World War* (1998; Penrith: Humanities eBooks, 2013), p. 14.

22 If, as Favret argues, the modern pattern for representing war at a distance is established by British writers during the Napoleonic Wars, this develops and changes in significant new ways in the Crimean War, with the use of eyewitness reporters, the expansion of press readership and the use of photography.

23 Held in National Army Museum. Reproduced on NAM website, http://prints.national-army-museum.ac.uk/image/424952/william-simpson-the-fall-of-sebastopol-1856 (accessed 17 March 2018).

24 Keller, *The Ultimate Spectacle*, p. 164. Anon., *Inside Sebastopol and Experiences in Camp: Being the Narrative of a Journey to the Ruins of Sebastopol* (London: Chapman and Hall, 1856), p. 165.

25 Robins, introduction to Dunscombe's *Diary*, p. 7. Matthew Lalumia, *Realism and Politics in Victorian Art of the Crimean War* (Epping: Bowker, 1984).

26 Information from *Oxford Dictionary of National Biography* entry on James Robertson, 1813/14–1888, and from Keller, *The Ultimate Spectacle*, ch. 4. Both Robertson and Beato took photographs that were exhibited and sold under the company name 'James Robertson'. Beato went on to have a long career as a photographer, whereas Robertson seems to have stopped taking pictures after the Crimea. Keller, *The Ultimate Spectacle*, p. 162.

27 This comes from a work entitled 'Inside Sebastopol', which is quoted in the *ILN* within an article entitled 'Interior of the Redan', discussing

Robertson's photos. *ILN*, 15 March 1856, p. 266.

28 Tolstoy was first translated into French and then English in the late 1880s. The Maude translations were published in 1901 and 1932. See Susan Layton, 'The Maude Translations of the Sevastopol Stories', *Tolstoy Studies Journal* 20 (2008): 14–26.

29 Joseph Michael Barry, 'Sebastopol is Won!', *Lays of the War and Miscellaneous Lyrics* (London: Longman and Co., 1856), p. 57.

30 Augusta Baldwyn, 'The Victory', dated 9 October 1855, in *Poems* (Montreal: John Lovell, 1859).

31 Keller, *The Ultimate Spectacle*; Ulrich Keller, 'Photography, History, (Dis) belief', *Visual Resources: An International Journal of Documentation* 26, no. 2 (2010): 95–111.

32 Daniel Pick, *War Machine: The Rationalisation of Slaughter in the Modern Age* (New Haven CT: Yale University Press, 1996).

33 Dunscombe, *Diary*, 13 September 1855, p. 157; 14 September 1855, p. 158. Dunscombe was acting as an Assistant Engineer. Due to the burden of work and the shortage of Royal Engineers, many infantry officers had to supervise work parties and simple engineering tasks, for which they got extra pay. Thanks to Major Colin Robins for this information.

34 Allan, Letter, 17 September 1855, p. 125.

CHAPTER 5: THE BALTIC CAMPAIGN

1 *The Times*, 13 March 1854, p. 9; rpt in Andrew Lambert and Stephen Badsey (eds), *The War Correspondents: The Crimean War* (London: Bramley Books, 1994/1997), p. 276. Further ships and crew followed piecemeal over the following weeks.

2 Andrew Lambert, *Battleships in Transition: The Creation of the Steam Battlefleet 1815–1860* (London: Conway Maritime Press, 1984), ch. 3. Historical material in this chapter comes from Andrew Lambert, *The Crimean War: British Grand Strategy against Russia 1853–1856*, rev. edn (Farnham: Ashgate, 2011), esp. chapters 12 and 13; Lambert and Badsey, *The War Correspondents*; Basil Greenhill and Ann Giffard, *The British Assault on Finland, 1854–1855: A Forgotten Naval War* (London: Conway Maritime, 1988); Andrew Lambert, 'Looking for gunboats: British naval operations in the Gulf of Bothnia, 1854–55', *Journal for Maritime Research* 6, no. 1 (2004): 65–86, https://www.tandfonline.com/ doi/abs/10.1080/21533369.2004.9668337 (accessed 16 June 2018). See

further John Grainger, *The First Pacific War: Britain and Russia, 1854–56* (Woodbridge: Boydell, 2008).

3 *The Times*, 13 March 1854, p. 9; rpt in Lambert and Badsey, *The War Correspondents*, p. 276. For the *ILN*, the new steam technology is entirely due to 'English genius and energy'. 'Departure of the Baltic Fleet', *ILN*, 18 March 1854, p. 242.

4 Delia Millar, 'Brierly, Sir Oswald Walters (1817–1894)', *Oxford Dictionary of National Biography*, online edn, 2004; Andrew Greg, 'Carmichael, John Wilson (1799–1868)', *Oxford Dictionary of National Biography*, online edn, 2004. Lambert, *The Crimean War*, p. 411.

5 The *ILN* was founded in May 1842 and was the first weekly newspaper to publish pictures. Patrick Leary, 'A Brief History of the *Illustrated London News*', ILN database, http://gale.cengage.co.uk//images/PatrickLeary.pdf. Matthew Lalumia, *Realism and Politics in Victorian Art of the Crimean War* (Epping: Bowker, 1984), ch. 4.

6 *ILN*, Supplement on Baltic Fleet, 18 March 1854, p. 242.

7 *ILN*, 18 March 1854, p. 242

8 *The Times*, rpt in Lambert and Badsey, *The War Correspondents*, p. 278.

9 'Departure of the Baltic Fleet from Spithead', *Daily News*, 13 March 1854, p. 5.

10 'The Sailing of the Baltic Fleet', *ILN*, 18 March 1854, p. 243.

11 'Departure of the Baltic Fleet from Spithead', *Daily News*, 13 March 1854, p. 5. See also 'Her Majesty "Leading" the Fleet', *ILN*, 18 March 1854, p. 242.

12 Lambert, *The Crimean War*, pp. 79, 161.

13 Priscilla Napier, *Black Charlie: A Life of Admiral Sir Charles Napier KCB 1787–1860* (Norwich: Michael Russell, 1995), p. 124. Lambert, *The Crimean War*, ch. 6. Andrew Lambert, 'Napier, Sir Charles (1786–1860)', *Oxford Dictionary of National Biography*, online edn, 2011.

14 Jonathan Parry, 'Graham, Sir James Robert George, second baronet (1792–1861)', *Oxford Dictionary of National Biography*, online edn, 2009.

15 Lambert, 'Napier', *ODNB*.

16 'The Banquet to Sir Charles Napier, at the Reform Club', *ILN*, 18 March 1854, p. 228; see also *ILN*, 11 March 1854, p. 207. Other papers were equally enthusiastic.

17 Reported in the *ILN*, 18 March 1854, p. 243.

18 *ILN*, 18 March 1854, p. 243.

19 Napier, *Black Charlie*, p. 129. See also H. Noel Williams, *The Life and Letters of Admiral Sir Charles Napier, K.C.B.* (London: Hutchinson,

1917), chs 20 and 21.

20 Lambert, *The Crimean War*, p. 107.

21 Ibid., p. 182.

22 Lambert and Badsey, *The War Correspondents*, p. 277.

23 'The Baltic Fleet', *The Times*, 18 July 1854, p. 9; in September, an anonymous correspondent reports that one ship has had a case of cholera and another of scarlet fever, but otherwise he reports the fleet is now generally healthy. 'The Baltic Fleet', *The Times*, 27 September 1854, p. 10. See also *Medical Times and Gazette*, 5 and 12 August 1854 for discussions of cholera in the fleet.

24 *ILN*, 27 May 1854, p. 481.

25 A screw is a ship driven by a screw propeller.

26 Lambert, *The Crimean War*, pp. 186–7, 192. Lambert, 'Looking for gunboats', p. 74.

27 'The Baltic Fleet', *ILN*, 17 June 1854, p. 565. Lambert notes that the press in Britain was quite critical of Plumridge's activities, but he also argues that their reports were often based on Russian propaganda. 'Looking for gunboats', p. 75.

28 Lambert argues that public opinion was felt as a real pressure by some naval leaders. *The Crimean War*, pp. 183, 185; Lambert and Badsey, *The War Correspondents*, p. 285.

29 Factual information about Bomarsund is drawn mainly from Greenhill and Giffard, *The British Assault on Finland*, chs 2 and 14; also Lambert, *The Crimean War*, ch. 13.

30 Greenhill and Giffard, *The British Assault on Finland*, p. 33.

31 Had it been completed, the fort was expected to hold 5,000 men and 500 guns. Greenhill and Giffard, *The British Assault on Finland*, p. 245.

32 J. K. Laughton, 'Sulivan, Sir Bartholomew James (1810–1890)', rev. Andrew Lambert, *Oxford Dictionary of National Biography*, Oxford University Press, 2004; online edn, Jan 2008.

33 *The Times*, 16 August 1854; rpt Lambert and Badsey, *The War Correspondents*, pp. 286–7.

34 Henry Byam Martin, Baltic Journal, National Maritime Museum, JOD/200/1 and 2, quoted in Greenhill and Giffard, *The British Assault on Finland*, p. 259.

35 Greenhill and Giffard, *The British Assault on Finland*, pp. 262–3.

36 'Destruction of the Fortifications at Aland' (5 September), *Daily News*, 13 September 1854, p. 5.

37 Editorial, *Daily News*, 21 August 1854, p. 4.

38 *ILN*, 26 August 1854, p. 173.

39 The men habitually go barefoot on board ship, but they would expect to wear shoes ashore. Unfortunately, the navy blundered and sent shoes to the Baltic seamen which were too small for almost all of them. Greenhill and Giffard, *The British Assault on Finland*, p. 252.

40 'Operations in the Baltic', *ILN*, 30 September 1854, p. 330.

41 *ILN*, 21 October 1854, pp. 386–7.

42 *ILN*, 8 September 1855.

43 Historical information on Sveaborg comes from Greenhill and Giffard, *The British Assault on Finland*, ch. 19; and from the UNESCO World Heritage website for Suomenlinna in Finland, which contains the remains of the Sveaborg fortifications, https://whc.unesco.org/en/list/583 (accessed 16 June 2018).

44 Matyushkin letter of 1854, quoted in Greenhill and Giffard, *The British Assault on Finland*, p. 328. Had Napier known its weaknesses, perhaps he could have attacked Sveaborg successfully after all, even without the specialist gunboats needed.

45 *ILN*, 25 August 1855, p. 235.

46 'The Bombardment of Sveaborg', *ILN*, 25 August, p. 235.

47 *ILN*, 25 August 1855, p. 235.

48 *The Times*, rpt in Lambert and Badsey, *The War Correspondents*, p. 300.

CHAPTER 6: THE END OF THE WAR

1 Edmund Richardson, *Classical Victorians: Scholars, Scoundrels and Generals in Pursuit of Antiquity* (Cambridge: Cambridge University Press, 2013), ch. 3. Edmund Richardson, 'Of Doubtful Antiquity: Fighting for the Past in the Crimean War', in Astrid Swenson and Peter Mandler (eds), *From Plunder to Preservation: Britain and the Heritage of Empire, c. 1800–1940* (Oxford: Oxford University Press for the British Academy, 2013), pp. 31–48.

2 Earle, Letter, NAM 1994-03-153; quoted in Alastair Massie (ed.), *The National Army Museum Book of the Crimean War: The Untold Stories* (London: Sidgwick and Jackson, 2004), p. 236.

3 Humphrey Sandwith, *A Narrative of the Siege of Kars: And of the Six Months' Resistance by the Turkish Garrison Under General Williams to the Turkish Army* (London: John Murray, 1856), pp. 298–301; diary entries 14–21 November 1855. See further William Williams, *The Siege of Kars, 1855: Defence and Capitulation* (London: Stationery Office, 2000).

4 For further details of the siege of Kars, and of other struggles in the Caucasus between Russia and Turkey, see Winfried Baumgart, *The Crimean War, 1853–56* (London: Arnold, 1999), ch. 14, and Orlando Figes, *Crimea: The Last Crusade* (London: Allen Lane, 2010), pp. 398–401.

5 John Sweetman, *The Crimean War* (Oxford: Osprey, 2001), p. 85.

6 Walter Lippmann, *Public Opinion* (New York: Harcourt, Brace, and Co., 1922), p. 248. See further Edward Herman and Noam Chomsky, *Manufacturing Consent: The Political Economy of the Mass Media* (London: Vintage, 1994/1988); Trudi Tate, *Modernism, History and the First World War* (Penrith: HeB, 1998/2013), ch. 5.

7 Sometimes this is done in ingenious ways, as we see in the propaganda campaigns of the First World War. Peter Buitenhuis, *The Great War of Words: British, American, and Canadian Propaganda and Fiction, 1914–1933* (London: Batsford, 1987/1989). Tate, *Modernism*, chs 2, 5.

8 Figures come from Andrew Lambert, *The Crimean War: British Grand Strategy against Russia 1853–1856*, rev. edn (Farnham: Ashgate, 2011), p. 343.

9 Editorial, *The Times*, 23 April 1856, p. 8.

10 *ILN*, April 1856, supplement, pp. 1–2.

11 Lambert, *The Crimean War*, p. 344.

12 *ILN*, 31 May 1856. The 'splendours of illuminations' are also reported at length in *The Times*, 30 May 1856, p. 6.

13 Baumgart, *The Crimean War*, pp. 212–13; See also Eric Hobsbawm, *The Age of Capital 1848–1875* (London: Abacus, 1975), p. 97; Richard Evans, *The Pursuit of Power: Europe 1815–1914* (London: Penguin, 2016/2017). For the effects of the war on individual nations, see Baumgart, *The Crimean War*, ch. 18.

14 Sweetman, *The Crimean War*, p. 88.

15 *ILN*, 12 April 1856, p. 381.

16 Ulrich Keller, *The Ultimate Spectacle: A Visual History of the Crimean War* (Amsterdam: Gordon and Breach, 2001), pp. 146, 164, 171.

17 For an extended discussion of heroic womanhood, see Stefanie Markovits, *The Crimean War in the British Imagination* (Cambridge: Cambridge University Press, 2009), ch. 2.

18 Lewis Carroll, 'The Path of Roses', *The Train* 1 (May 1856); rpt in Lewis Carroll, *Jabberwocky and Other Nonsense*, ed. Gillian Beer (London: Penguin, 20012), pp. 176–9.

19 The Florence Nightingale Museum is devoted to educating a wide public about her life and work, http://www.florence-nightingale.co.uk (accessed

17 March 2018).

20 William Howard Russell, Letter to *The Times*, 11 April 1857, p. 8.

21 Mary Seacole, *The Wonderful Adventures of Mrs Seacole in Many Lands* (1857; London: Penguin, 2005). Seacole has been commemorated recently for her contributions to nursing in the Crimean War, though she was not strictly speaking a nurse; rather, she presented herself proudly as a doctoress and herbalist before the war. In the Crimea she was primarily a sutler, selling food, and also offered medical support where she could.

22 See further Helen Rappaport, *No Place for Ladies: The Untold Story of Women in the Crimean War* (Brighton: Victorian Secrets, 2007/2013).

23 Ibid., ch. 3.

24 Holly Furneaux, *Military Men of Feeling: Emotion, Touch and Masculinity in the Crimean War* (Oxford: Oxford University Press, 2016), pp. 181–4; Glenn Fisher, 'Thomas Walker 95th Regiment', *The War Correspondent* 26, no. 3 (2008): 23–4.

25 Furneaux, *Military Men*, p. 182.

26 Ibid., p. 184.

27 *The Athenaeum*, 10 January 1857, p. 54.

28 Queen Victoria, *Queen Victoria's Journals*, 19 June 1855, http://www.queenvictoriasjournals.org/ (accessed 17 March 2018).

29 Jan-Melissa Schramm argues that the soldiers in the Crimean War were seen as scapegoats, in the sense of 'the innocent one who perishes on behalf of many'. Soldiers were sacrificed to a cause that not everyone felt was worthwhile. For Schramm, the nation was left in need of communal healing after the upheavals of the Chartist protests and the suffering of the war. Schramm traces the ways in which this need for healing is played out through individual repentance and hard work in British novels by Dickens, Eliot, Gaskell and Trollope in the 1850s and 1860s. Jan-Melissa Schramm, *Atonement and Self-Sacrifice in Nineteenth-Century Narrative* (Cambridge: Cambridge University Press, 2012), p. 32.

30 Lambert, *The Crimean War*, p. 21.

31 Imperial War Museum, The Liberation of Bergen-Belsen Concentration Camp, April 1945, photograph collection; Richard Dimbleby, report on the liberation of Bergen-Belsen, BBC radio, 1945. Denise Chong, *The Girl in the Picture: The Story of Kim Phuc, the Photograph, and the Vietnam War* (London: Penguin, 2001).

Index

9 781848 858619